To Paul —
the man who
makes me look
great — except
for the way
I look today!
Best to you and
your family!!

Nann Thill
(the hullabalooer)
2013

HULLABALOO!

THE LIFE AND (MIS)ADVENTURES OF L.A. RADIO LEGEND DAVE HULL

by Dave Hull

with Bill Hayes
& Jennifer Thomas

Foreword by Bob Eubanks

FINAL WORD PRESS

Published by Final Word Press, P.O. Box 3008, Redondo Beach, CA 90277 www.finalwordpress.com. Contact: info@finalwordpress.com or 310.991.7893

Although the authors and publisher have made every effort to ensure that the information in this book is correct at press time, the author and publisher do not assume and hereby disclaim any liability to any party for any loss, damage, or disruption caused by errors or omissions, whether such errors or omissions result from negligence, accident, or any other cause.

ISBN: 978-0-9884126-0-6 (Hardcover)

First edition

Library of Congress Control Number: 2012950224

Printed in the United States of America

Edited by Jennifer Thomas
Jacket and body design by Jennifer Thomas
Rear flap photo of Dave Hull by Lisa Hull Hemstreet
Rear flap photo of Bill Hayes and Jennifer Thomas by Christine Fay
Mouseketeer photo, p. 366, © Walt Disney Corporation
Photo of Dave Hull and Bob Eubanks, p. 454, by David Schwartz
All other photos courtesy of the Dave Hull Archive

There's a guy we all know well
We're sure glad he was born
He can send you in a spell
when he honks his little horn <Honk, Honk!>
Dave Hull, Dave Hull the Hullabalooer
Dave Hull, Dave Hull the Hullabalooer
The sunny, funny, fuzzy, scuzzy Hullabalooer.

We're not much on fancy words so we'll just drop a note
To say you were sensational on your "junky" float
Dave Hull, Dave Hull the Hullabalooer
Dave Hull, Dave Hull the Hullabalooer
The sunny, funny, fuzzy, scuzzy Hullabalooer.

He's the kind of guy who is handsome in every way
He's the one we listen to on KRLA...K-R-L-A!

Someday when we're old and gray and all our days are dull
We'll look back in memory to those carefree days with Dave Hull
Dave Hull, Dave Hull the Hullabalooer
Dave Hull, Dave Hull the Hullabalooer
The sunny, funny, fuzzy, scuzzy Hullabalooer.

KRLA (The sunny, funny, fuzzy, scuzzy Hullabalooer)...
KRLA (The sunny, funny, fuzzy, scuzzy Hullabalooer)...
KRLA...K-R-L-A!

<Honk, Honk!>

—"Dave Hull The Hullabalooer," the Scuzzies, 1965

This book is dedicated to my wife, Jeanette,
and my only daughter, Lisa,
for encouraging me for years to write this book.
They insisted my story be written so that others
could enjoy the foibles of my professional life.

When I wasn't sure I had much to tell, they disagreed.
They had lived my story with me through all these decades!

It's now up to you to judge whether they were right...

Table of Contents

Foreword

BY BOB EUBANKS

Bob Eubanks is the ultimate on-the-air, on-camera, onstage, and behind-the-scenes Renaissance man. He has done it all. We all know him from his long runs as host of The Newlywed Game *and the Annual Rose Parade (the entire spectacle would wilt without his commentary!).*

Eubanks' autobiography, It's in the Book, Bob!, *is a ride through not just his life but through every frantic facet of Hollywood's highs and lows.*

Bob managed public relations for rock legends that flew "Eight Miles High" like the Byrds, promoted the "Silver Wings" of country-western common-man-poet Merle Haggard, and has touched the lives and careers of just about every artist in between.

He hocked his house so Southern California could watch the Beatles twist and shout at the Hollywood Bowl and Dodger Stadium—later adding the Rolling Stones and Bob Dylan to his concert-promoting mix. And he ran the Cinnamon Cinder chain of teen nightclubs.

Bob Eubanks was also one of KRLA's "Eleven-Ten Men" when a young disc jockey named Dave Hull sat behind that mic in Pasadena, California, for the first time and entered into a Renaissance of his own—a crazed awakening powered by horns, laughter, and a whole lot of hullabaloo!

On a Sunday afternoon, June 6, 1963, I was doing a weekend shift at KRLA and not loving it. I had been told that a new guy would be doing the six–to-midnight evening shift and I was to welcome him to the land of the Eleven-Ten Men. I didn't like the idea that I was working on a Sunday, and I couldn't wait for the new dude to arrive so I could go home.

At about 5:30 p.m., in walked this very energetic guy carrying a cardboard box full of the craziest items I had ever seen. He introduced himself, and I showed him how to run the board and hurried to my car. As I was driving out of the parking lot, I caught the end of the hourly news and then a top ten record came on. Ten seconds later, I heard this terrible crash and Dave Hull the Hullabalooer said, "How do you like the show so far?"

From that moment on, KRLA was never the same. What Dave Hull did for Los Angeles radio cannot be duplicated. Not by Rick Dees, not by Ryan Seacrest, not by anybody. The Hullabalooer literally took over the town. He became the Fifth Beatle. He became the most popular radio personality that Los Angeles had ever seen. Dave did some crazy things that you will read about in this book. Some of my favorites are stowing away on the Beatles' airplane; giving out John, Paul, George, and Ringo's telephone numbers; and "cutting a deal" with an employee at Capitol Records so KRLA always had the Beatles' albums first.

He's crazy, he's insane, he's talented, and most of all, he's a good human being.

Sit back and relax, and read all about a one-of-a-kind radio icon: Dave Hull the Hullabalooer.

Acknowledgments

I have many people I am grateful to for their roles in my life, my career, and the creation of this book.

First and foremost is my family.

To my wife, Jeanette, my daughter, Lisa, and my sons, Mike, Mark, Clark, and Brian, who had to put up with my crazy shenanigans daily!

To my sister, Nan, and to my brother, Gary—the man who dialed that phone to KRLA to get me a job, and off of his couch!

To my mother, Edna Loretta Hull, for taking me to the national radio show that sparked all this hullabaloo.

And to my father, John Franklin Hull, M.D., who taught me so many valuable lessons.

Next...

To John Barrett, who told me before that first Sunday night on the air in L.A. to go into *that* studio and "prove me right."

To KRLA's Dick Moreland, who understood that many of my foolish ideas might amount to something special—while others felt my foolishness would end in collapse.

To Bob Eubanks and Richard Beebe, the duo who understood and respected what I was trying to accomplish.

To Linda Thor, whose leadership and devotion created the largest and most unique celebrity fan club in the country at the time. And to her co-leaders, Kim Sudol, Jan Jackson, and Marcia Levine, along with every single member of the club for their commitment, creativity, and their loving assessment of my character ('cause I'm a real character!).

To the Scuzzies—including the late Suzie Cappetta and the entire Cappetta family—for ensuring that my loony legacy would live on in song.

To Wes Parker, Gold Glove winner and 1965 World Series champ, for his outstanding encouragement, loyalty, and friendship which continues to today.

To Dennis Ousley and J.J. Solari whose comedic personalities added so much flavor to an already bizarre "on-air" atmosphere.

To Rich Marotta, who helped Beebe and me through some funny L.A. Raiders situations.

To Bill Earl, who chronicled our KRLA history with amazing accuracy in his book, *Dream-House*.

To Gary Kleinman, who helped turn my KGBS *Dial-A-Date* and KMPC *Lovelines* features into a hilarious NBC nightly television show.

To Bob Colvin, my one and only agent, who brought respectability to my commercial voiceover career.

To Don Barrett of L.A. Radio People, who kept my name prominently alive.

To Bill Hayes and Jennifer Thomas, who understood my brand of hullabaloo and used their time and talent to help me realize my vision for a book.

To Chris Lewis, for his friendship and enthusiasm during this daunting literary endeavor!

And to Charlie O'Donnell, who made the trip to Palm Springs on the eve of my retirement just to say good-bye.

Last but certainly not least...

I want to acknowledge all of my fans. Your loyalty not only continued through all of my extraordinarily good times, but also during all of my clumsy unthoughtfulness. *You* are what made my fifty-seven-year career a truly memorable success.

– Dave Hull

When the 1960s burst out of the fifties, it wasn't exactly like a caterpillar easing into a butterfly; it was more like a firecracker exploding into an atom bomb. I was a proud part of that booming generation, cruising around Southern California in a variety of hot rods with my closest friends—AM radio, rock 'n' roll, and especially the voice and fun of Dave Hull the Hullabalooer. Who could have guessed that forty-plus years later I would have the honor of helping this legend look back—and look ahead—on a life that had such impact on so many people? To Dave Hull the Hullabalooer, my deepest thanks for adding so much to my life once again.

– Bill Hayes

Thank you, Dave, for entrusting us to capture the spirit of your life, laughter, and legacy. It has been an honor and a privilege to immerse myself in your hilarious tales of hijinks and hullabaloo!

A sincere thanks, also, to the friends and family who helped make possible this labor of love, through their encouragement, support, and free food! We love and appreciate you.

– Jennifer Thomas

"Mark Twain or some other guy once said:
'Never let the facts interfere with the story' ...
or something like that!"

—Dave Hull, 2012

Who in the Hull...?

"NEVER TRUST ANYONE IN SHORT PANTS"

Roots and Radio Fever: 1933–1953

On the Air, KRLA, 1965

Operator: Operator, may I help you?

Dave: Uh, yes, hello, long distance information?

Operator: What city?

Dave: Give me Memphis, Tennessee.

Operator: Thank you, just a moment.

Dave: Help me find the party that tried to get in touch with me...

Operator: All right... *(Calm, pleasant, polite)*

Dave: She could not leave her number but I know who placed the call...

Operator: Okay, just a moment. *(Still calm...polite)*

Dave: 'Cause my uncle took the message and he wrote it on the wall.

Operator: *(Very slight, somewhat nervous laughter)*

Dave: Hello, long distance information?

Operator: Yes sir, may I help you? *(Frustration growing a bit)*

Dave: Give me Memphis, Tennessee...

Operator: Yes sir, this is Memphis... *(Not so calm, not so polite)*

Dave: Help me find the party that tried to get in touch with me...she could not leave her number but I know who placed the call... *(Enthusiasm starting to rise)*

Operator: Sir, who are you calling, please? *(Frustration clearly amping up)*

Dave: 'Cause my uncle took the message and he wrote it on the wall! *(Dave's rollin' now!)* Help me information, get in touch with my Marie!!! She's the only one who'd call me here from Memphis, Tennessee!!!

Operator: Sir...

Dave: Her home is on the south side *(Laughter and enthusiasm now building to a wild crescendo!),* high upon the ridge, just a half a mile from the Mississippi Bridge!!!

Glide perfectly into a seamless segue, right into the Johnny Rivers version of Chuck Berry's "Memphis"...

Stuff like that exemplifies the tone—the edict of insanity that pretty well defined my fifty-six-year career behind soundproof glass, mountains of electronic gear, and silver Electro-Voice mics.

Folks like that poor operator from Memphis may not have exactly *aspired* to where she found *her*self—behind a busy switchboard trying to be nice to a crazy man—but *I* had a very early focus in my life.

Radio!

It was in my blood, on my mind, and in the hottest and brightest gooey gray-matter vacuum tubes psychically plugged into my cerebrum—that magical part of the brain that cooks up creativity *and* humor. And those tubes burned white-hot for me at a very young age.

I was born in Alhambra, California, on January 20, 1934. Just seven years later, I *knew* I wanted to be a "radio announcer."

**Just seven years after my birth,
I *knew* I wanted to be a radio announcer!**

"Shut Up and Watch the Show!"

My mother, Edna Hull, took my older sister, Janann, my younger brother, Gary, and me to see a national radio show from Columbia Square in Hollywood. The announcer came out onto the stage to warm up the audience. He told us that at exactly 6:00 p.m.—*our time*—we would be broadcasting back to New York, where it would be 9:00 p.m. Eastern Time. And to Chicago where it would be 8:00 p.m. Central Time.

Nationwide!

I was captivated.

He told us that we should laugh, applaud, and have fun throughout the entire program—and again he told us that we would go on the air at *exactly* 6:00 p.m.

There was apprehension!

Tension!

We would be *on the air*—live!

This was radio!

At just thirty seconds before the hour, the announcer began to tell a joke. And as he told the audience the story, their eyes were glued to him. But *my* eyes were glued to the clock. I became extremely anxious as the huge red second hand circled toward the top of the hour. I thought, *He'll never make it.*

The punch line to the joke came at *exactly* one second before the hour, and the audience burst into laughter. Immediately—to the perfect backdrop of crowd reaction—the announcer said, "From Hollywood, CBS Radio presents *Meet Corliss Archer*!"

It was the greatest thing I'd ever seen!

I told my mother *that's* what I wanted to do.

"Shut up and watch the show!" she told me.

At family gatherings, whenever I related the story about my mom (Edna Hull, left) telling me to "Shut up and watch the show!", my mom would always deny it. But it was the absolute truth!

Even though my mom wasn't *quite* as enthusiastic as I was, those little psychic tubes of joy and destiny had already started to glow deep within my frontal lobe and in those special synapses that control an individual's *zaniness quotient*.

Just twelve years later, I would be *on the air.*

Along the way, many factors served to set that *tone.* That *tone* that carried my work into the fun-fringe of radio. My family and the *adventures* (and misadventures!) of my youth were integral ingredients in a potent soup of life that eventually boiled down into a wild-man stew—a stew that helped feed appetites for entertainment and laughter for over five decades. Cravings for someone to act with pure abandon, expressing that wonderful and rare feeling that life is there to be experienced, enjoyed, and let loose of in a crazed chaos of honking horns, rock 'n' roll, berserk silliness, and stunts.

So let's go *way* back.

Closing the "Holl" in History

Starting a new country kind of falls into that "acting with abandon" category. Two of the Hull family ancestors were part of America's first *pre-radio* wave of citizens. James Wilson, born in Scotland in 1742, grew into one of the more *dignified* branches of our family tree. He was the last signer of the United States Constitution and the Declaration of Independence. He became a prominent professor of law at the College of Pennsylvania and one of the country's first Associate Justices to the United States Supreme Court in 1789.

When asked by President George Washington to become the nation's first Chief Justice, Wilson reportedly declined, telling the Father of Our Country that he would be "honored to serve on the court," but that his fellow court members should choose their *own* first Chief Justice. That became the policy of the first court.

Our second most prominent member of the family was Isaac Holl. Good ol' Isaac joined the Revolutionary War forces as a Private First Class and—according to family legend—didn't quite close the top of the "O" in his last name while signing his induction papers. Consequently, the family name would be permanently and bureaucratically changed from Holl to Hull.

That actually worked out well in the long run—I've gotten a lot of mirth-mileage out of the wacky twists I've put on "Hull"!

The Hollabalooer just wouldn't have had that same ring to it—that *tone*.

There was other "pioneering" in my family as well.

Like the world's second largest laundry!

On my mother's side of the family were the Murphys and Wolffs. That major-league laundry was owned by my great uncle, Thomas Wolff. He also headed the national American Red Cross from his home in the Philippines. But during World War II, he and his wife, Caroline, were interned by the Japanese in Santa Tomas prison near Manila until General Douglas MacArthur and his allied forces liberated the nation.

And then there was my dad.

Although he died when I was just twelve years old, my dad was one of the most remarkable men ever—having a profound impact on my life.

The Old Lamplighter

John F. Hull was born in Keota, Iowa, near the end of the nineteenth century in November of 1874, the second child of Benjamin and Eliza Hull.

He put himself through the University of Iowa by being a lamplighter. Dad truly lived that 1940s song, "The Old Lamplighter." Whenever he saw people in the park—young sweethearts enjoying the romantic dark—he wouldn't break the mood by lighting the lamp. That's exactly what the Browns sang about in that tune, and I always wondered if my dad was the inspiration for it.

John Hull became a doctor in Iowa City at the age twenty-four, after graduating medical school in just three years—extraordinary, especially for that time. He was the 136th doctor in the United States. He mounted his caduceus—the snake symbol that only M.D.s are allowed to have—onto the back of his horse-drawn wagon.

In 1917, Dad took a covered wagon out West and became just the second physician in all of Southern California. When you got sick, you went to either Dr. Chamberlain or Dr. Hull.

My pioneering pop, one of the earliest M.D.s in the U.S.— EVER!—displayed his caduceus (only the 120th issued) on his horse-drawn wagon.

Dad joined the Army Medical Corps during WWI and was stationed at Fort Riley, Kansas, as a captain. After his discharge, he returned to Alhambra, going on to head the staffs of both Garfield and Alhambra Hospitals and join the team at Good Samaritan Hospital in Los Angeles. Years later, Dad would also help found The California Home for the Aged in San Gabriel.

My father definitely blazed many medicinal trails. Several years after he died, my mother asked if I would like to have his medical books.

Of course!

And they turned out to be not just dry journals. The books were blow-by-blow briefings of battlefield blood. This was history!

As a surgeon during WWI, my dad had to be up on surgical procedures of the time—*and* the shortcuts necessary during the in-field fighting. It was frightening! It was like having a tech-primitive Model T Ford—then having to *push it*!

After reading the journals and being amazed at human *resilience*, I called the curator of books at the Huntington Library in San Marino, near Pasadena. As opposed to the *Twilight* series and *The Internet for Dummies*, the Huntington's shelves include a Gutenberg Bible, the first two quartos of *Hamlet,* the manuscript of Benjamin Franklin's autobiography, and the first seven drafts of Thoreau's *Walden.*

I figured those would be good company for my father's books.

The curator invited me to bring them in so the research department could take a look at the material.

And look they did!

The set contained several complete volumes on the "amputation of limbs by chisel and mallet while biting bullets and drinking liquor"! *And* volumes on the use of a new experimental anesthetic substance called "ether."

Since medical students from all over the world use the Huntington for their research work, the library offered us a special place for the donation of the entire works. They titled the display: "Early American Surgical Procedures provided by the late John F. Hull, M.D."

My father and greatest influence, John F. Hull, M.D.

The section still exists today and I'm guessing it will be there long after those vampire books in those other libraries are laid to rest for the last time.

Anaesthetizing Alhambra

After making house calls as a general practitioner well into 1919, Dad wanted to put up a shingle in town. But few buildings had vacancies in growing Alhambra.

During his search, he visited the Alhambra First Bank building at First and Main. Next to the bank was a landing with doors that opened straight to a stairway; upstairs were about a half-dozen or more offices.

Dad thought this layout made for a perfect rental location. He introduced himself to the bank manager and asked what they were doing with the offices upstairs.

"We're using them for storage—records and furniture," he was told.

"I'd like to lease a few of them," my dad explained. "And I think I can also get a dentist to come to Alhambra."

In those days, Alhambra had *no* dentist at all!

"No, we're not interested," the manager said.

Dad was amazed. "You've got an opportunity to get a general practitioner physician and surgeon in here *and* to house a dentist, and *you don't think you can do it?!*"

"No, we're not interested," the bank manager reiterated.

So Dad bought the building.

"I'm the new landlord," he announced a few weeks later. "And I want all the stuff in those offices out of here. Get it done as quickly as possible!"

He opened his office there, along with a Dr. McCaig, the first dentist in Alhambra.

And Dad jumped into World War II, *too*—he became an air raid warden.

When the sirens would go off, he'd put on his helmet and his gas mask, climb into his car with the very small blacked-out headlights (so the car couldn't be seen by enemy airplanes!), and go out and make his rounds.

A Liberating Lesson

My father's service in two World Wars and his medical pioneering was all pretty darn impressive! I, too, felt that industrious desire! Yes, it was time!

I was seven or eight when I had a "talk" with Dad—I told him I was going to get a job.

"That's good; that's admirable," he said.

Then he asked what I was going to do.

I told him I hadn't quite figured out *that* part of it yet.

"Would you open up a lemonade stand or something like that?" he asked.

"No, I think I'll work for the *Alhambra Post-Advocate* delivering newspapers."

Well, they wouldn't hire anybody under twelve. But I found one of those free ad papers, the *Alhambra Shopping News*, which would.

It was my first shot at "big business"!

I knew it would be tough out there, but I didn't know *how* tough.

The circulation manager told me that my papers would be bound and waiting for me to fold at a corner several blocks from my home at four-thirty in the morning. This would give me time to walk the entire route and get back home in time for school.

No problem.

But what the manager *failed* to tell my dad and me was that the papers would be bound with heavy wire—metal bands that could have been used to gift wrap the Golden Gate Bridge.

I'd brought a pair of scissors to cut the expected *twine*!

My father dropped me off at the corner and neither of us noticed the industrial-strength, Bethlehem Steel–endorsed strapping around the bundle. And these papers had to be liberated from their iron shackles, folded, and delivered to *every* house in the neighborhood by the start of school at eight-fifteen.

There was, of course, only one thing to do.

Yup, I cried.

My sobbing was heard by a man across the street. Like everyone else in the world except for my dad and me, he'd been asleep. But he was up *now*! Still in pajamas, he surveyed the scene of desperation and tragedy; then he went to his garage, got a pair of heavy wire cutters, opened the papers, and sat down on the cold curb to help me fold them all.

When Dad came home for dinner, he asked my how things had gone on my first job.

I told him.

My dad immediately phoned the circulation department, told them *exactly* what he thought of this, and advised them that they would need another delivery boy tomorrow morning.

Another *adventure*. More *learning*: Expect the unexpected in business! Big or otherwise!

Leftover Parts

Ultimately, tools and mechanics were just never my focused forte.

By the time I turned ten, those newspapers-in-bondage were a thing of my far distant past; I already had the radio tubes pulsating in my head and in my future. But when I was eight or nine, my father gave me a pocket watch and asked me to disassemble it and reassemble it—just to see if I was mechanically inclined at all.

It was kind of a last-ditch, hope-for-the-best aptitude exercise.

I asked him what if I took it apart, but couldn't put it back together?!

He told me it didn't matter; it hadn't run for years.

That was a good thing.

It's never promising when you reassemble something and have parts left over. I finished with three stray pieces: two tiny springs and a tiny notched wheel. After seeing what had been left out, Dad told me it might be best for me to consider doing something that *didn't* involve working with my hands.

"Can You Hear Me NOW!?!"

Thankfully, my "hands-off" vocation was already in the broadcasting cards.

But before *that* hand was dealt, *other* high-level media distractions presented possible paths to fame, success, and artistic satisfaction.

Besides the prophetic "radio announcer" revelations at the CBS Radio event, I also landed the lead in a play at Granada Grammar School. It was to be performed in a grand manner, nearly identical to that of Shakespearean Globe Theatre epics—at the band-shell bowl in Alhambra Park.

I was to fall in love with a young woman in the play. I had to deliver the line "I love you" to this woman.

It was important, sensitive, and, yes, soulful.

"I love you..."

"We can't hear you, David!" yelled the instructor from the back of the "bowl." "You're going to have to speak up!"

So I went through my lines again.

"I Love You..."

"That's not *big* enough!" she directed. "I can't hear you back here in the back!"

So I went through my lines *again*.

"I LOVE YOU!" I shouted, as *un*loving and as loud as anyone could ever say it.

"That's perfect!" she said.

After the rehearsal, she came up to me. "You've got to learn to speak up!"

"How can I deliver a line meaning that I love someone by *shouting* it?" I asked.

"Well, the people way in the back have *got* to hear you!" she said.

I looked at her. "Why would you do this to a person who's trying to give you their best effort; having me *scream*—when the people you're worried about are the *last* people who came in? Why should we work to the people who were so late they got put way in the back? They didn't even care enough to get here early to get better seats!"

The woman didn't know what to say.

And I never worked for *her* again.

Mind over Maggots

The pioneering and the adventures—*and the learning*—never stopped as I grew up.

I had never seen my father cry until he came home early one day from the hospital. When my mother saw him coming up the walkway in tears, she ordered us all to our rooms, which was customary for her in stressful situations.

It wasn't until several hours later that I was told that my father had lost one of his patients in childbirth; that the patient had died.

I was curious. I asked my father, what was death?

He told me it was "metamorphosis."

I told him I didn't understand, so he said we should look it up in the dictionary. He found the definition:

met·a·mor·pho·sis [met-*uh*-mawr-f*uh*-sis], noun
the transition between species.

I told him I still didn't understand.

He told me that the worms in the garbage die like everything else and then are reborn as flies. (As a side note, we briefly contemplated whether flies and maggots could communicate with each other, and I told him "probably not.")

I asked Dad if death meant the *end*? He asked me if I could spell the word "end." I was really excited because I could easily spell that word, and I looked it up for us. I was somewhat stunned with something the dictionary said: *The "end" is the "beginning"*...

I was about to experience my first allegory.

Dad explained that when we left my grandparents' house and headed home, it was the *end* of our visit and the *beginning* of our trip home. He explained that the end of *everything* was the beginning of something new—including death.

"Dad, do we have to make that trip of death alone?" I asked.

"Millions of souls in the universe could die at the same moment," he speculated. "So why *couldn't* they all make the trip together?"

At that young age, I finally felt comfortable trying to understand what death might be all about.

Funny Papers

My conversation with my dad coincided with another *pioneering* moment—the first friend I made in kindergarten taught me early on that I could make people laugh. He sought me out daily and used to call me "Funny Papers" when we played in the sandbox.

But he died before first grade was over.

Glen Sandal was his name. The picture of our graduation at Granada Grammar School gives all the names of the students around the table—at the end, with an asterisk, it says, *Glen Sandal, deceased.* My first best friend.

Our principal announced to the class that he had died overnight. No reason was ever given. I guess they thought since we were so young, no explanation was necessary.

I was really bummed out. I mean, *There goes my sandbox guy.*

Humor Is Mightier Than the Pen

The only time I was ever disciplined in elementary school was when I reached my fountain pen through the crack in the folding desk seat in front of me and stuck the girl sitting there, with it. Of course, she screamed out loud and our teacher asked her what happened.

Before she could answer, I stood up and said, "I just stuck Elizabeth Camino in the butt with my pen."

The whole class broke out in laughter—except Elizabeth.

Off I went to the principal's office. Since I had never been in trouble before, the principal asked me what I was doing there.

I told her what I had done.

She asked me why I would do such a thing.

I was contemplative. Serious. Introspective.

"I don't know *WHAT* possessed me!" I blurted.

She laughed out loud and sent me back to class.

It may have been just a bit more of *setting that tone...*

And it preceded true greatness—*true genius*—just ahead.

A "Short" Speech

I became the first elected student body president *ever* at Granada Grammar School—winning with one of the shortest speeches in political history.

The morning the candidates were to speak to the entire student body in the school's auditorium, I had absolutely nothing prepared.

Nothing.

Since we had never held an election like this before, I thought that we candidates would just stand up and be recognized. But when the other guy (who was introduced first since his last name began with a G and mine began with an H) stood up and began speaking into the microphone about what he planned on doing should the student body elect him—how he would institute world peace, feed orphans, and suckle lost kittens—I immediately knew I was in serious trouble.

I learned early on the power of humor—especially in a pinch!!

His speech was about five minutes long and was very well prepared—just *possibly* written by his parents the night before.

Now I had to think *fast*.

The other candidate never wore long pants *anywhere*. After our principal introduced me, I simply waited for the applause to die down and then pointed over to my rival and said: "Do you really trust *anyone* who wears short pants to school?"

The auditorium went wild with laughter and applause. Our principal finally had to step to the microphone and ask everyone to please quiet down.

"David has more to say," she told the assembly.

Things got settled and I stepped back up to the microphone; everyone was expectant.

"Thank you," I said—and sat back down. *That* brought the entire audience to their feet.

Again!

An hour later it was determined that the election was a landslide in my favor!

Adventures. *Tone...*

The Show Must Go On...Right Now!

The early 1940s offered very few places to go for entertainment. There was *no* Disneyland or Six Flags Magic Mountain, only Palisades Park at the end of the Santa Monica Pier or Knott's Berry Farm, which was only a restaurant and berry stand by the side of the road.

Besides those two places, my dad once took my siblings and me to "Gay's Lion Farm" in El Monte. But we were met there by a huge sign saying "Closed for the Duration"—the World War had closed many entertainment spots for fear that an air attack would kill thousands.

But we did have those Saturday afternoons at the movies!

My brother and I were really close. On Saturdays we were allowed to walk about five miles to the Granada movie theater. You had to be there at noon, because the box office opened at twelve o'clock straight up and they had two or three serials—Tom Mix and all that kind of stuff, and a dozen cartoons.

It cost a nickel for three hours of fun!

Now, we're talking the forties, and it was quite an outing because Mom would give us each a dime. You had your ten cents, and out of that, Gary and I would buy our tickets and have five cents each left for popcorn.

One Saturday we got there and the prices had been raised—admission nine cents!

We'd been given a dime, so we could get in, but no popcorn!

"Geez," I said, "this is really going to cut into us. Next week we're going to have to bring *fifteen* cents. I wonder if we can get that out of Mom."

Gary said, "Go in and get us some seats. I'll be down in a minute."

He returned minutes later with two sacks of popcorn.

"Wait a minute," I said. "Where did you get the money for *that*?"

"I didn't *buy* them. I just grabbed a couple of sacks and filled them both up from the overfill thing!"

That was Gary.

Gary also found *the button*.

He noticed it in action just once before discovering the true essence of its *power*!

After the last person was in, the guy at the front who sold the tickets would go up to the wall in the theater, pull the curtain back, and push *the button*. This magic key would ring a bell up in the projector's office. That told the projectionist that all of the people had come in and he could start the newsreel or whatever was going to play first.

From that point on, as soon as we'd go in, Gary would pull the curtain back, push the button, and everything would start.

The heck with everybody else still out front—that's their problem! They should get here early!

Making a Name for Myself

The stories about how I won my elementary school's election became legendary—so *naturally* I was asked to run for Freshman Class President when I entered high school at Alhambra High (home of the Moors!) in 1948. Our campaign badges and signs read *"GO TO HULL for Freshman Class President"*—a foreshadowing of the phonic funniness to come.

I won the presidency hands down, and four years later I won a spot on the senior council.

But "politics" wasn't exactly my thing; I began to gravitate toward music.

I became the drummer in the school's jazz band, the Gordie McGinley Quintet. Along with other gigs, we would be asked to perform at school assemblies. All five of us guys became quite popular on campus.

The Gordie McGinley Quintet had *one* paid performance—we were hired for the entire summer at a bar up in the mountains at Big Bear Lake. They had no place to house us, so they put us up in this old abandoned hospital—at least it had beds! We only lasted about four weeks though, before the club we were playing at ran out of money.

Gordie McGinley, the pianist, was really the most talented guy. The rest of us, well...we had bass; a sax player; Dwayne Wettle playing horn; and me on drums. The Monterey Jazz Festival never called us. Neither did the Playboy Jazz Festival—or even the King Pin Lounge in the bowling alley in Culver City. But at least we had those glory days at the bar in Big Bear and those wild nights in the abandoned hospital—*Gordiemania*.

Gordie reportedly went on to become an FBI agent, partially because of how good he got at speaking Spanish and its various dialects. In high school, he and I would speak fluent Spanish to each other—and we knew every cuss word, every terrible word, and could talk faster than the native speakers!

It was said that when Gordie joined the FBI, they sent him down to Cuba and embedded him in the jungle for about ten or fifteen years, keeping his ears open for Fidel Castro.

I met Gordie again during a class reunion some years later, but he didn't seem to remember me. It may have been the effects of his tension-filled years in the Cuban jungle—or perhaps just some selective–memory blocking because of my drumming.

Hull and Metzger, Metzger and Hull

Besides my *glory years* with Gordie's quintet, there was also *Metzger and Hull*.

Jack Metzger and I became close friends in high school.

After knowing him a few months, I would spend time at his house often. As I headed upstairs to his room one day, *my* sister, Janann, stuck her head out of a door down the hall.

"What are *you* doing here?" she asked me.

I told her I was there to see Jack, my best friend.

"How can that be?!" she asked.

Turns out, she was there to see *her* best friend: Jack's sister, Shirley.

My best friend's sister was my sister's best friend.

Jack and I went to Alhambra High; Janann and Shirley went to Ramona Convent, several miles away. For months, apparently, my sister and I had gone to the Metzger home separately, no one realizing the connection. Seems there was a bit of a communication gap between siblings!

Although we evidently didn't interact much back then, we're all good friends today. We really *do* talk to one another—and not just through doors down hallways!

Laps and a Bloody Axe

Jack and I ran around together the whole time we were at Alhambra. Jack was a giant of a guy; he was six-foot-six *then*. Nobody messed with Jack Metzger.

He had a '52 Buick—a white Roadmaster. When anyone in Alhambra saw the white Buick Roadmaster coming, they knew it was Metzger and Hull. It had to be, because we were inseparable.

One evening, his dad wanted to use the big car for a "night out."

"Do you guys mind using my truck?" he asked.

"No problem...it's transportation."

But we didn't notice what was *in* the truck. It didn't really matter, after all; we were just using it to go to Hamburger Heaven.

Jack is driving, and he's running *just a tad* over the speed limit. We get pulled over, by *Officer Bruno*. Officer Bruno, with the Alhambra Police Department, used to be a star football player at Alhambra High. We *all* knew and recognized Bruno.

"Do you know what you did wrong?" he asked.

He's *explaining* it to Jack while I'm just sitting there.

No real problem.

But then he shined his light into the bed of the truck.

That's where he found the axe.

The axe with blood on it.

"Turn your car around and follow me to the police station in Alhambra!" Bruno told Jack.

We did.

We didn't know what we'd done, but we did see Bruno take the axe and put it in his cruiser.

When we got there, the sergeant came out and he and Bruno talked.

Then the sergeant came up to the truck; he apparently had something to say to us.

Something somewhat important.

"I'm arresting you for murder!"

I looked at Jack.

"Have you murdered anyone?" I asked.

"No. *You* haven't murdered anyone, have you?" he asked me.

"No."

"How can you arrest us for murder if we haven't murdered anyone?" I asked the cops.

"Because you've got a bloody axe!"

"I want to call my mother!" I said.

"You've both got one phone call," they conceded.

"I'm calling my ma!" I repeated.

By now it was about eleven-thirty at night and my mother answered the phone.

"We've been arrested," I told her. "Jack and me. We're at the police station. Will you come and get me? Because they're thinking of impounding his dad's truck."

"What have they arrested you for?!" she asked.

"Murder..." I answered.

"Murder?! Tell that officer I want to speak to him on the phone!" she demanded.

So I give him the phone and all I hear is just, "No, ma'am...yes, ma'am...I understand...yes, ma'am..."

She told him she was coming down to the station, she was going to get her son, and that her son had never murdered anyone!

She's on *her* way; now Jack gets *his* call.

Jack's father answered.

"Dave and I have been arrested for murder," he told his dad.

"Who'd you kill?" his dad asked. He was *trying* to be funny.

"We didn't kill *anyone*! The cops found a bloody axe in the back of the truck!"

"Oh my God! Let me speak to the officer."

All we heard *this* time was, "Yes, Mr. Metzger...I understand... okay..."

"I cut the heads off of chickens this afternoon so we could have chicken dinner at the house," Jack's dad told them. "And I used the axe to do it. It's blood, but if you test it, it's not human blood; it's *chicken* blood!"

They let us go.

This is the kind of *problem with authority* that followed me a bit during my scholastic career—from the play director to Officer Bruno to *Coach Cushman*...

"Take a Lap, Hull!"

When I went out for football, I really wasn't interested in the *game* that much—it had a lot more to do with meeting girls! Years later, my sons turned out to be great football players, but I was a mediocre guy on the field. The main reason for my lack of All-American status, of course, was that I'd spend a lot of time over at the fence...*talking to the girls.*

"Hi-i-i-i Dave..."

It wasn't like I'd do that during a game or anything—it was always *before* practice—but it did take up a lot of time!

Coach Cushman was the head JV coach and he *hated* to see guys with their heads over the fence fooling with the girls, so he used to scream at me: "Take a lap, Hull! Take a lap!"

It got so that *every* time I came out on the field, he would scream at me, "Take a lap, Hull!"

It became the routine—it also became *motivational inspiration* for the whole team.

"Hey, you gonna to take your lap today, Hull?"

"What are you gonna do when he tells you *today*, Hull?"

"I'm going to run my ass off!" I'd tell them.

Every time I'd leave the fence with the girls or *any* time I'd just come out of the locker room, I'd hear, "Take a lap, Hull!"

Authority...

My poor brother, Gary, also wound up sweating to the heat that I created.

He went out for football after I did and Coach Cushman had quite a way with the "rookies."

He'd say to all the seniors, "I want you to meet the guys who think they're going to take your place. I'm gonna introduce them to you, one by one, and I want you *new* men to let these seniors know that you're here to take their spot."

He went down the list, and when he got to Gary Hull, he stopped..

"Did you have a brother who played here?" he asked.

"Yes, sir," Gary replied, "my older brother, Dave."

Coach Cushman didn't even pause.

"Take a lap, Hull!!!" he screamed.

**"Take a lap, Hull!":
My football career at
Alhambra High had a lot
more to do with meeting
girls than winning games!**

Turning the Dial

It had been several years since those little psychic radio tubes began to burn in my soul, but radio was becoming more and more a part of everyday life. Teens are always drawn toward music and personalities, but for me it was taking a heftier hold.

Especially when it came to the personalities.

Everyone's favorite radio station was KLAC–AM 570. They played pop music day and night, and had some true legends "spinning the wax"!

Dick Haynes—*Haynes at the Reins*!—would start the morning.

The great Al Jarvis and his *Make Believe Ballroom* was midday.

Alex "Pick Up a Couple of Bucks" Cooper would fill the afternoons, along with Bob McLaughlin.

Gene Norman, broadcasting from his jazz nightclub on the Sunset Strip, would take us into the night.

And there were more.

Peter Potter and his *Platter Parade* and Jim Hawthorne with his famous "Hogan-twanger" (a marvelous musical instrument made from a wooden box and hacksaw blades!) were big favorites of mine.

Even as a preteen, I loved the personalities. I wanted *interaction*— to be at least a little part of it all. I wrote to McLaughlin requesting an autographed picture; I told him how much I enjoyed his show!

I waited weeks for a response.

Nothing.

Finally, my mother said, "He's probably busy answering hundreds of requests. Write him again!"

So I did!

Nothing.

I was devastated. But that was another of those learning adventures, of sorts—another dial of life being turned that would set that tone. It would teach me how important fans are; how through-the-heart close their love and support is—and that was something that never left me as my life's main event took the stage on both sides of that microphone.

My all-time favorite hit song throughout my years at Alhambra High School was #1 in 1945: "Till the End of Time" by Perry Como.

At graduation in 1952, my favorite was the #1 Joni James hit "Why Don't You Believe Me?"

I graduated from Alhambra High in January of 1952. I was about to take a pretty big leap from the coast and palm trees of Southern California to the port and plains of Casablanca, French Morocco, in North Africa.

I was also about to begin a *true* path to becoming an actual "radio announcer." The tone had indeed been set!

Deutzenfoyer!!

AN AIRMAN TAKES TO THE AIRWAVES

Armed Forces Radio: 1953

"Almost everything I've done, I've done through my own creativity. I don't think I ever had to listen to anyone else to learn how to play drums. I wish I could say that for about ten thousand other drummers."

—Buddy Rich

"I feel truly honored to be in such distinguished company. The mold was broken when this guy [the Hullabalooer!] *came onto the broadcast scene—definitely one of the best of the best."*

—The Real Don Steele

On July 27, 1953, a ceasefire stopped the fighting in Korea. With the conflict winding down, I enlisted in the Air Force right out of high school and was sent to Parks Air Force Base near San Francisco for basic training.

The audio-ambition portion of my life was about to have its volume turned up!

Amplified by my highly successful high school career as a gifted drummer, the military soon learned that I could hear the "decided differences" in Morse Code symbols and could match the right ones together perfectly. *So,* my Air Force career flew south in a hurry—literally (but not figuratively!) to Biloxi, Mississippi, to the Air Force's Accelerated Code School.

-.- / .-. / .-.. / .-
Dah-di-dah, Di-dah-dit, Di-dah-di-dit, Di-dah
(Morse Code for KRLA)

After seven months of advanced training, I was one of just three candidates out of 350 who could type incoming code correctly at nearly seventy-five words per minute—all while carrying on a separate conversation with my instructor.

My ear moved me even further from home. The Air Force found a highly classified position for me at Nouasseur Air Force Base in Casablanca, French Morocco, North Africa. My job was to receive and transmit highly secret crypto-coded messages to others on our North African network.

One day, the officer of our section came to me and told me I actually needed to *slow down* my transmissions, because *someone* in Rabat, French Morocco, was having trouble understanding them. Several months later, we learned that this *someone* was arrested as a foreign spy!

I beat a good rhythm with my Morse Code, but I was about to up my tempo!
P.S. Yes, that's me, third from left!

A Spell Is Cast

I was a wizard on that J-38 "straight key" for my code transmissions, but the real *key* that I wanted to open my life's work with was radio.

And we had an Armed Forces Radio station at Nouasseur.

I was about to learn a lot about radio in a hurry. I would quickly learn that the magic of "being in the right place at the right time" casts a serious spell in this business. I would also learn that the magic of "being straightforward and not being afraid to ask for what you want" casts a spell of its own.

And I would learn that the absolute fire-breathing voodoo of improvisation can vex, hex, jinx, or charm the whole thing!

And *improvisation* would become *my* magic word.

I walked right into the station on the base and asked the sergeant in charge just *how* I could get on the air and become an announcer.

The magic was electric—a spell was weaving through the wavelengths.

One of their evening announcers, it seems, had *just* rotated back to the States following his tour of duty.

"You can go on *tonight*," the sergeant told me. "You can do our fifteen-minute classical music show. It starts at eighteen hundred hours."

This little spell was becoming an exorcism! It had worked a tad more rapidly than I'd anticipated.

I told him I had never actually *been* on the air before and wouldn't know what to do or say.

"Don't worry," he said. "All the music is lined up and I'll give you a script for the whole show. All you need to do is go back to the barracks and rehearse until we go on the air."

On the air!

There were a couple of things he didn't mention though. The first was that this was the base commander's favorite nightly radio show...

I took the script back to my barracks. A spooky sorcery was taking hold!

The other thing he'd neglected to mention was the inclusion of foreign language "inserts" throughout the show. The program *this* night was to feature classical passages written in German— a language I had never spoken and couldn't understand or pronounce.

I told myself that I had two choices: (1) return the script to the station and give up my life's ambition of being on the radio, or (2) go into the station that evening and fake it.

My career began when I chose the latter.

On the Air

1800 hours...

I turn on my mic...

The base commander, Brigadier General James L. Jackson, tuned in. On this particular night, he was sharing his fifteen-minute daily dose of musical bliss with a high-ranking European officer who was his houseguest. An officer who spoke German...

The musical intro went well.

My opening remarks went well.

Then I came to the German section: I was seeing names, words, and phrases I had never even *thought* about pronouncing before. So I began to *creatively manipulate* the long German phrases. It was a deft speaking in tongues. I was bold. I was confident. *I was ridiculous!*

"I hope you enjoyed the fruitive *Glosternorman* Fugue by Stephan von *Strastengorber* played by the *Trastorfort* Symphony Orchestra of Stuttgart, Germany!"

The speed of light—and sound—were once again proven as physical laws, as the station's phone lines lit up *immediately* with calls coming in from all over French Morocco and the Mediterranean. Listeners were laughing out loud.

This poor airman who was working as the station's operator was fielding the calls as best he could, but he really had no idea how to handle it.

Throughout North Africa, thousands speak German, French, Spanish, and Italian fluently; none of them could understand a word *I* was saying.

One of the "already lined up" pieces of music would finish.

"That was the *Der Firsten Storgernun* sonata," I would say, "with the contrasting tempo and style performed on the *Deutzenfoyermin* violin."

The operator was buried! He told some of the callers that this was a "pilot" for a new comedy show. Others expressed a deeper interest, admitting that they had never exactly listened *so intently* to our classical music show before.

"Who is this guy and where did he come from?" some were asking.

"This guy has no clue!" others were saying. "But we love it!"

"Is this guy gonna be doing this every night?"

Finally the airman/operator rushed into the studio, hollering at me, "I don't know what you're doing...but do *more* of it!"

"And now the beautiful music of Alfred Dormenorfen..."

Someone else was enjoying the show, too—General Jackson's guest! And the commander also got word of all the phone calls and the sudden windfall of listeners. This wacky airman had brutalized his show, but we were getting an audience!

The calls were nonstop. It was an eternal fifteen minutes!

Within a few nights, the program was officially mine.

I was *on the air*!

Dave Hull's One Simple Theory

From then on, the phones never stopped ringing. They'd light up almost any time I'd say *anything*. We'd get calls from all over North Africa, from Rabat and Marrakesh—wherever our troops were. It was kind of like an early version of Adrian Cronauer's wild aural outreach in *Good Morning, Vietnam*!

I had three favorite songs in 1953
when I was in Casablanca, and they all hit #1:
"Vaya Con Dios" by Les Paul and Mary Ford,
"You, You, You" by the Ames Brothers,
and "Have You Heard?" by Joni James.

In 1954, I really liked two #1 hits:
"Little Things Mean a Lot" by Kitty Kallen
and "Oh My Papa" by Eddie Fisher.

In 1955, my fav was another #1:
"Sixteen Tons" by Tennessee Ernie Ford.

It was at this juncture that I paused a little to reflect. I had already learned about radio's "right place at the right time" and "being straightforward" magic. But now I saw the development of something else that would stay with me throughout my entire radio career: I called it "Dave Hull's One Simple Theory."

It's a basic and gritty theory that says: *You take whatever is thrown at you and you make the most of it!*

I took what I was given here in Casablanca—*on the air*—and had fun with it. I learned quickly that "making stuff up" could please the listeners, even if they knew darn well it wasn't the truth. It was all about the *presentation*!

I would rely on my One Simple Theory often.

Deutzenfoyer!!

The Commander Speaks

A few weeks later, someone was needed to do an on-air interview with a high-ranking U.S. official from the Department of Defense: Assistant Secretary Franklin G. Floete.

I volunteered.

Airman Hull with the Assistant Secretary of Defense, in an interview transmitted all over North Africa, talking about our defenses in the region. It was *big*!

And according to Secretary Floete himself, our interview was the best he experienced throughout his European Tour. He even mentioned this fact in a subsequent interview in the worldwide military journal *Stars and Stripes*.

That word got back to General Jackson, too.

The general called the station and asked to speak with Airman Hull. Lieutenant Andrew Gary was the station's officer in charge, and he summoned me *at once*.

(Lieutenant Gary was quite a guy. Later, he would write my mother telling her he had "never heard anyone like me on the air who did nothing 'by the book'...but it worked." He also offered to find me a position at a major radio station in South Carolina following my discharge *and* enroll me in college at his alma mater—all at his expense—so I could finish my education and support myself at the same time. It was an offer that I didn't accept, but to this day I appreciate his generosity.)

Well, when Lt. Gary summoned me, I was on top of Madouna Hill, the highest point on the base, deciphering code. He dispatched a vehicle—*and* a sergeant with five stripes on his sleeve—to come get me.

My two-striped stock really soared when Assistant Defense Secretary Franklin G. Floete raved about my interview with him.

"The commander wants to speak to you in his office!" the sergeant shouted to me as he drove up. He was in a staff car from the motor pool and didn't seem happy at all that *he,* with his five stripes, had to drive *me,* with only two stripes, back to the commander.

The word of the *summoning* spread fast and everyone at the station was convinced that this was the end of my short but *impactful* career.

We got to General Jackson's office and a staff sergeant told me to present myself at attention.

"Airman Hull reporting as ordered, Sir!"

"At ease...relax...have a seat."

I was *a bit* surprised.

"I have an idea!" he told me.

Hmmmm...

His broadcast-brainchild was to create a program called *The Commander Speaks!* which would follow my show each night. He was all excited to hear my thoughts.

The Commander Speaks!

Now, as I mentioned, I've only got two stripes on *my* sleeve and *he* has a star on his shoulder. (Accessorizing your wardrobe *really* matters in the military!)

"What a great idea, Sir!" was my enthusiastic—and very quick—response.

"Does the radio station have a studio where I could record the show every day?" he asked, gearing up to be *on the air.*

I told him that it wouldn't even be necessary to leave his office—*I* would bring the recording equipment to *him*!

Some of the other guys at the station were eager to help set up the general's recording equipment, but when they found out how heavy and bulky the mixers, tape recorders, microphones, and speakers were (especially in those days!)—the daily chore became all mine.

But it paid off. General Jackson had my critical Air Force Secret Code designation changed from a *highly classified crypto-code radio operator* to the more fun-loving and career-building classification of Air Force Special Services. I would now be working at the radio station full-time*!*

And I would learn more about that magic in the media. This time the magic would be seen in its *power.*

I was thrilled to go from crypto-code radio operator to full-time radio *personality*!

A Hot Story

> Q: *"What's the weather like out there?"*
> A: *"It's hot. Damn hot! Real hot!*
> *Hottest thing is my shorts—I could cook things in it.*
> *A little crotch-pot cooking."*
> Q: *"Well, can you tell me what it feels like?"*
> A: *"Fool, it's hot! I told you again!*
> *Were you born on the sun? It's damn hot!"*
>
> —Adrian Cronauer asking Roosevelt E. Roosevelt
> about the weather in *Good Morning, Vietnam*

Summer in the Sahara Desert is everything that it sounds like it would be—and more! It's the *tepid* equivalent of winter in Antarctica.

> The biggest scorcher ever noted was on September 13, 1922, in El Azizia (also known as Al 'Aziziyah), Libya, when the mercury hit 136 degrees Fahrenheit. El Azizia is near the Sahara desert, so it's no wonder the place gets so hot. Temperatures have likely gotten even hotter in the actual desert, but weather stations aren't there to record it.
>
> —The *official* word on summer in the Sahara

Those temperatures that could "likely" get hotter than the official 136 degrees *did*. It was over 140 when the *slight issue* of the enlisted men's swimming pool being "out of service" began to heat up.

The pool had become infected and had been shut down for days and days of cleaning.

Conjuring up some of that "being straightforward and not being afraid to ask for what you want" magic, I informed General Jackson that the NCO swimming pool was currently inaccessible, and that the enlisted men—like *myself*—were suffering greatly. I suggested that we could and should write a program about a "stepped-up campaign" to get the pool operational again.

The commander certainly didn't want to infuriate his NCO corps! Morale in the military is so important, and heat like this—*like the core of the sun!*—can make tempers short. So the general decided to visit the Officer's Club to speak to his fellow officers about inviting the enlisted men to use *their* pool a couple days a week during the heat wave. And he asked me to put some thoughts about this down on paper while he was gone.

Perfect! No problem!

It was while I was using the office's old Underwood typewriter that I suddenly realized that *I* had become *The Commander Speaking*. The morale of thousands of men under General Jackson's command could and would be affected here. The base newspaper would cover the *ongoing situation* over the weeks while the cleaning work was being done.

This was power!

Respect and praise marched in for the general—a respect and praise that would last.

And, yes, *I* had become *The Commander Speaking*!

Some Magical Connections

One of the other ways that the radio magic of "being in the right place at the right time" would wield its witchery was seen in my relationship with an airman named Jim Washburne. Jim worked at the station with me and was the son of "Country" Washburne, the singer/songwriter who wrote the monster worldwide hit for Jim Reeves, "One Dozen Roses."

> *"Give me one dozen roses,*
> *Put my heart in beside them,*
> *Send them to the one I love…"*

That little song put a fair amount of royalties into the Washburnes' pockets and bought them a huge home in the high-rent district of Balboa Island near Newport Beach, California.

"Country" would go on to have an incredible career with Spike Jones, Ted Weems, and others.

Jim would later play an important part in *my* career—especially at KRLA.

One other spark of magic would zap me over in Africa, and it had nothing to do with radio. The *enchantment* of love was beginning to creep into my young life.

It was the early 1950s and servicemen's recreational facilities were very limited on the base. Many of the young airmen—including me—were just a few years older than the high school seniors who hung out at the civilian's club on the base (children of on-base civilian employees). We young guys would fit right in there!

If we could get in…

To get in, you had to be invited by a member. We didn't exactly have that kind of formal invite, so we sort of *snuck* into the club and became fast friends with several of the senior girls.

I got quite interested in one very popular girl whose father headed the Corps of Engineers. She was popular because she could drink a six-pack of beer in the time it took the guys to drink just two cans. At the time, her talent was pretty darn impressive!

But we were all so young. Alcohol wasn't a problem then. It wasn't until she returned to the States—and we got married—that I learned how damaging it could be.

A Hard-Won Triumph

My return home was coming quick but I extended my tour of duty in Casablanca by an extra six months. I had a reason—a few, actually.

I *loved* working at the station. That was my main reason.

I was also experiencing that love of a different kind with my girlfriend.

Plus, staying over for six months allowed me to choose any Stateside base I wanted for my final ten months in the Air Force. I chose March Air Force Base, just outside of Riverside, California, so that I could be near my family in Alhambra for the remainder of my service.

An additional bonus was that extending my overseas tour of duty allowed me to have my new car shipped back to the States at no expense to me! While in Casablanca, I had bought a brand-new 1955 Triumph TR-2 sports car.

The deal started off well, but ultimately the car salesmen in Casablanca are closer to the seedy bar patrons at Rick's than, say, slick showmen like Ralph Williams or Cal Worthington. Now, Ralph and Cal may have done some *creative* deals in their time, but they weren't even in the same league as the *merchant* who held the keys to my Triumph!

I paid cash; fifteen hundred dollars for that little TR-2. They were selling for about seventeen hundred elsewhere, but I flashed the green and we worked out a good deal.

However, when I went to pick up the car, the salesman *informed me* of a minor amendment to our arrangement.

"It's going to cost you another thousand dollars," he said, "for the necessary paperwork to be able to get your car shipped to America."

Here's looking at you, kid...

"Wait a minute," I told him. "I've already paid for this car!"

"But you *need* this paperwork," he said, holding a footlong brown form of some kind, written all in Arabic, reminding me a little too much of Captain Louis Renault working out his "beautiful friendship" with Bogie.

Well, I made a strategic business decision right there on the spot. I thumbed my nose at him.

I got in the car.

I kept the car.

It was *my* car!

And I made the right decision—at least for now. When I put the Triumph on the boat, paperwork didn't matter. I was a serviceman with extended time overseas, so that means I had foreign-service privileges. Whatever I had possession of was going home with me—and the U.S. government was paying for it!

But the shipping vessel had to go through the Mediterranean and back out the Straits of Gibraltar, picking up other cars from other servicemen in Italy, Sicily, Germany, England, and all kinds of other places.

It would be a while before I'd see my car.

I had been given three months of leave, though, so I could wait—no problem.

A friend of mine at the radio station was from Jamaica, New York, on Long Island. His parents were very attached to their only child; his room was vacant while he was overseas. So he arranged for me to stay there.

Perfect!

They welcomed me into their home and didn't charge me a thing. All I had to do was to wait for that car.

The wait wound up being about a month.

I was grateful for their hospitality, but I wouldn't advise anyone to ever go to Jamaica, New York—unless, of course, you're waiting for a car to arrive from North Africa without any real paperwork that would actually make the thing legal.

Okay, I finally get *The Call*!

"Your car has arrived!"

It was my version of a New York minute—out the door, across busy streets, running down those grimy subway station stairs, through the turnstile, and onto that port-bound train.

At the harbor office, I was shown a map of my car's *projected* location. The place was the size of the Great Barrier Reef—tens of thousands of cars parked on *hundreds* of square miles. The map was scrutinized to provide me a carefully calculated geographical estimate of where my little car *might* be stationed.

"It looks like it's about three or four miles from the Port Authority office here," I was officially and officiously informed.

After walking for forty-five minutes and looking at the rows and rows and rows of cars, I figured I'd find Amelia Earhart before I found the Triumph. Much to my surprise, the TR-2 materialized first! And it was absolutely filthy—*with four absolutely flat tires.*

So...I turned around and started the *long walk back* to the Port Authority office, keeping my eye out for Amelia's Lockheed Electra, just in case.

After finally coming full circle, and catching my breath to explain that I couldn't drive the car back to the office because the tires were a hundred percent dead, the attendant in the office posed a question to me:

"Do you have the paperwork showing ownership of the vehicle?"

I immediately thought back to my enterprising friend in Casablanca with that long, brown, Arabic-official scroll.

"I left it in the glove compartment," I told him, sweating a bit, now in more ways than one.

He noticed that my shipping information stated that I was a returning serviceman. No problem. He just stamped my paperwork "CLEARED" and told me he'd get me a ride to the car with a tow truck he'd call. They'd fill all of my tires and show me the way out of the motor-city maze.

With nice, newly rounded tires, a month's worth of trans-Atlantic dirt on my sports car, and directions to U.S. 40 (later to become I-70), I was on my way.

Buckeye Banishment

I swung back through Jamaica, said good-bye to my friend's folks, and grabbed my belongings—just a duffel bag that I stuffed into the car, along with a few ham and cheese sandwiches—and headed west.

I was now on U.S. 40, making great time, when I stopped in Zanesville, Ohio, for gas.

Zanesville is the home of the famous "Y-Bridge," a bridge that spans the crossing where the Licking and Muskingum Rivers come together. Well, it may have been famous, but *I'd* never heard of it, so I asked the gas station attendant (they actually had attendants in those days who would pump your gas and even *talk* to you!) how I could get back on the road heading west. He said to take the bridge just up ahead and "turn left in the middle of it."

Turn left in the middle of the bridge?!

I figured he was a wise guy who didn't like Californians.

The car was all gassed up, so I hit the bridge and there was the sign: Zanesville, one way; Los Angeles and other points west, the other way. The attendant was right—you *can* turn in the middle of the bridge!

I was on the road again!

For a while.

Just east of Columbus, I noticed red lights in my mirror. My progress was going to be slowed a little, I figured.

I pulled over and was greeted by an Ohio State Trooper who found my hand-painted license plate "interesting." I explained that I was a returning serviceman and that's the way things are done in North Africa. They paint it on at the port and that becomes the number that's stamped on the car.

And now it's stamped on my registration.

This hand-painted number...

The officer was bewildered. He thought he had a good one. He thought he had a live one—some simple young punk he could roust for having a poor excuse for a phony plate—not this nasty nest of bureaucratic baffling he'd just stepped into.

I then produced my cleared Port Authority paperwork and told him—pleasantly, yet in a *businesslike* manner—that according to officials there, I had thirty days to secure my proper licensing in my home state of California.

He seemed not to like my extensive legal knowledge. He clenched his teeth and told me to "get the hell out of Ohio"—which I did. In fact, he followed me all the way to the Indiana state line. I made Missouri in record time and it was a nonstop run to the coast.

California here I come...

A New (Mexico) Plan

Right back where I started from...

This was perfect. I'd be at March Air Force Base, in my own backyard, until my service career officially culminated.

After my three months of leave, I reported to the base on a Saturday morning and was told by the Officer of the Day that I had orders to report *immediately* to my "new duty station" at Walker Air Force Base in Roswell, New Mexico! I would be taking over as editor of the base newspaper, there.

This wasn't in the plan at all.

On top of the relocation issue—as I told the officer—I had never edited a newspaper in my life!

This really didn't produce much empathy in him.

"That's how the military works," the officer responded. "They *never* send you where you *ought* to go!"

But he did have a little good news—I had *another* thirty days of leave! That's not bad. A total of a hundred and twenty days off, and I was still getting paid.

I turned right around and headed back home. Mom met me at the door and freaked out, thinking I must be in trouble.

She asked what had happened. I told her I was becoming a "New Mexican."

Facing the Atomic Blast

I would soon discover one nice thing about having to report to the Land of Enchantment: in those days you could register a vehicle there without previous registration or even a bill of sale. Nobody would need to see my footlong brown registration papers written all in Arabic, after all.

What people *would* need to see very soon, however, was an Air Force newspaper outside of Roswell, New Mexico, edited by *me.* Pecking away at that old Underwood at the base in Casablanca, lobbying for the rapid removal of fungus in a swimming pool was one thing—this was sure to be a bit more intense.

The newspaper was called the *Atomic Blast,* as the first test of an atom bomb had occurred in New Mexico in 1945 and Walker had served as home base to the Enola Gay, the B-29 that planted its payload on Hiroshima. Plus, as everyone knew, aliens had landed in Roswell in 1947 and were still being held there for interrogation.

I wondered if all these slightly explosive things were an omen of what was in store for *me.*

Editing a newspaper was alien to me as I headed to Roswell to launch my career at the *Atomic Blast*!

What REALLY Landed in Roswell

LUCKY LAGER DANCE TIME AND OTHER ALIEN ENCOUNTERS

KGFL, KSWS: 1955–1956

RAAF Captures Flying Saucer On Ranch in Roswell Region
No Details of Flying Disk Are Revealed

The intelligence office of the 509th Bombardment group at Roswell Army Air Field announced at noon today, that the field has come into possession of a flying saucer.

—*Roswell Daily Record,* July 8, 1947

The *Roswell Daily Record* is a famous newspaper. Maybe not *quite* as famous as let's say, the *New York Times* or the *Washington Post,* but it was the journalistic juggernaut that broke *The Story*! In the annals and archives of extraterrestrial enthusiasts, its Pulitzer-potential status is inarguable.

It had been just eight short Earth-years since the *Record* had scooped the news world with their Page One declaration about the alien landing, so I figured its staff could teach me all I'd need to know in my new Perry White job as "Chief" of the *Atomic Blast*.

I was once again summoning that magic of "being in the right place at the right time" and "being straightforward and not afraid to ask for what you want."

Once I was settled into my barracks at Walker Air Force Base, I went into town—into greater Roswell. I found the address of the *Roswell Daily Record* building and banged on the door. The door—the portal into this print paradise—was a little less impressive than the entrance to the *Daily Planet's* globe-topped skyscraper at the corner of Fifth and Concord Lane in Metropolis. On top of that, it was Saturday and the rather *un*impressive door was locked.

But I could see one guy inside, working on a linotype machine. For all of you too young to remember the pre-computer dark ages, a linotype was a machine about as big as twelve pizza ovens, with a keyboard attached to it. One man would sit behind this thing and type newspaper copy, while hot-lead molds of his typed words were created.

So here's this guy running this mass of molten metal-infused machinery, trying to get out his weekend editions, and now I'm banging on his door.

He did a good job of ignoring me.

But I was persistent— and I think that *he* thought

I might have some copy for the edition he was working on—so he finally came to the door.

Straightforward, not afraid to ask for what I want...

I told him that I really needed to learn the newspaper business— *this weekend*. I explained in fine detail, which he may or may not have really wanted to hear, all about how the Air Force had appointed me editor of the *Atomic Blast* and how I needed to make sure I didn't bomb out on Monday.

"Hmmmm..." he considered, exhibiting surprising care and compassion. "You know, the same thing happened to me when I got *this* job. I had no idea what to do, either, until the publisher here took me under his wing years ago.

"Okay, there's a cot in the back room if you get tired; meantime, watch everything I do."

I did.

I watched him put the papers together from start to finish. He taught me how to write a *news* story with all of the important information in the lead paragraph. He taught me how to write a *feature* story, where all of the important information is at the end.

By the time my weekend watch was put to bed, he had taught me the basics of everything I needed to know. He even got me running the linotype machine *and* the printing press.

He was a grizzly old guy, but what a teacher!

And everything he showed me *worked*!

Within six months of my becoming editor, the *Atomic Blast* won the Eighth Air Force's "Newspaper of the Year" award! Of course, the *New York Times,* the *Los Angeles Times,* and the *Detroit Free Press* all won Pulitzers that year, but we were pretty darn proud of what we did at the *Blast*!

Take Me to Your Leader

As newspaper king, I felt not only like Perry White, but like Jimmy Olsen, William Hearst, and Gutenberg all rolled up into one brilliant ball of bylines and bullets.

I was even able to pass along some of what the grizzly guy at the *Roswell Daily Record* had done for me.

I had an enlisted man come to me—*Mr. Editor* me. He had a college degree and far more journalistic ability than I had, but he was of much lower rank.

He had been assigned to the paper as a sports reporter. I— *Mr. Editor* I—made him Sports Editor! I told him I would never micromanage him; he would be in charge of the entire Sports section—both its content and layout.

I told him it was his baby and to make us proud!

I always hated micromanagers and I wasn't about to become one myself.

So the newspaper thing was working. But radio still had my creative heart.

Roswell's most popular music station at the time was KGFL, and I'd been listening to it on the base. Well…listening to *some* of it. One of their personalities was *un*listenable! This guy was terrible!

He had no humor at all. *Zero!*

And he had a raspy, grating voice that made a fingernail-blackboard wail sound like Pavarotti.

I knew I could do a better job than him.

A *much* better job!

I called the station and spoke with the general manager, Walt Whitmore—who was also the station owner's son. I told him that I could fly air-wave circles around the guy he had on at night.

My proclamation was met by a few beats of silence.

"If you're so good," he finally said, "what are you doing in Roswell, New Mexico?"

He had a point.

But I explained about being stationed at Walker and told of my illustrious broadcasting career on Armed Forces Radio. And to prove I was better than his current guy, I offered to come in and record an audition tape.

So Whitmore invited me in the next morning and said he would have a studio all ready for me.

Once inside, I began recording my demo—making mistakes, cussing loudly, starting over, playing records, and reading the news. I took the finished tape into the manager and asked him to listen to it. He told me he didn't need to. He showed me the switch he'd thrown that let him hear everything that went on in that studio.

"And don't worry—your 'colorful language' isn't anything I haven't heard before," he reassured me.

He also admitted that I was right: I *was* better than that the guy with the nighttime slot. Whitmore fired him and hired me—I was *on the air* again, nine p.m. to midnight.

This being Roswell, Walt and I got to know one another. He did tell me—strictly in a news context, of course—that he had been there in '47. He had rushed to the alien crash scene that night, tape recorder in hand. Unfortunately, he didn't get the juicy "Take me to your leader" sound bite he'd hoped for.

But what he *did* get was a command by Air Force personnel to keep his mouth shut as to what he saw.

I was a star at the *Atomic Blast* and my voice filled the flickering Roswell skies.

Sunshine on My Deutschendorf

> After the intelligence officer here had inspected the instrument it was flown to higher headquarters.
>
> The intelligence office stated that no details of the saucer's construction or its appearance had been revealed.
>
> —*Roswell Daily Record,* July 8, 1947

So now my voice fills the Roswell night, I'm a shining supernova at the *Atomic Blast, and* I'm married.

In the short time between my daily duties at the base and my job at KGFL, I had been using most of my afternoons to telephone Dell, that attractive young gal I had left in Casablanca. Within two months of my return, she was back in the U.S. and we were wed in Front Royal, Virginia. We returned to Roswell and set up house off base.

On that now famous/infamous date of July 8, 1947, KGFL received Air Force Officer William Blanchard's first press release about the crash of the alien spacecraft. But things like that little ET encounter report didn't exactly have a "good beat that you could dance to." So by 1955, KGFL was rocking Roswell with Elvis Presley, "Fats" Domino, Pat Boone, Bill Haley and His Comets, the Platters, and other artists who would become legends and Rock and Roll Hall of Famers.

And I was always on the lookout for other new artists to "break."

I needed a steady supply of new records.

I knew about a record store down on Main Street in Roswell—but what I *didn't* know anything about was "payola." Luckily, the 1955 hinterland home of Roswell radio wasn't the 1958 New York power market of WABC where Alan Freed got busted and the "P" word was born.

He was busted, of course, for accepting *favors.*

And here I was, going down to the record store to ask for a *favor.*

I asked the owner for some freebees to play during my show. He said sure—so long as I gave the store an on-air plug. No problem!

It was innocent! And I'd okayed it with my boss, Whitmore.

As I got the new tunes, I'd keep the "hits" and throw away the "misses."

One day, a red-haired freckle-faced kid about twelve or thirteen came riding up to KGFL on his bike, asking for any old records we might have. Some of the staff were annoyed, but I told them to give the kid the misses, plus the cracked and the scratched hits. The kid seemed delighted.

Real delighted as a matter of fact.

Turns out we had fed platters and wax to a music-hungry freckled stray cat—and he started prowling back around week after week.

"The kid's back again!" the staff members would yell as he rolled in on that bike, his taste buds whetted for tunes. He became like a tow-headed mirage, materializing out of the desert heat!

I never really talked to the kid, but someone did find out his name—Henry John Deutschendorf. It was a hard handle, more suited to a member of European Parliament, or maybe a scientist who discovers asteroids. It wasn't exactly what you'd call a bright-eyed country kid with a smile and a passion for rock 'n' roll.

No wonder he changed it to "John Denver" a few years down the record-lined road.

Although I never officially met him later in life, I still thank him for relieving us of some of our trash—and just maybe the classic doo-wop, R & B, and rock beneath those scratches and pops helped influence his rocky mountain high and that sunshine on his shoulders.

UFO: Utterly-Out-of-Control Flying Object

> Mr. and Mrs. Dan Wilmot apparently were the only persons in Roswell who saw what they thought was a flying disk.
>
> They were sitting on their porch at 105 South Penn. last Wednesday night at about ten o'clock when a large glowing object zoomed out of the sky from the southeast, going in a northwesterly direction at a high rate of speed.
>
> —*Roswell Daily Record,* July 8, 1947

I may have *landed* in Roswell, but every day you're there you hear about stuff *flying*. And after all, I was an Airman in the Air Force.

I wanted to fly!

I always wanted to become a pilot. I wanted to be able to tell myself that I could take a plane up in the air and bring it down to the ground—*safely.*

I wanted to do a better job than the aliens, too. The "powers that be" have supposedly been studying *those* wrong-way drivers for going on seventy years now! Could you imagine if the same thing happened to me?! It would take them a lot more than seventy years to figure out what makes *me* tick!

Anyway, I called Roswell airport and asked if they had a flight school. They did. *Where do I sign up?!*

After about six weeks of supervised soaring through Roswell's little green men–laden skies, my instructor said to me, "You're on your own!"

I asked him what he meant.

"You've been flying this plane for two weeks now, essentially without my help," he explained. "It's time to put this plane down and let me out."

"Am I ready for this?!" I asked.

"You've been ready for a while," he told me. "I'll be watching from the runway. Everything will be fine!"

Oh boy!

We landed; *he* left.

I'm headed down the runway...I lift up. Now I'm going into my downwind leg. I'm on my final approach, and I look down and there he is. It's then that I truly realize: NO ONE is sitting next to me!

I put that plane down in a perfect three-point landing—it was beautiful. I had flown "solo" for the first time in my life.

"That was great!" my instructor told me. "But you should continue to practice landings for a few more weeks before you take my cross-country classes."

I took his advice.

Now, in those days, renting a single-engine Piper or Cessna was about forty-five dollars an hour—nothing like it is today. I decided to rent a plane one afternoon and shoot some landings.

It seemed like a great—and educational—idea.

At the time.

Again, there was no one sitting next to me. I was in charge! I was the pilot! *I was flying!*

I was also the one who forgot to check for other aircraft while waiting to take off.

At Roswell Airport, you didn't have radio communication. This was 1955, and in Roswell, at least, you worked simply on handheld lights. When you shot landings, you were on your own. You just kept your eyes open.

I was ready for my solo liftoff, but I had only turned my plane halfway around—it was halfway too little to clear aircraft taking off from other runways. I *failed to notice* the DC-3 leaving for Albuquerque. It was hard to miss, but I managed it. As my plane raced forward for takeoff, I couldn't believe what I was seeing. The big, dual-engine passenger plane crossed directly in my path, no more than five hundred feet away!

I got up in the air and looked down at the control tower. They had a red light on me, flashing. Wherever my plane went, they followed me with that flashing light—that *powerful* light. Day or night, you could see it. You could probably have seen it on the Moon!

It has a very specific meaning: *Return at once!*

I did.

When I landed, a jeep appeared hauling a lighted sign that flashed the order: *FOLLOW ME.*

I did.

I was taken to the tower where an FAA man was waiting. He wasn't happy. He was, in fact, furious!

"Give me your license!" he yelled.

I did.

He held it, looking at it. He was just fuming! It was an awkward few minutes. I was thinking that those aliens probably didn't even *have* a license. I at least had something on *them*.

"If I *ever* see anything like that from you again," he said, shaking as he handed back my license, "I'll tear this in half!"

Well, that wasn't going to happen. I never flew again.

Besides, radio was always where my heart was...

I Found My Thrill

I had certainly made an impression on the FAA guy and that poor pilot of the DC-3, but on the brighter side of things, I was also making an impression in the Roswell radio market.

At KGFL, I continued what I'd been doing at Armed Forces Radio—having fun. And I built upon it. I saw how listeners related to enjoying the guy who is enjoying what he's doing.

I also understood that I wasn't cut out in any way for objective-reporting radio. Unfortunately, that was a revelation *not* shared by the sports director at KGFL.

He asked me to work a basketball game one night with him at the nearby college, New Mexico Military Institute (NMMI); his regular color man couldn't make it.

During the course of the game, I must have been channeling the Celtics' Johnny Most!

> **Dave:** *He's going the length of the court! And he scores!!!*
> *What an incredible reverse lay-up!!! It's amazing*
> *to see a young player make a shot like that!!!*

"You did great!" the sports director told me after the game. "Why don't you be my color man next season?!"

I told him I would think about it. But I had already made up my mind. I wanted to play Fats Domino records! I wanted to get *my* thrill on Blueberry Hill, not get bored with scores and stats.

For one very upsetting week, he tried to convince me to give up being a DJ; but I kept blocking his shots. I was much more suited for humor than for fielding facts.

Then he charged into a fast break with the NMMI:

> *Now he's speaking with the college athletic department!*
> *He goes up for a shot: "How 'bout a contract?!"*
> *In and out—heartbrrrreeeak!*
> *He goes for a three-point play: "I can bring on the rookie as my color man!"*
> *It ricochets off the rim—but he gets the rebound!!!*
> *The terms are being set...He charges in for lay-up!*
> *IT'S GOOD!*
> *"The contract is ready!" he tells me.*
> *The crowd goes wild!*
> *<TWEEEEEET!>*
> *Stop the play!*
> *Time out!*
> *Personal foul!*

I told him and the school to forget it. This game was over. I wanted to play rock 'n' roll and I wasn't gonna report their sports or anybody else's!

I rebounded my own shot and inbounded my career. I was again on a breakaway toward *my* goal!

The sports guy was singing a Fats Domino tune of his own: *"Ain't That a Shame..."*

The A-Rod of the Desert

After being on the air at KGFL for several months, things improved even further—for me *and* for the discerning music and radio lovers of Roswell, New Mexico.

In 1956,
I and the desert jackrabbits who made up
the majority of my listening audience in Roswell
had two favorite tunes.

One was the #1 hit by Gogi Grant,
"The Wayward Wind."
The other was the Platters' #1,
"The Great Pretender."

One day after one of my more insane shows, I received a call from John Barnett, the owner of KGFL's cross-town rival, KSWS radio and television.

"I want to hire you over here at KSWS radio!" he said. "I'm prepared to pay you the highest salary in the history of Roswell, New Mexico, radio! Would you like to come and talk to me?"

Are you kidding? *Of course* I wanted to meet with him. This was big!

The station's offer was to give me $98.50 a week to take over the nightly show, *Lucky Lager Dance Time*!

Well, I couldn't pass up the best radio offer in Roswell, New Mexico's history, now could I? And I would immediately become the highest paid *radio personality* in Roswell's history. I was kind of like Alex Rodriguez—the "A-Rod" of the desert airwaves!

As I settled into the job at KSWS, another important part of the *warmth* of radio touched me: the interaction you have with the other personalities—how so many of them connect with you and you with them. And how, throughout your career, you cross paths with some of them over and over. *And* how you become close to others of them, but never see them again once *things change* at a station.

Those constant changes are a big part of radio that *doesn't* change.

At KSWS I met Earl Vandervort. He was an announcer with one of the most beautiful voices I had ever heard on the air.

Earl became instrumental in my career—he gave me the confidence and drive to follow my talents as far as I could.

Earl had come to Roswell after being the voice of the Easter Sunrise Services on the Mutual Radio Network. He had one problem, though: he always drank heavily before his noon newscast. Of course, there *may* have been a deeper reason for this than just a taste for alcohol: the more he drank, the better he got!

When it was time for his on-air news segment, I would get him started with a musical opening and an introduction. Then I'd leave *my* studio and run down to *his*. I'd quietly slip inside and begin pulling his pages for him one by one. When he got to the weather—his final segment—I would leave quickly and get back up to my studio for his closing.

I remember so well his telling me not to stay any longer in Roswell than I had to.

"There are far better places to work, Dave," he would say.

And he was right.

Not long after his warm words of wisdom, I would leave for my first "big market" experience!

Earl would also leave KSWS and become the track announcer for Ruidoso Downs, the world-famous horseracing track, just seventy-four miles west of Roswell. Rumor has it he lasted only three days—or maybe it was just three *races*—before he was found drunk underneath the bleachers and fired.

I never did see him again. But I still thank him for believing in me so strongly and encouraging me to shoot further out into the stratosphere than Roswell, New Mexico.

It was just another bittersweet, inevitable part of radio—that part where constant change *never really changes.*

In September of 1956, my active duty in the Air Force came to an official end, released honorably as a staff sergeant.

My job was now official and singular. I was a "radio announcer"!

I was—and would be—*on the air* for nearly six decades.

The Hullabaloo Begins

FOLLOWING THE LITTLE GREEN MEN TO DAYTON

WONE: 1957–1960

Recently, Wright-Patterson AFB has become very well known among UFO researchers and theorists due to its connection with the Roswell incident of July 1947. This is one of the locations, alongside the Groom Lake/Area 51 installation in Nevada, where wreckage of a crashed UFO as well as alien bodies were shipped. Wreckage of the craft was shipped directly to Ohio aboard a B-29 after the mysterious crash and placed in the infamous Hangar 18.

—abovetopsecret.com

In 1981, a writer named Jean-Charles Fumoux wrote a book about it.

A researcher named Tommy Blann did a secret interview with a "Colonel X" about it.

In the 1960s, Senator Barry Goldwater—the man who lost to LBJ for president in 1964—was denied access and information from Wright-Patterson Air Force Base about it.

And that's where *I* was soon headed: to Dayton, Ohio, home of Wright-Patterson, Hangar 18, and Phase Two of the whole Roswell *incident*. I'd be on my way, fresh from Roswell, right behind the aliens!

I had been working my usual shift at KSWS one afternoon in late August, when Ron Woodyard, the owner of one of those "big market" stations—WONE in Dayton, Ohio—was listening to me as he passed through New Mexico, heading for a vacation in California.

He stopped at a pay phone in the summer desert heat and called the station. He may have been sweating out there in the dust and the sun, but he had something even more red-hot on his mind.

Our KSWS operator put his call straight through to me. You had very few "buffers" in those days—listeners could call a DJ just "to chat"!

"You're the funniest thing I've ever heard!" he told me. "And probably the most entertaining guy on radio in the entire Southwest! How'd you like to come and work for me at WONE in Dayton?"

He didn't have to add any more coins to that *hot line*; my answer came quick.

"How long will it take you to get to Dayton? I want you to take the afternoon show and the nighttime remote broadcast outside the city."

I told him I'd be in Ohio before *he* got back. "I've only got ten thousand jackrabbits listening to me out here—and most of them won't miss me at all!"

"I'll call my program director, George Dunlevy, and tell him to expect you," Ron said. "I'll hire you for two hundred a week."

Now we're getting somewhere, I thought. *Now we've hit the big time!*

The Hullabalooer Gets His Name

My trip to Dayton in my 1957 Chevy Bel Air included my wife, Dell, now pregnant with our first son, Mark, (our second son, Clark, would arrive a few years later), and our German Shepherd, Blitz—who nearly took the head off one of the gas station attendants who approached my window. Still, it was probably a lot better than the aliens' commute into the Buckeye State—all those poor little guys jammed together in the belly of that B-29!

But apparently my arrival generated some of that same *uneasiness*, at least in "ufologist" circles.

My old boss from KGFL in Roswell, Walt Whitmore, had already made some nervous news with his out-of-this-world reporting. And I stirred up some interplanetary pots with my jet-quick takeoff from Roswell. I left so fast most of those ten thousand hurried hares hadn't even realized I was gone yet.

When word of my Air Force career and my super-secret crypto-clearance got around, I noticed a lot of raised eyebrows and a few sideways glances around the station—I think they may have been checking for my "third eye" or antennae!

But the airwaves of WONE were the only ones I wanted to fly in. It didn't take me long to get into the swing of things there.

WONE–AM 980 was far and away the most popular music station in Southeastern Ohio, even before I got there. This was the late 1950s—an easy, white-wall-tire era. It was a *Happy Days* world with sock hops, dances, and personal appearances by daffy DJs and teen idols under jelly rolls and Pomade.

Radio and music was as big and as wild-wide as the cars out on the new interstates. Imagine a single year giving pure American culture "All Shook Up" by Elvis, "Whole Lotta Shakin' Goin' On" by Jerry Lee, "Wake Up Little Susie" by the Everly Brothers, *and* the 1957 Chevy Bel Air! The next year, the new '58 Buick would have more chrome on it than any car ever produced before or since. It was hard not to be excited in those days!

Of course, it was *always* hard for *me* not to be excited!

I hadn't been in WONE's lineup for long when a woman traveling through Ohio sent me a hotel postcard:

I've just heard your show and I just can't stand all that hullabaloo on the air!

This brought me back to my dictionary days with my dad—when we'd look up words like "metamorphosis" and "end." I looked up "hullabaloo."

hul·la·ba·loo [huhl-*uh*-b*uh*-loo], noun
a tumultuous uproar; a clamorous noise or disturbance.

> **Dave:** How 'bout a horn, bub?! <Honk!>
> How 'bout a horn, huh? <Honk!>

Sounds have always meant more to me than words; because with sounds you can imagine more. If you hear the words, well, you've heard them—no imagination needed. But with sounds, you can make a listener imagine something entirely different.

Hullabaloo...

My mind immediately tuned in to my horn-tooting, banging of things, and crashing of stuff on the floor. This is *me*!

This woman may have thought she was making a *dig,* but what she was really doing was excavating gold! Just add two letters and spin:

Dave Hull the Hullabalooer!

Maybe my horns and crashes and laughs were a bit much for *her,* but a lot of people didn't buy those snazzy Chevys and mirror-shined Buicks, either. I understand a fair amount of Rambler station wagons and four-cylinder Renault Dauphines were sold, too. But the Chevy hardtops and the monster-bad Buicks had "the Hullabalooer" and rock 'n' roll cranked up on *their* AM tube radios. Those dull little sedans poking down the road were probably tuned to André Kostelanetz and Lawrence Welk!

My favorite songs in 1957
were the #1 hit "Tammy" by Debbie Reynolds
and the #1 hit by Pat Boone, "Love Letters in the Sand."

In 1958, I really liked a new group, the Everly Brothers,
and their 45 of "All I Have to Do Is Dream,"
as well as the Teddy Bears' "To Know Him Is To Love Him"
and the Platters #1 hit, "Twilight Time."

By the end of 1959, my favorites were
"Venus" by Frankie Avalon and
Santo & Johnny's "Sleep Walk"—
both made #1.

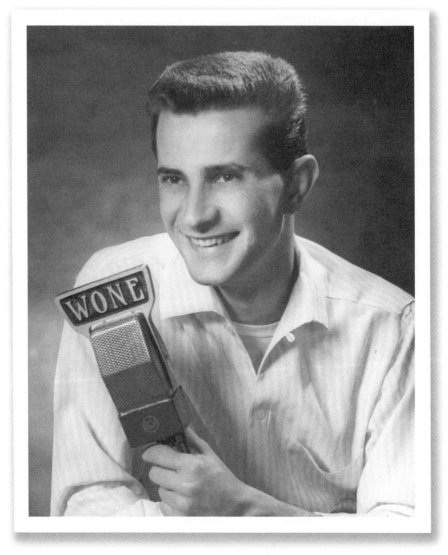

I hadn't been at WONE for long, when I got my "Hullabalooer" nickname from a listener suffering from uproarious tumult-osis and acute clamor-itis!

Fun Begets Fun (and Fortune!)

Sundown in Dayton took me to one of the largest furniture and appliance dealerships in Ohio: "Barnett's in Bellbrook." Each weeknight I went down there and broadcast live from the second floor, pitching the store's merchandise.

Teens came from everywhere to watch the show. The program also got to be a giant hit with young married couples just starting out, ready to furnish their new homes with Barnett's Frigidaires, Sylvanias, and plastic-coated green sectional sofas.

There I learned that if *I* could get enthused about a product, I could get *the listeners* enthused about that product. It was an extension of that "fun begets fun" principle that I had stumbled upon in Casablanca and Roswell.

And a lot of people got *enthused* about furniture and appliances in Dayton.

Dave Barnett would become a millionaire in a few short years.

After working Monday through Friday nights for a year, Barnett told me he would double my weekly salary of two hundred bucks with *another* two hundred—*in cash*—if I would broadcast from the store on both Saturdays and Sundays, too.

Four hundred dollars a week!

That was a *huge* amount of money in 1958, and WONE's sales manager, Al Frolich, went nuts! It was always difficult to sell weekend airtime in Southern Ohio during the cold, snowy winter months, but Barnett's in Bellbrook was rolling, as was Barnett's stake with WONE! Sales at the store soared to a point that trucks bringing in new

CLOSE COVER BEFORE STRIKING

7:45-9 P.M.   980 Club   3-6 P.M.
WONE Show
DAYTON, OHIO
WONE - 980 KC
DAVE HULL
Compliments Of
Baldwin 4-6501

EVANS BUYING SERVICE • DAYTON

Dave Barnett became a millionaire, and I all I got was this lousy matchbook!

appliances and furniture wouldn't even have time to be unloaded into the store showrooms. Buyers, their kids in tow, would flock to Bellbrook, climb aboard the trucks, and make their purchases right on the spot.

I was also learning to adapt to situations even better than I had in the past—Dave Hull's One Simple Theory. I had to keep everyone happy and entertained—the live crowd in front of me, the listening audience at home, the kids in both places, and the adults who would potentially be buying all this stuff!

I did it; and we all had fun.

The Crash of Caveman Cavey

Barnett's was big. I was big. WONE was big. Al Frolich was big.

And I was about to learn what being big can mean in terms of *exposure* and interaction with fans.

I was making good money, so I figured I'd cash in on a little of *stardom's* rewards by buying a new car—a 1958 Chevy convertible! One of my fans, a Bellbrook teenager who came *every* night to watch and listen to the show, offered to get together with a few of his friends and wash and polish my new car. *But* they would have to drive it to his house to do all that work.

On the surface, this was a wonderful and glorious example of fan worship and my true coming of age in that rare niche of the personality-elite.

But beneath that glittering surface, it was one of the worst—and easily most predictable—demonstrations of poor judgment since Henry produced the Edsel.

Sure, take it away...

The kid's name was John Cavey. An hour later, he came back to Barnett's.

Walking.

Without the car.

I was still on the air as he explained to me how they had scattered the transmission all over the turnpike while they were "trying to shift gears at high speed."

John did swear to me that he wasn't the one behind the wheel— or the gearshift—at the time of the explosion. And I believed him; he was the only one of the four boys to make the several-mile walk back from where the car now sat—amongst metal fragments that had once been my transmission—to give me the news.

The car had just six hundred miles on the odometer. It really hadn't even had time to get dirty. I had it towed back to the dealer and they replaced the transmission—after all, it *was* under warranty.

Years later, I passed through the mountain town of Frazier Park at the summit of California's Grapevine. There I was, at the top of the Tejon Pass, the gateway to Bakersfield and the great San Joaquin Valley. I was walking down the main drag, soaking up the local-village culture, and...I smelled pizza! I stopped and peered into the window of what was obviously the finest pizza establishment in Frazier Park.

I looked at the *chef* slinging dough and ladling sauce. *I know him!* I thought. I looked at the sign above the door: *Caveman Cavey's*!

John the Transmission Torturer!

I went right in and we talked—and he still insisted he wasn't the one behind the wheel that fateful night! But he did give me a discount on a large pizza, with the works.

"Man, He's Got a Machine Gun!"

Besides the kids and the newlyweds, I had plenty of other fans who were getting caught up in the hullabaloo at Barnett's. One bunch included the deputies at the Montgomery County Sheriff's Department.

"We come down to listen to *you*," one of them said. "You ought to come out into our field with *us*!"

I loved the idea!

My schedule at WONE was afternoons from 3:00 to 6:00, and then it was right to Barnett's in Bellbrook from 7:15 to 9:00. But I still felt like I needed a little something else.

And I would get it!

The deputies asked if I'd like to ride with Sergeant Conrad Munson, the shift commander. After a few weeks, I fell in love with the work and was sworn in as a deputy by then-Sheriff Bernard Keiter.

I definitely had something to do *now*. I'd work the graveyard shift with Munson from 11:00 p.m. to 7:00 a.m. I'd go to bed around 8:00 a.m., be up at 1:30 p.m., start my afternoon show, go to Barnett's until 9:00 p.m., and then head out to the sheriff's station. Every day, Monday through Friday.

For a year, I was *really* busy. I had some extra money to spend and some great stories to tell on the air, but I never did really *solve* a thing in the way of manhunts, murder, or mayhem!

But there *was* that one night...

Munson and I were driving out in the boonies in Montgomery County, when we heard this roar coming from a T-intersection about a half-mile ahead of us.

"Jesus, there's a stop sign up there and those cars are just barreling right through it!" Munson said. "I think we've got some racers, Dave!"

He was driving, so I asked him if he wanted me to hit the flashing red lights.

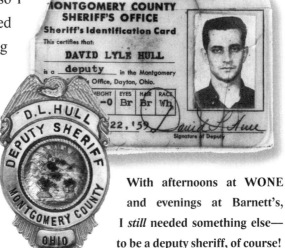

"No, no, we're gonna fall in behind," he said.

So we did. They were drag racing all right. We watched for a while and finally Munson said, "I think we got enough

With afternoons at WONE and evenings at Barnett's, I *still* needed something else— to be a deputy sheriff, of course!

on these guys. Hit the lights! *And* I want you to take the carbine out on the back seat."

Conrad had just bought a new carbine. It wasn't an AK-47 or anything, but it had a banana clip; it looked rather scary!

We got everyone pulled over and out of their vehicles. There were about eight or ten of them in four cars.

There were two of us.

I was back a ways, with this gun propped against my gut, when one guy started to give Conrad some lip. He went back to his car and opened his door, reaching for something...

"You stay right where you are!" Munson yelled. "I want to see your hands! C'mon up here, Dave, and level that gun on him!"

The mouthy guy looked up at me.

"Man, he's got a machine gun!" he yelled. "The guy's got a machine gun!"

None of them moved another muscle.

I never solved anything and I was never able to say to anyone "Go ahead, make my day" or "Just the facts, ma'am," but for that one night, I was "the guy with the machine gun"!

Closed Pockets and Open Ears

I may not have had a big, high-caliber weapon, but I *was* armed with double-barreled integrity when I experienced two more face-offs—right there in the studios of WONE. Two more encounters with mouthy guys engaged in a different kind of "stop-sign running"; guys who were *also* way over the line.

By 1959, I definitely knew what "payola" was; my visits to that little record store in Roswell were long over and the government crackdown that would short-circuit Alan Freed and others was already shocking the industry.

On November 24, 1959, the little standoffs I had at WONE made the *Dayton Daily News:*

Dayton DJ Offered 'Payola'
Told the Guys to Get Out, WONE Spinner Says

A Dayton disc jockey today said he was offered "payola" to spin rock 'n' roll records in 1958 and again early this year.

"But I've never taken a dime," Dave Hull of WONE declared. He was one of 11 local disc jockeys queried who admitted being approached...

"I told the guys to get out," he declared.

DJ-ing is all fun and games until someone offers you payola...

I had been on the air in Dayton for three years. Along with everything else I'd been doing, I'd become the program director for WONE's sister station, WONE-FM. I was learning the industry more and more. I would also learn that you never know just who might be out there listening.

Ron Woodyard had been listening in Roswell—along with those ten thousand jackrabbits—when he gave me the opportunity to come to Ohio. That woman in the hotel room was listening when she backhandedly gifted me with the title of "Hullabalooer."

In 1960, my third year at WONE, yet another set of influential and open ears would be listening to my "tumultuous uproars" and "clamorous noises."

I would divert from my spacemen-city tour. The probes into my alien affiliation would retract.

But I *would* be headed to the land of Mercurys, Meteors, and Galaxies...

DETROIT, DETROIT, DETROIT!!!

A DIRTY WHITE SHIRT
AND A HANDFUL OF MUDDY MONEY

WQTE, WTVN: 1960–1962

The set of *non*-rabbit ears that had been listening to me on WONE belonged to Ross Mulholland, part owner and manager of WQTE–AM 560—"Cutie Radio"—in Detroit. Ross was a brilliant radio guy and had been an outstanding morning man for many years before he got into the ownership end of things.

It was "déjà vu all over again."

As with Ron Woodyard back in Roswell, Mulholland had been listening to me on *his* way to a vacation in Florida.

Again my phone rang with one of those "right place at the right time" offers.

Mulholland told me that he was putting together a staff of "prominent people from around the country" for WQTE, and he asked *if I would consider being his morning man!*

"Are you nuts?!" I said. "Of course I'll consider it!"

Within weeks, my family and I packed and headed for what was then the fifth largest radio market in the country. Dayton had been the *thirty-sixth* largest. I was making a cosmic leap that left the aliens and the bunnies and even Barnett's Frigidaires far behind.

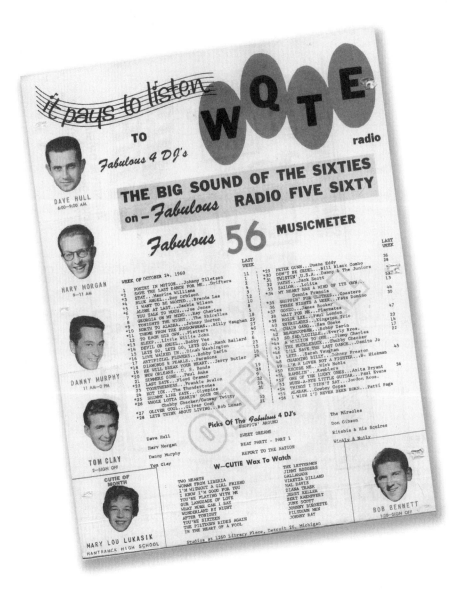

My cosmic leap to WQTE in Detroit—the fifth largest radio market in the country—put me on the expressway to fame and fabulousness!

I had two favorite songs at WQTE—
both #1 hits:
"Itsy Bitsy Teenie Weenie Yellow Polka Dot Bikini"
by Brian Hyland
and Marty Robbins' classic, "El Paso."

Highway to Hull

I would speedily find out that even Roswell with its jackrabbits and Dayton with its transmission-torturing kids were a bit more tolerant than the Motor City of "all that hullabaloo."

Detroit took me into the real urban world. It had freeways—*busy* freeways—which meant, yes, traffic reports on the radio. That just didn't happen in Roswell; no one cared if a litter of those long-eared furballs had a rear-ender in the tumbleweed lane at rush hour. And the biggest traffic problem I ever encountered in Dayton was my *own* new car sitting in the middle of the road with a scrap pile of shrapnel for a gearbox. But in Detroit, people *needed* to know the shifting state of their roads. And the main focus of frantic flow and grinding gridlock was the John Lodge Expressway

Now, on their own, traffic reports just aren't funny. But with some *hullabaloo*...

> *"We have some slowing on the John Lodge Expressway at Jefferson...*(cue sounds of fenders and bumpers falling off of cars)*...and, oh, looks like we have heavy traffic at Wyoming Avenue...*(more horrible metal clanks and bangs)*...Hey, watch out!...*(more debris and destruction)*..."*

The problem *was* that these cars I had falling apart all over southeastern Michigan's freeway system were *made* there in Detroit! I was twisting a very sensitive knife.

This was like demanding a well-done steak at the old Carl's Chop House. *And then putting ketchup on it!*

I learned a tough lesson in discretionary humor.

Things would get even messier.

During my short stint at WQTE (with DJs Tom Clay, left, and Harv Morgan, right), I learned about discretion in humor—and in "creative" advertising.

The Barren Demagnetized Desert-Land of Silence

The actual broadcast license for WQTE was issued to Monroe, Michigan—the home of Monroe Shock Absorbers. But the station also had studios located in downtown Detroit—where I worked—in the Earl B. Brink Building. (The Brink family was one of the owners of the station.)

By law, we were required to identify the station at the top and bottom of the hour, with our call sign and *legal* location—Monroe. However, we were allowed to mention Detroit by saying, "WQTE: Monroe-Detroit"—but with *equal* inflection and emphasis on both cities.

However, our production director—a brilliant young guy from Miami—had a different thought. He directed us to produce station breaks that made WQTE sound, well, a little more *important*:

> *"This is WQTE! With studios in the Earl B. Brink Building!*
> (Whisper) *Monroe...*
> (And now loudly) *DETROIT! DETROIT! DETROIT!"*

"Cutie Radio" had become the dominant rock 'n' roll force in the area, so naturally, we were a target for our competitors. A big enough target that they may have been inspired to file a complaint or two with the FCC over our *creative* station breaks. And FCC complaints are serious—the feds never fool around!

But *I* wouldn't have to face down any airwave Elliot Nesses.

The Edsel automobile lasted for three years in Detroit—from 1958 to 1960. I didn't make it that long.

On what began as a quiet Saturday morning, when the programming had been transferred to our Monroe studios for the weekend, the entire Detroit staff was let go. *Fired!*

I only lasted a third as long as the biggest bust in automotive history: a crazy car with a toilet seat for a grille!

Management even called in security guards to make sure that we all gathered our personal belongings and were on the Brink Building's express down-elevator *within ten minutes*!

"Wait! Wait just a second!" said our production guy to the impatient, rushing guards. "I need just a few more minutes! I have some personal stuff in the main control room!"

Well, he was in there for more than a few minutes. So I went in to see if I could help him. Those security guys were getting restless!

In the main control room, I found him running around, wielding a large, round mechanical device.

"What the hell are you doing?!" I asked him.

"I'm waving the magic wand!" he explained with an anxious quick-smile.

It was an electronic degausser—an *erasing device*. And he was "fencing" with this exorcising-Excalibur in front of all of the production elements—the jingles, the commercials, even the public service announcements.

The demons behind our dismissals were being burned.

The next morning at sign-on, I tuned into the station—*just to see*. And hear.

The national anthem played a few notes. Then there was a *pause*. Then a few more notes. Then another *pause*.

"One moment please…" came from the newly-hired announcer—one of our *replacements*.

He then tried to play a public service announcement—probably to take up some air time while the tech guys tried to figure out what was going wrong.

A few words of the PSA began. Then it all stopped—again. Another *pause*...

The "magic wand" had worked. Not one of the new announcers was heard *that* day— the station went into immediate auto-mode, and uninterrupted music played and played and played. Everything else had been sent to the barren demagnetized desert-land of silence.

There was also silence as I switched off the dial and began to pack things up at home. Silence as I thought about how

Before my untimely firing, I was a whiz on the reel-to-reel. But the station learned the hard way that the *real* power was in the "magic wand": the electronic deguasser!

those "constant changes" in radio had come a lot quicker this time. And silence in my family.

It was just a few days after WQTE's mass-firing that Dell decided to take our two young sons, Mark and Clark—our second son had been born just a few weeks earlier—to Arkansas to join her mother.

She never returned.

We divorced the following year.

A Hiring Hullabaloo

Change and being in that right place at that wonderfully right—and so often surprising—time. That was radio.

And so was laying bare your talent-soul to get a new job.

I had appointments to interview back in Dayton at WONE's old cross-town rival, WING, and in Baltimore at WBAL. My also-fired program director from "Cutie" had an interview in Washington, D.C., and one at WTVN in Columbus. I was heading to Ohio first; he was traveling back East. To save us both some time, travel, and most importantly *money,* he took *my* résumé and materials for my second interview to Baltimore and I took *his* stuff to Columbus.

I stopped off at WTVN on my way to Dayton and waited for someone I could give my old program director's application to. After a few minutes, Gene D'Angelo, the general manager, came out of his office and asked if I had been helped.

"Not yet..."

He asked who I was and what I wanted. I introduced myself as the former morning talent at WQTE in Detroit and explained my mission to drop off materials for another guy scheduled for *his* interview.

He looked at me.

"Hmmmm..."

He said *he* was looking for a morning man, and he seemed a lot more interested in hearing *my* tapes than the ones I had brought of my former PD.

He put my demo in his tape recorder as we stood there.

About two minutes into my demo tape, he began laughing out loud. He told me to take the tape and résumé—*now!*—and head to the Taft Hotel in downtown Columbus, owned by the prominent Ohio

Taft family. He said I'd find Bob Yeager, WTVN's program director, staying there.

"Tell him he can stop looking for a morning personality! I'm hiring *you* myself!"

It turned out that Gene D'Angelo's daughter is actress Beverly D'Angelo—Ellen Griswold in National Lampoon's *Vacation* movies with Chevy Chase.

When I got to the hotel room, I recognized the guy who answered the door: Jim Runyon, a popular disc jockey from Dayton who had worked for our competition when I was at WONE.

"Dave! Damn, it's good to see you!" said Jim. "What are you doing here?"

"Gene D'Angelo just hired me as your morning man."

I entered the room and he introduced me to Yeager, quickly telling him in bright, tube-glowing terms about how big I had been at WONE. I'd been worried about just showing up at the PD's room and telling him I was his new guy—that the station manager had gone over Yeager's head. But Runyon, whom Yeager had just hired, defused the tension. After *that* introduction, I figured I'd be appreciated no matter *who* hired me. Also, my hiring made their newly assembled staff complete.

I was also feeling a bit uncomfortable about the "right place at the right time" *stealing* of this job from my old buddy at WQTE. It was sort of a "Speak for yourself, John" type of thing! But then I found out that *he* got the job at the station where he dropped off *my* résumé in Baltimore! Such is the fine-tuning of radio!

No-Offense Nonsense

Jim Runyon would later join a station in Cleveland to become the announcer for "Chicken Man," a five-minute syndicated comedy vignette written and produced by Burt & Ernie Productions that would become a national hit. They actually wound up hiring me to do voices for a lot of funny stuff they wrote.

Jim Runyon (right) helped ease tensions after I (yes, that's me on the left!) accidentally stole my old PD's hoped-for spot at WTVN.

So I was now in Columbus, opening each day for WTVN–AM 610. I was feeling comfortable with each new day of experience.

Looking back, I probably hadn't been ready for that heavyweight morning slot at WQTE in Detroit. That may have been why I made the automotive faux pas with the crunches and crashes.

It wouldn't happen again.

Discretion in humor...

WTVN gave me the chance to really hone my style of having fun and creating nonsense out of the topical news stories of the day *without offending anyone!*

I became instrumental in producing the major on-air promotional stunts and gimmicks used all through the broadcast day. I learned to write copy for promotions developed for our commercial clients.

I was becoming a major-market personality.

WTVN quickly became the dominant market outlet, beating the area leader for the prior ten years, WCOL, by an audience of two-to-one.

A Two-Tune Affair

It was the early 1960s—still an age of *Father Knows Best, Ozzie and Harriet,* and *Leave It to Beaver* innocence.

The top ten records on WTVN's "Official Tunedex" from July 13, 1961, included "Dum Dum" by Brenda Lee, "Heart and Soul" by Jan and Dean, and Chubby Checker's "Let's Twist Again." Ozzie and Harriet's rising-star son, Ricky Nelson, came in at number thirty-six with the two-sided hit "Travelin' Man"/"Hello, Mary Lou."

The Tunedex also featured Vickie Hixson from West High School as the "Teen Queen of the Week"; my selection of "School Is Out" by Gary "U.S." Bonds in that week's "Personality Piks"; DJ Johnny Dollar as WTVN's "Music Man of the Week"; and the *good clean fun* of the station's "Pool Parties for Fun Under the Sun this Summer."

Johnny Dollar was a guy we could always bank on to deposit a lot of *moola* into the human interest and drama accounts of the station.

He gets a lot of credit for being the main asset in a touching and musical love story that floated out over the airwaves on AM 610.

One of the biggest songs of the day was "Johnny Angel" by Shelley Fabares; "Wake Up Little Susie" was a classic by the Everly Brothers from five years earlier. These two tunes became the soft weapons in a romantic duel between Dollar (whose real name was Jim Pidcock) and a girl he had been dating named Susie Lowery (her real name was, well, *Susie Lowery*).

Johnny Dollar (right, shown with teen idol Brian Hyland) was the leading man in a musical story that resulted in "Johnny Angel" overload at WTVN!

Johnny would begin each show with "Wake Up Little Susie." The lovely Miss Lowery would counter by getting every teenage girl she knew in Central Ohio to call in and repeatedly request "Johnny Angel"!

It was an on-air affair that wound up with the two of them *Going to the Chapel* and getting happily hitched—but not until all of us on the staff and the entire listening audience of WTVN had heard those two tunes a million times!

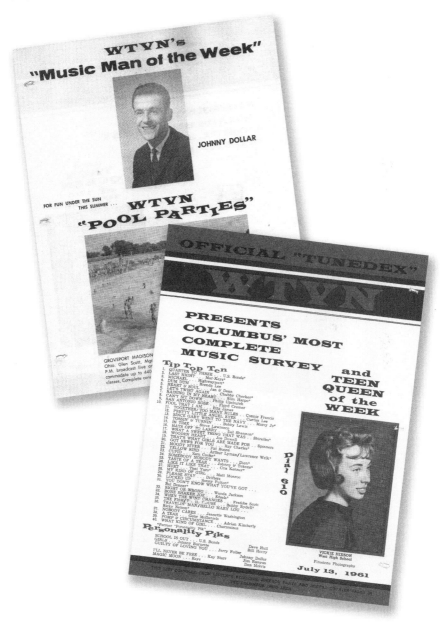

Crazy Rinkside Seats

These truly were the "happy days" that Richie, Joanie, and the Fonz would look back on in the seventies and eighties. Dances and sock hops were some of the most important events in teenagers' lives, with radio personalities—and their sound equipment!—in great demand, doing remote broadcasts and "spinning the platters" anywhere teenagers gathered.

One of my favorite performance hot spots was a roller skating rink in Mechanicsburg, Ohio. Thousands would flock there every week, even on the snowiest of nights, to dance for hours.

I was onstage there one night, pumping out the tunes, when this attractive young woman came through the doors and headed directly towards me. She wasn't there to dance. She came up the bandstand steps and told me she was there to promote her latest record. She had copies of the 45 in one hand and photographs of herself in the other.

She was going to do a short performance.

"I'll use the mic, but *turn it off…*" she told me.

The world of lip-synching had arrived.

"How should I introduce you?" I asked.

"America's foremost female singing star, Patsy Cline!"

It was the first I'd heard of her.

Cline brought the house down with "Crazy." She signed photos, thanked me, and left to monster applause from the teen dancers.

It was just two years later that her plane went down in that Tennessee countryside, killing her and veteran country music performers Cowboy Copas and Hawkshaw Hawkins.

Knight of the Slightly-Out-of-Round Table

There was *another* attractive woman—the most amazing I had ever seen—who came into my life while at WTVN.

It was a cold, wintry day and I was just leaving the studio. This *angel* was walking down the street towards me. I know I'm better at honking horns than creating poetry, but I really *have to say,* the morning sun was like a halo of light behind her!

As she got closer, I knew I had to speak to her.

"Hi! How are you?"

"Fine..."

...to which I cleverly and charmingly came back with: *"I should SAY you ARE!"*

She wouldn't speak to me again for nearly six months. She'd cross to the other side of the street when she saw me coming.

I guess my romantic lines were right up there with my poetry!

WTVN had its studios on the seventh floor of a big bank building. Everyone who worked in the building's offices did their banking there. And downstairs outside was this little food stand called Charlie's, where all the people would get their coffee, snacks, magazines, cigarettes, and everything.

Including my angel.

And like everyone else, she'd head down there with her cash and change handy to hit Charlie's.

On one particular day, it had been snowing. In Ohio, outside the doors to many public places is a steel grate about the size of a coffee table for you to wipe your feet on before going in; otherwise you could find yourself sprawled out on a slippery tile floor.

Here comes my angel—I'm coming the other way. I suddenly see her stumble and drop all of her money into this grate!

This is perfect!

I'll be a snowy Sir Galahad.

"Everybody, STOP!" I screamed, standing in the doorway with my hands up, like Superman facing down that speeding locomotive. "No one comes through this door! This woman has just lost *ALL* of her money!"

Well, all sorts of professional people were walking to and from their offices—doctors and lawyers, people who could appreciate this fiscal tragedy. I knew they were thinking, *Okay, that's cool. We'll wait.*

I opened the doors wide. Then I reached down and strained every muscle I had to get that heavy damned grate lifted up. And I was working this "construction project" with a white shirt on. And a tie— we had to wear ties at the station. I reached into the mire.

I plunged my hands into the muddy, snowy sludge and came out with a fistful of change. I dove in again: another fistful of change. Well, I did that over and over, and retrieved fistfuls of change after fistfuls of change from the long-buried treasure of others who had also fumbled their funds *over the past ten years!* It was a grimy, mushy Mother Lode! And I placed all the damp and dripping booty into the rapidly-expanding purse of my Guinevere.

By now my sleeves were cold-soaking wet. And filthy. But I kept going.

And nobody moved to get through the door. *Until* I was finished with my excavation.

"All right, gentlemen!" I finally said, dropping the mud-moat grate back into place. "Commence walking through!"

I actually received some polite applause and a few pats on the back.

But not from my angel.

She was really ticked! *She was embarrassed!* She goes into Charlie's, mortified and mucky, with a barrel-purse of soggy money that doesn't belong to her—all given to her by a filth-encrusted Sir Galahad whom she can't stand.

After the mud settled, I began to think. She'd *already* been crossing the street to avoid me. I couldn't imagine what she might do *now*!

But I didn't give up.

I'm going to find out about her; I'm going to find out her name, I thought.

I knew where she worked—I had seen her coming out of Galbreath Mortgage, a large mortgage company owned by John Galbreath, also the owner of the Pittsburgh Pirates.

Her name was Jeanette Morrison.

I began going up to her office and peering at her through the window—making funny faces.

She didn't like this at all. Her girlfriends would say, "Look, he's back!"

So one day, I went straight in to talk to her. I was direct, asking her what time she got off work and how she got home.

Five o'clock...and I always take the bus...

I told her that my car would be waiting for her out front at five o'clock and that she would *never* have to take a bus again!

At precisely five o'clock, she came out to my car. It was parked at the curb, with me gallantly standing by the open passenger door. I looked as dashing as a knight, as regal as a Viceroy.

Most of her coworkers were staring out their windows at the pomp and circumstance. Some of the shine of the magnificence dulled, however, as car horns began blaring, urging me to "move along."

Jeanette and I began dating within a few weeks and have been together ever since.

My favorite in 1961 was
"Runaway" by Del Shannon.

In 1962, I loved the all-time classic
from Ray Charles, "I Can't Stop Loving You,"
and the Elvis Presley hit
"Can't Help Falling In Love."

Very near and dear to my heart
was Ketty Lester's "Love Letters";
it became "our song" for
Jeanette and me!

Hit the Road, Jack

The day I *really* knew Jeanette was meant for me was one Saturday morning. I dropped by her apartment and stepped inside to the voice of Milton Cross on her radio, announcing the New York Metropolitan Opera. I had always enjoyed the classics, ever since attending a few Saturday Children's Concerts at the Los Angeles Philharmonic

Auditorium as a youngster. (Years later, our children would laugh at me for listening to classical music during the day and playing rock 'n' roll at night!) Here was a woman after *mi* own *cuoro*!

But when we *first* finally met, she had an attorney boyfriend by the name of Jack. He'd look out his office window and see us walking together. When I'd see *him*, I'd look up and wave.

And every morning on the air, I played one of Ray Charles' best: "Hit the Road Jack"!

For a while, Jack would still give her a ride to work sometimes. And the radio would be on...

"Are you listening, Jack?" I'd say on the air. "Jack, are you listening up there?"

"*...don't you come back no more, no more, no more, no more...*"

And shortly after that, he never did.

Off-the-Hook Lessons

There's always something new to learn in the radio biz.

The news director for WTVN was Al Crouch, an outstanding on-air journalist hired away from a giant news station in Houston. But he was physically a short man and had a Napoleonic complex.

One morning just after I finished my show, Crouch ran into the studio and screamed at me that a two-story home on the west side of Columbus was fully engulfed in flames with several children trapped inside! Columbus was sending every available piece of fire and police equipment to the scene.

This was big!

He *ordered* me to accompany him in the station's van. He told me he was going to teach me a few things about news reporting.

Radio stations had little mobile communication in 1961—and the invention of cell phones was a long way off. So reporters had to stop and use pay phones to call in their scoops.

As we neared the street where the home was on fire, Al stopped the van by every phone booth along the way and told me to get out and remove the mouthpieces from the receivers!

I did as I was told—unscrewing the bottoms of the receivers again and again, taking out the mouthpieces, and putting them in my pocket.

When we got to the *story,* we watched reporter after reporter run to a booth, lift the receiver off the hook, drop in their dimes and quarters, and then talk—and then *yell*—into the phone. But no one on that other end could hear them.

No one.

Then they'd realize they'd been had.

We had the key connections in my pocket. So we'd place one back into the closest phone and ring in our bulletins.

Al Crouch later received an award from the city for having the best local news coverage of the year.

It was another of those lessons I'd remember for the rest of my life.

And there were always more lessons—and *adventures.*

And more ways I could be propelled to the pinnacle of show-biz glamour!

WTVN had a contest, *Win a Day with a Disc Jockey*. Listeners had to write "Why I want to spend a day with a DJ." A female listener— a *not-so-attractive* female listener—wrote that she wanted to spend a day with *me* because I sounded like a "grease monkey" and she needed her car repaired. I guess all the horn honking, metal clanging, and large things crashing to the floor gave me that *image*.

And yes, she won.

So I spent an entire day with a slightly "full-figured" girl trying to fix her Rambler. And, yep, like my dad's old watch, when I was done, there were a few small parts left over.

Ladies and Gentlemen...
Mister Johnny Mathis!

WELCOME TO THE SOUTH IN THE SIXTIES

WVKO, WFLA: 1962–1963

WTVN was number one in the market—it had been the AM king of Columbus for *three years*. But in a *"What the...?!"* kind of move right up there with the creation of "New Coke," Zima clear beer, rabbit jerky, and emu burgers, the brass at WTVN decided to *change things*. To introduce *something new*. They replaced the hip sounds of artists like Del Shannon, the Shirelles, and Ray Charles—loved by all the teens in Central Ohio—with soft crooning, cooing, and out-of-vogue swing from the likes of "Old Blue Eyes," Bing, Rosemary Clooney, and the forties big bands.

The switch from wild to mild wasn't flying with most of AM 610's "Music Men," and I was one of the first defectors. I was quickly offered the position of morning personality and production director at WTVN's rival, WVKO.

A short time later, the station's operations director, Al Fiala, resigned to become Director of Programming at WICE in Providence,

Rhode Island, and I was promoted to *that* position. I was growing professionally.

I was able to institute a completely new sound on the air in both news and programming, by hiring better personnel from other stations in the market and adding several popular recording artists to the playlist that Fiala thought weren't important.

I always felt it was necessary to have an open mind when it came to new music and pop trends. Al, on the other hand, was staying safe with artists like Elvis, while ignoring breakthrough records like Ray Charles' "Georgia"!

And he simply didn't understand the concept of instrumentals—even though singles like "Sleep Walk" and the Ventures' "Walk, Don't Run" were smash hits and remain as classics to this day. Al just didn't like "that twangy guitar" in "Sleep Walk." But others apparently did. That "twangy guitar" tune has remained very much awake and alive for decades. It has sold millions of copies, been used in the soundtracks to countless modern movies, and a version of Santo & Johnny's composition won a Grammy Award for Brian Setzer as 1998's Best Pop Instrumental Performance. Santo & Johnny—and their twang—were inducted into the Steel Guitar Hall of Fame in 2002.

The new playlist that I started to spin at WVKO was spinning listenership to new heights.

And we had personalities-plus!

When I left the newly mellowed WTVN, I took a few of their most popular jocks with me—including Susie Lowery's main squeeze, Johnny Dollar, and Dale Tucker, who used the air-alias "Dale Kirby." Throughout much of '62 and '63, WVKO was rolling. It was all good. I was expanding my radio abilities, knowledge, and clout.

And all of it was getting better!

WVKO had personalities-plus and my playlist was spinning us all to new heights!

Now, I had been in the newspapers before—I mean, heck, I was the *editor* of the *Atomic Blast*!—but my mention in the *Columbus Citizen-Journal* really stopped the presses. TV-Radio Editor Jo Bradley Reed really brought out the star-quality that I was shining with at WVKO:

> "Why don't you ever say something about me?" joked WVKO's Dave Hull when we met recently. "I've been in town since Jan. 1, 1961, read your column every morning, but have yet to come upon my name."

> Apparently Dave announced on his program that "Jo Bradley Reed has never said anything about me," because the next day's mail brought cards from Sue, Cookie, Mary, Irene and Kathy, who are ardent fans apparently of the handsome 28-year-old bachelor...

This glowing mention also featured one of my WVKO promo photos, with me in a stately *Churchillian* pose.

The same column also noted that Art Linkletter would be in Columbus to star in the Kenley Players production of *Father of the Bride* and that Ed Sullivan was celebrating the fourteenth anniversary of his television show and that he is five feet ten inches tall.

I was in important company!

But, as was certainly expected, Ms. Reed's comments about *me* sparked the *most* attention and attraction! Her column the following week included this very astute observation by a reader:

> Mrs. John B. Barton, Worthington [Ohio], writes: "Has no one suggested to you that WVKO's Dave Hull, whom you represented in picture last week, has a remarkable sameness in features with pianist Peter Nero?"

Wow! First I was rubbing elbows-in-print with Art Linkletter and Ed Sullivan; now it was *really* hard to believe that I'd been mentioned in the same breath with the man about whom Ray Charles once said: "Peter Nero plays his buns off!"

Art, Ed, Pete, and the Hullabalooer—I had risen to a potent plateau!

I rose to a potent plateau at WVKO—even rubbing tanned Florida elbows with Miss Teenage America!

The Last to Go

I was pretty much on top of the radio world in Columbus until the owner-manager of WVKO, Bert Charles, took me aside to *talk*.

"I'm selling the station to an African-American radio group out of Detroit," he said.

Hmmm...

I had been in radio in Detroit, of course, and I knew the station group who was buying WVKO quite well. They were an excellent broadcasting company from Inkster, a small Motor City suburb. But WVKO would switch to what was referred to then in the radio industry as "race music." The term "soul music" was still very new, not having actually been used until 1961 to describe "gospel-style music with secular lyrics."

The entire WVKO staff would also be *adjusted* to represent the African-American community.

Except Bert. Bert would stay on as part of the purchase.

And here's how it's all going to go down...

"Dave, you're the operations director," Bert told me. "You're going to call the staff together and you're going to fire them, one by one. And I'm going to take a vacation. It's going to be *your* job."

"I'm not going to do it like that, Bert," I told him. "You go on vacation. Fine. I'm your operations director, yes. I *will* tell the staff that we're being bought out and that everybody here will be replaced—but I'm going to let *them* decide when they want to go.

"I'm going to have *them* tell *me*. I'll call this group in Inkster— at WJLB. I know them. They're from a rough town, but they're businessmen and they're really good at their profession. I can work with their operations director and I'll tell him the truth. After our meeting, as our people tell me they want to leave, I'll call him and have him send in the subs."

I could tell Bert was pondering all that I had just said—and I knew he *really* didn't want to be there.

"All right, you handle it your way," he finally said. "But I'm going on vacation!"

"How long do you think you'll be?" I asked.

"At least a month."

He wanted no part of this.

On Monday, I sent out a memo. Everybody was required to be at a 10:00 a.m. meeting. I got off the air at exactly 1000 hours and knew I had to jump right into this fire.

Be prepared for a formal change at the radio station, the memo read. *You MUST attend!*

They did.

Sales, clerical, administration, news, disc jockeys—they were all there; even the gardener.

It took me about ten minutes to explain who the Inkster group was. I explained that the sale had already gone to the FCC, meaning it would probably be consummated within six months. I then explained that the new owners would be bringing in their own staff. The key point was obvious, but I spelled it out anyway: *"Every person in this current staff, including myself, will be let go and replaced."*

When I explained that each person would be allowed to *choose* when they wanted to leave, the requests started rolling in at once:

"I'd like to leave on the eighth of the month."

"I'd like to leave on the twenty-first."

It went on and on. Everybody claimed a day.

Then someone asked: "When are *you* going to leave, Dave?"

"I'm going to be the last one to go."

I put my name down at the very end, because it was my job. I had to sit there and watch them all go. *One by one.*

And I had one month to do it, before Bert Charles came back.

But situations like this always have two sides to the story. And emotions can run hot on both.

The first of the WVKO staff to leave was our beautiful and talented receptionist. I made my first call to the Inkster group operations guy, and he sent in their first replacement.

The woman who came in from Detroit *did not* want to be there. She was born and raised in Inkster and she evidently saw Columbus as an evil dungeon somewhere between Alcatraz and the shackle room in the Tower of London. Plus, she was not exactly overjoyed at having to pack up her things, gather her kids, and uproot her family—just like *my* staff was now being forced to do.

She was a loud pariah with an attitude from the moment she arrived. *This* was a problem we didn't need in an already edgy environment.

But thankfully, like nauseating viral gastroenteritis, within two days she was gone.

Things got more in tune from that point on.

Our second person to go was one of our salesmen—a very good salesman. He left because he landed a position at another station almost immediately.

I was on the phone with the Inkster boss daily.

Here are the people I need...

I need a salesman on this date.

I need a clerical person on this date.

I need a guy to do the gardening on this date…

And he and I were getting to know one another pretty well.

"I'll be the last to go," I explained to him, "and *you're* going to replace *me*."

"Yeah, that's good," he said. "Because I have a lot of things to do *here*, and I know you have a lot of things to do *there,* too."

He was a genuinely nice guy.

I was now down to about four days before Bert Charles would be back in Columbus. The changeover was nearly complete. Just a few of the old WVKO staff remained—Johnny Dollar, a couple of the other DJs, and me.

Then it was *just me.*

I made the last call to the operations man at Inkster.

"It's time," I told him.

"I know…"

My Career Heads South

I'd been in Ohio now for several years—very good years—but this was radio, with its ever-constant it's-time-to-move-on change.

But along with that change—at least for those of us who were lucky, blessed, or just in "that magic place at the equally magical right time"—usually came a phone call.

Rrriiiinnnggggg…

This time the call came toward the end of WVKO's transition, while the remnants of my staff were making the final walks off the end of that AM plank—right before I made that last call to the boss at Inkster.

"Dave! This is Dick Lawrence from WFLA in Tampa," the voice on the other end of the line said. "I've seen it in the trades—I've heard around the business that the whole staff of WVKO is going, including you. I'd like to know if you'd come work as my assistant program director and take over morning drive?"

It was a great call and a great offer, and *very* ironic.

You see, Jeanette had become a little *tired* of me, my crazy radio life, and the Ohio weather, and had left with her son, Michael— heading for, yes, *Tampa, Florida*!

I accepted Dick Lawrence's offer and became the morning man and assistant PD at the 50,000-watt powerhouse of the Sunshine State, WFLA.

Now, there is change and then there is *change*.

My southern migration would bring much more than just a switch in scenery, stations, and studio.

I had gone from Southern California to Africa to Roswell to Ohio to Detroit and back to Ohio. But I was still in my twenties, and I was still learning about life. This part to come would teach me a lot.

"I've decided to come down," I told Dick over the phone. It actually took me a couple of days to officially determine I was coming aboard WFLA.

I knew I wanted to go to Tampa, because of Jeanette, but I was concerned about the responsibility of being both a major-time-slot personality *and* the assistant program director. I knew I would be under a lot of pressure.

And I was right.

"Good!" said Dick to my acceptance. "And I've got just the place for you to stay. I've got a place on Davis Island. You can move in with me until you get yourself squared away where you want to go."

Hmmm... I thought. *I don't want to move in with Dick Lawrence! I want to be close to Jeanette; not on Davis Island.*

"Well, gee," I said to Dick, "that's something to consider. I, uh, really do appreciate that, but I think I've made other arrangements."

I pack my stuff, get in my car, and head for Tampa.

I call Jeanette...

I'm coming!

But I was concerned with the "pressure" I was getting from Dick.

First of all, this was 1963. The fuse may have been lit, but the societal upheaval and moral changes of the *mid*-sixties hadn't even started to explode yet. *The Beverly Hillbillies, The Dick Van Dyke Show,* and *Andy Williams* were ruling the television world. "Sugar Shack" by Jimmy Gilmer and The Fireballs and "Surfin' U.S.A." by the Beach Boys were the top two records of '63. It was still an innocent and protected world.

Many things were still not talked about, addressed, *or accepted.*

And I ran right into one of them.

Unbeknownst to me, Dick Lawrence was thought to be gay by many in Florida and that may have had something to do with his quick-willingness to have me share his place on Davis Island.

But I never did. And Jeanette and I resumed dating.

My relationship with Lawrence also proved fine, however—very professional.

At least *then.*

It's Not for Me to Say

But there was still that learning process—a process that extended well beyond the radio station.

It began at the speed of sound.

I had been on the air for just a couple of days when I played a Johnny Mathis record. During the three- or four-second lead-in intro I said, "Ladies and gentlemen, Mister Johnny Mathis..."

Boom! Out comes the vocal.

Well, Johnny hadn't even finished the first line of "What Will Mary Say?" (the somewhat prophetic lyrics, *"I must be going [don't go]..."*) when the phone rang. It was a listener.

"Hi there, Dave," said the drawling voice—his conspiratorial tone giving me a chill, like the boss's sicky-sweetness in *Cool Hand Luke.* "Hey, buddy," he said, "we shur 'preciate your show and we welcome ya to Tampa an' all...but listen now—down here, we never call a *n*----- 'Mister.' D'ya understand that?"

This was a first.

I had worked in Detroit. I had worked with the Black staff of Inkster to get them situated at WVKO—and they'd worked with me. I'd played music by Black artists for *years*. And this *voice* is telling me *this*?

After I've been working here just two days?!

I've got to get out of here!

I told Jeanette what happened.

"I've got to get out of here!" I said aloud.

I continued to work, but I just kept *thinking*—trying to figure out this *situation*.

I've got a problem. I can't be me in this environment. I can't be funny. I can't be serious. I've got a problem. What is this all about?

To muddy the pristine Tampa waters even further, in just the few months I was there, WFLA was kicking the butts of the competition. My dual role as drive-time personality and Dick's assistant *seemed* to be working. The WFLA pop-music/light-adult-hits format—with *regionally-censored intros*—was apparently *also* working.

Things also worked when I was put in charge of developing all of the commercial and promotional campaigns. And WFLA was Western Florida's biggest and most powerful station. I created serious, topical business promotions, and I learned to discipline myself—*again*—as to when "politically accepted" humor and fun could be used alongside them. And I made it all successful.

My favorite songs in 1963 were
"Go Away Little Girl" by Steve Lawrence
and "Our Day Will Come"
by Ruby and the Romantics.

A Sound Move

At this point in my career, the station changed from reel-to-reel tapes to eight-track cartridges. And then—very quickly—to small, multitrack cassettes. I used them all. This may seem foreign to those working in the industry today, surrounded by digital equipment and computers that do *everything* for them, but primitive as it may have been, it prepared me for using all kinds of effects in my future on-air commercials.

All of this experience was pure gold when it came to readying me for the largest radio market in the country—a market that seemed really remote at the time.

As that short spurt of time in Florida passed, even with the station's success, I knew the personalities of myself and Lawrence were diametrically opposed to one another. He was a micromanager; I came from the school that allowed people of talent the opportunity to develop themselves—not simply be told what to do. I've always believed that creativity *cannot* be dictated from behind a desk, but rather is a God-given *gift* that must be cultivated over time.

Most talented people *know* what will work, and what won't. And that "being told what to do" thing can not only squeeze the creative juices dry, it can spin seriously out of control and flush everything down an over-managed drain.

I was still *spinning* all the parts of this "situation" around in my head, when Dick told me that he was going to Dallas to put together WFLA's jingles.

Jingles aren't produced by individual stations. They're contracted out to one of several different musical companies, most of which are in Dallas, Texas. WFLA chose PAMS because their jingles were exactly what we needed. (PAMS still exists today, and a big part of their business is in nostalgia—marketing classic jingle tracks on CD from the fifties through the seventies!)

> *Come on in, the music's free,*
> *Yours, musi-cal-ly—*
> *W-A-B-C*

The right company can come up with just the right "hooks" to feature whatever it is a station wants to highlight. In this case, it was our new pop music format. The jingles were short, to the point, and Dick was sure they'd work.

While spinning the wax at WFLA, I was also spinning this whole Southern snafu around in my head.

Meanwhile, he left *me* with a full agenda of a dozen things he wanted done.

"Have everything finished by the time I get back!" he *commanded*.

"No problem, Dick!"

I had this done, I had that done.

This promotion, that promotion.

The new sounders were all done, *thanks to me*—newly produced openings and closings for the station's promotional ideas and gimmicks, public service announcements, hourly news openings, and station IDs.

The news had to be switched to another time. I did it.

Even the music playlist had to be changed.

I did it.

I got everything done.

Except for one thing...

Control freaks are good at noticing that *one thing* that doesn't get done—with no thanks or appreciation for what *does* get completed and accomplished.

As soon as he landed back in Tampa, Lawrence picked up his car and turned on the station.

And he listened.

He heard eleven of the things on his list, but not the twelfth.

"I didn't hear the stolen car report!" he said when he arrived at the studio. "Did you get it done?"

"No, I didn't, Dick," I said. "I just didn't have time. In the week or ten days you've been gone, I've been working my—"

"I don't care!" he shouted, and he started screaming at me in the middle of a row of cubicles that led directly to the general manager's office.

Everyone in the cubicles was watching—and hearing—this rant.

Dick was trying to make a fool out of me, berating me.

I've got a problem...

I've got to get out of here...

I'd had it.

As loud as I could, I told Dick: "You'd better find a new morning man quick! I quit!"

Here comes the general manager out of his office!

"Dave, now, you could be overreacting," he said.

"No!" I told him. "The person you ought to be talking to about overreaction is Dick Lawrence. I'm out of here! As of this moment! I want a check drawn at once!"

As I headed for the employee parking lot, I heard applause coming from the cubicles. I'll never know *for sure* whom they were applauding for because I never returned. I never even looked back.

It was a good move.

Maybe the real magic in this business has always come from looking *forward*. I may not have known it, but as I pulled out of that parking lot at WFLA, I was now looking forward to Los Angeles and KRLA—to times and places and broadcast experiences that would never be equaled in all of radio history.

Ever.

Entering the Dream-House

"Did You Hear Him?! Did You Hear *That*?!"

KRLA: 1963–1969, The Beginning

So many people we have talked to have all answered the same when asked who was [your one favorite] *overall personality...who really represented the greatness of KRLA, the Dream-House, the home for heroes. The greatest "hero" of them all had now joined KRLA in June 1963, replacing Bill Keffury in the four-hour six-to-ten p.m. Sunday show and filling in once in a while during the week. Dave Hull had entered the Dream-House.*

—Bill Earl, *Dream-House*

The sound of the applause as I left WFLA had stopped ringing in my ears; it was rapidly replaced by the rising scream of reality.

I needed a job—and it wasn't going to be in the South! And it wouldn't be for another megalomaniac micromanager, either!

Meanwhile, Jeanette had grown just slightly tired of me—*again!* Her focus was really on raising her son—she didn't need *me* to raise, too. So she and Mike left Tampa for Greenville, Texas. A friend of hers down there needed some help, so it was a good and timely opportunity for a westward shift in Southern hospitality and scenery.

I would do sort of the same thing, but with a destination—and *destiny*—a lot further west.

One of the top tunes of 1963 was Bobby Bare's crossover hit "500 Miles Away from Home." It was a homesick lament that I took to heart—and I was *twenty*-five hundred miles away from home. It was time to go back to California.

Jeanette found her opportunity in Texas; I found mine with my brother, Gary. He had an apartment right on the sand in Seal Beach—a Southern Cal surf city on the coastal border of Los Angeles and Orange Counties.

I called Gary with my tales of Southern woe and we quickly established that he could use a roommate for his beach digs—*me!* And, if I would pay all of his expenses *(in advance)* he'd fly into Tampa, help me load up my car and a rented trailer, and share the drive home.

It took us over a week to get the job done, but it was worth it. That magic of *looking forward* was already casting its spell, although I still wasn't aware of its power or what kind of rabbit I would be pulling from the hat. The real wizardry was still a ways off.

Saved by the Spell?

I settled into my brother's place and spent about a week regrouping and enjoying the beach sun.

Meanwhile, Gary heard about a nearby apartment that might suit the needs of two handsome and extremely suave bachelors a bit more. We went over to look at it, and what we found was a *party house*— complete with an inside bar with a thatched roof décor. I immediately had the urge to do the limbo, and I fully expected to see Harry Belafonte dance out of the bedroom in a straw hat singing "Day-O." Palm fronds were *everywhere*!

The landlady advised us to sign the rental papers right away—there was another group of guys interested.

But Gary and I wanted to think about it.

Well, the other guys slid in right behind us, signed on the dotted line, and grabbed the rights to Jamaica west.

A short time later *something happened* within the infrastructure of that apartment and a fire started. Those dried-out palms went up in speed-flames and all of those guys were killed.

That was very close. I began to really wonder about the nature of this magic, about that rabbit in the top hat, and about the future.

I needed a little more regrouping and a few more weeks in the Seal Beach sun.

"Did You Call KRLA?"

Gary began getting antsy about my extended life of tanned leisure. Finally, *he* reached in to grab that bunny by the ears!

"Start calling some stations here in L.A.!" he *suggested*.

So I did.

I started at the top of the market with number one: KFWB. But the program director there, the super-eccentric broadcast pioneer Jim Hawthorne, wouldn't return my messages and his secretary got to the point that she wouldn't even pick up the phone when I called into their switchboard.

And it was the same answer—or *non*-answer—everywhere.

Another big record from 1963 began to creep into my psyche: Skeeter Davis' "End of the World."

"Did you call KRLA?" demanded Gary. "They're just about a mile away from Mom's house in Alhambra."

I told him that nobody here in L.A. wanted to talk to me, and besides that, I had already accepted a morning show at WICE in Providence, Rhode Island. I had received the offer from Al Fiala, the operations manager who had hired me at WVKO.

"Providence, Rhode Island?! W-*ICE?!*" Gary's reaction to this news was a bit frigid. "Do you know how cold it gets there?!" he went on. He wasn't actually *asking*—but more making a statement. "And they have huge nor'easters there, too!"

I told him *again* that no station in L.A. wanted to even *talk* with anyone outside this market. "And besides, KRLA wouldn't want *me*, they're a *country* station!" I'd rather be spinning Little Stevie Wonder 45s than Little Jimmy Dickens!

KRLA—AM 1110—began in 1942 with the call sign KPAS (the "PAS" referring to its City of License: Pasadena, California). In 1945, the station changed to KXLA and went country—*real* country!

KXLA became the home of the "Ol' Pea-Picker" himself, Tennessee Ernie Ford. Ford worked the morning shift and appeared live as a vocalist on KXLA's *Dinner Bell Roundup* show with another classic country crooner, Cliffie Stone.

From 1950 to 1959, AM 1110 broadcast the down-home voice and sounds of Cal Worthington—a true good ol' boy from Shidler, Oklahoma, who later climbed to multi-zillionaire status by becoming *the* ultimate car dealer. Cal's huge cowboy hat and "his dog, Spot" commercials are world famous. Of course, his dog, Spot, was never actually a *dog*. Over the years, Spot was a tiger, a seal, an elephant, a chimpanzee, a bear, and a hippopotamus—most of which he would ride on! Once, Cal even went the "inanimate" route—actually, *very* animated, but not living: "Spot" was an airplane that Cal stood atop as it flew!

One of America's most inventive comics, Stan Freberg, also had his share of broadcasts on KXLA.

And now my brother wanted me to work *my* way into *that* mix?!

To play things like "Yellow Bandana," "You Comb Her Hair," and "Will Your Lawyer Talk to God?"

No!

"They don't play country music there anymore!" Gary told me. "They've gone pop."

Pop? No more Ferlin Husky?

"And if you won't call them," he threatened, "*I* will!"

I didn't.

He did.

And as soon as the line started ringing, he handed the receiver to me!

The magic of being in the right place at the right time...

On that day, KRLA's longtime receptionist wasn't at her desk to answer the phone. Her daughter had gotten sick at school, so she had run out to go get her.

Program director "Reb" Foster picked up the phone.

The magic of being straightforward and not being afraid to ask for what you want...

I told him who I was and where I had worked, and I asked if he had anything available.

This may *sound* very "straightforward," but telling radio honchos who you are and where you've worked involves a lot more than just a recitation of "facts." They need to really *know* you—to at least get an idea of who you are and what you've done. *Fast.*

And it always helps to have *names*.

I told Reb that I knew his general manager, John Barrett. At one point, I had sent Barrett and his then–program director one of my tapes and a résumé. That program director was Jim Washburne, my old buddy from the Air Force and Armed Forces Radio! The Barrett-Washburne team *had* offered me a chance to work for both of them at WKBW in Buffalo, New York; but before I could say yes, they both quit and headed for California. That's when *I* hit Florida.

This all quickly caught the ear of Reb Foster as he held the phone that he never answered.

Something a bit more important than his receptionist's absence was on Foster's mind. His weekend man, Bill Keffury, had just been notified by his draft board in San Francisco that he was being called up for military service. This was 1963; "conscription" was in effect and was taking many young men into the armed forces—and eventually to Vietnam. The draft touched everyone from college students to disc jockeys to the heavyweight champion of the world.

Foster and Barrett had *just* had a meeting. Keffury was about to swap his microphone for an M-16—so who was going to be filling the air time *this Sunday night* from six to ten p.m.?

That's when Reb answered the phone.

"How long would it take you to get to our Pasadena studios with all of your demo materials?" he asked me.

Seal Beach to Pasadena.

Up the Long Beach Freeway.

I told him I would be there within the hour.

I *flew* in my Tampa-tired little car; screeching onto the grounds of the historic Huntington Sheraton Hotel where the studios were.

John Barrett knew who I was before I walked in the door, of course. He told me to sit down, and together with Reb Foster, we listened to everything I had brought with me.

It was tricky—for them and me. Again, this was 1963. Personality selection for broadcast in that much-more-innocent, "It's My Party," "Puff the Magic Dragon," clean-cut-like-Bobby-Vee world had to have a lot more *discretion* than it does now.

On-air voices had *influence.*

It was a time when children actually listened to what their parents and other adults had to say—*and* they respected the police. Girls wore skirts and blouses to school; no pierced belly buttons hanging out! You didn't see purple spiked hairdos either, sticking out of the heads of *either* gender. And guys' pants still covered their boxers!

The records we played had lyrics about "surfer girls," hot rods, and summer love. Violence, profanity, debauchery, perversion, and hookers and pimps hadn't yet gouged their way into mainstream musical *entertainment.*

But Barrett and Foster listened to me—and they sized up my personality. *Will this guy fit in with our format and what KRLA is doing?* KFWB was far and away number one. So these guys were thinking that someone "different" like me might be just the perfect thing for the station—*but*...they had to be cautious.

They asked me to step outside.

The jury didn't deliberate long.

Barrett called me back into the office. He stood up from behind his desk, shook my hand, and—pointing to the studios—said, "We've hired you for Sunday night! Now go in there and prove that we were right in our decision!"

I was locked in.

Ironically, though, Bill Keffury never did get drafted. He was classified 4-F a few weeks later for physical reasons. I felt bad when I heard that, but *this was radio.*

After Barrett gave me the news and I spoke one more time with Reb, I headed back to Seal Beach. Somewhat slower this time.

And I thanked Gary.

He'd been right! I was pretty darn happy about the job. *And* the fact that I wasn't going to have to play anything even close to the twang of Rex Allen's "Don't Go Near the Indians"!

A Hull of a First Impression

It was Sunday.

6:00 p.m.

Barrett, Foster, and KRLA's production director, Dick Moreland, were all listening.

I played about two seconds of the first record. Then I broke in over the mic and said, "Well, how do you like the show so far?"

I found out later that it broke them all up!

"Did you hear him?! Did you hear *that*?!" They're all phoning each other to make sure the others had heard it!

Dave Hull had indeed entered the Dream-House.

So...how do you like the book so far?!

The Eleven-Ten Men

You Can't Just Sit Behind a Desk

KRLA: 1963–1969, The What-*We*-Want Years

It was apparent very quickly that KRLA was the enchanted rabbit that had leapt from that *forward-looking* hat. KRLA was magic and would produce magic for years to come. Those mangy desert jackrabbits way-back-when in Roswell couldn't hold a carrot to *this* kind of wax-spinning sorcery.

As the new guy on weekends, I entered into a major-league lineup that included "Emperor" Bob Hudson, Casey Kasem, Bob Eubanks, Ted Quillin, and Arlen Sanders. Dick Moreland and Reb Foster were doing double duty: they were on the air *and* in management. Newsman Richard Beebe was making a name for himself with his unorthodox sixties-slant perspective on the increasingly crazed events of the day. And very soon, Chi-town superstar Dick Biondi would be part of the crew.

These were *names*.

Legends.

And the station itself was heading toward that same elite status.

The ethereal "Dream-House" depiction of KRLA as a "home for heroes" with "music to strengthen your heart" was *already* starting to come true in 1963. KRLA's Dream-House feel was caressed in a poem that was part of a contest-winning painting of the "Eleven-Ten Men" in 1967. It was also the title of Bill Earl's lovingly detailed 1989 history of KRLA's thirty most prominent years. By the time that poem and painting were unveiled, the station was *clearly* legendary. Countless "dreams" had been fulfilled, experienced, and created.

But now it was still 1963 and my time in the soon-to-be Dream-House was just beginning.

THE MOOR

ALHAMBRA HIGH SCHOOL
ALHAMBRA, CALIFORNIA
Vol. XLVIII, No. 8
Tuesday, November 5, 1963

Moor Grad Realized Old Dream When He Became KRLA Deejay

By GARY BENJAMIN, 'MOOR' Sports Editor

A long dream to come back to the Los Angeles area and have a radio program was fulfilled last summer for AHS grad Dave Hull, as he started his nightly, nine to midnight show on KRLA, radio Los Angeles.

For the past 11 years Dave has been doing radio work for the Air Force and, later, commercial radio before coming to Los Angeles.

IT ALL STARTED when he was ten years old and went to see the radio show, "Meet Corliss Archer." Ten seconds before the show began, the announcer told a joke. When he got to the punch line, the show began and the audience broke into laughter.

"That's what I want to be, a radio announcer," Dave told his mother after the show started.

"Shut up and watch the show," returned his mother.

DURING HIS HIGH SCHOOL career, Mr. Hull was freshman class president, member of the Senior Council, and a Legislature representative for two years. His athletic endeavors included playing junior varsity football.

He holds a high regard for his favorite teacher, Miss Jane Beeman, who he feels runs the greatest class at AHS.

"She has complete control of the class, yet she can make them feel at ease when talking on certain subjects," remarked the '52 grad. "I learned more from her than any other teacher."

EX-MOOR NOW DEEJAY — Southland teenagers listen nightly to the popular "Hullabaloo" conducted by ex-Moor student Dave Hull over station KRLA. He recently visited his old high school haunts and met some of his former teachers.

STILL IN the Air Force, he was "mustered out" of the armed forces at Walker Air Force Base, located at the "end of the world" in New Mexico. Doing night work for KGFL, he beamed his show to 10,000 jackrabbits on the barren desert.

was offered a job with WFLA. He decided to have a paid vacation so he went to work for both radio and TV.

"After four months in Florida, I came out to the coast hoping to find a job. When I arrived I went

My job at KRLA was a dream come true...
but the Dream-House was just being unlocked!

My weekend gig was in a nice little groove. But I was still relatively new and unknown—just a few months in. And being heard only on Sundays and in a few random substitute spots, I hadn't exactly reached the household-name recognition level of the prime-time Bobs—Hudson and Eubanks—or Casey Kasem. So when Dick Moreland decided to leave his daily nine-to-midnight shift in favor of moving further into management, I *wasn't* the one to move up.

Yet.

That was when Dick Biondi was hired. Biondi had been "the most popular disc jockey in the Midwest," with his signature screams wailing out of Chicago's WLS–AM 890. He had been one of the first DJs to play Elvis, Gene Vincent, Bo Diddley, and so many other timeless artists.

Biondi had an impact!

But he had left WLS earlier that year over a dispute involving the quantity of commercials played during his show; he had since been on a bit of a hiatus.

Not anymore.

Biondi powered into KRLA and Southern California like the "Big Blow" blizzard rolling in off Lake Michigan. But for a variety of reasons, things never really warmed up between KRLA's audience and Dick. It just didn't work. After only two months, Biondi headed back East and started a syndicated show called *Dick Biondi's Young America*. Dick would return to KRLA two years later and things *would* get cozy and work well. But right then, a chilly gap had opened in that nine-to-midnight spot—Foster and Moreland had another opening to fill.

Now, they wanted me to take it.

And I wanted it, too!

Homework Hotline

My first regular shift on the air was a great chance to exercise Dave Hull's One Simple Theory about "taking whatever is thrown at you and making the most of it."

I was in the nine-to-midnight role.

During those hours, high school kids were still up and listening—listening while they were struggling along with their homework. You could almost see them: books and papers spread all over their beds, their transistor radios close by—tuned to AM 1110.

On that first night, I guess the homework struggle got a bit too much for one girl and she called in to the station. She was stumped for an answer to an assignment question, and she was way ahead of her time—reaching out for a *Who Wants to Be a Millionaire* kind of "lifeline."

I put her and her question on the air.

And the phones started ringing!

The calls coming in weren't from other high schoolers as much as from teachers and professors! Mostly from nearby Caltech! It seemed like those guys were just *waiting* to show the world that they knew more than anyone else.

Okay, the lifelines had been cast! We had taken the girl's number and we called her back.

Now, I've got the professor on one line and our little student on the other. These were the days, however, when the super advanced technology of being able to put two calls on the air at the same time was as out of scientific reach as a landing on Jupiter! *My* precision inter-call equipment consisted of an old-time bulky phone receiver!

But with the help of my highly trained and skilled engineer, I could at least go back and forth between the prof and the girl as we got to the root of the answer.

Her question centered around a math dilemma—which the Caltech brainiac naturally solved. *In great detail!*

But...

What the professor offered was both logarithmically and quantum physics-*ally* far beyond anything that the high school student's teacher would have slightly expected. It was like asking for a book report on *Moby Dick* and having an actual white whale delivered to the gymnasium pool.

The next day, the high school teacher gave the student her deserved A+. But then the teacher *encouraged* the student to explain to the class just how she was able to come up with that answer.

Homework Hotline raised listeners' GPAs from 2.0 to 1110! The show was in a class by itself!

Like the pure, ethical, and moral Hullabalooer listener she was, the student told the truth. The teacher then urged the *entire class* to listen and learn math from nine p.m. to midnight on KRLA!

We knew at once that we had a winner. *Homework Hotline* was born!

Amid my standard hullabaloo, we began solving hundreds of problems weekly, with grade-raising testimonials coming in night after night.

$a^2 + b^2 = c^2$

$\sin(\Theta) = a/c$

WAOOUAH!

$\Pi = 3.141592653589\ldots$

A Creative Collective

As I became an important ingredient in that magic potion—that imaginative-collective that was KRLA—I found myself thinking back to the stifling micromanaging of Dick Lawrence at WFLA in Tampa. And how creatively tragic all of that was. I said it then and I've said it throughout my career: As a radio boss you *have* to let your on-air guys develop their own personas. You *can't* just sit behind a desk and tell them, "*This* is what I want!"

That's when you—and your station—will fail.

That didn't happen at KRLA.

And that's why we were now blowing up the airwaves. KRLA became the dominant station in L.A. throughout so much of the soaring-sixties decade, simply because each one of the on-air staff was totally different from the others. Each had—and was *allowed*—his own act and separate personality.

The Legendary Lineup

Bob Hudson became "Emperor Hudson"—*and* "Beautiful Bob"—in the mornings. We all thought he actually believed he *was* the Emperor of California. He had a cadre of actors and performers who played all the parts of the "Emperor's Commandos"—a loyal and crusading bunch that claimed forty thousand followers!

Emperor Bob would ride around town in a gold-colored Rolls Royce, wearing an ermine robe, holding a scepter, and waving to people as he drove by.

His show's closing line each day was, "Get off the freeways, peasants! His Highness is coming!"

Following Beautiful Bob was our version of a *GQ* cover model. Ted Quillin had come to KRLA from early country radio with gifted, announcer-school, golden-voice perfection.

Ted's sign-off line was a sultry, "Mama, come get your baby boy."

His "mama" may not have shown up every day, but plenty of other women would—just to catch a glimpse of Ted as he left the studio.

One day, I heard one of them say that she had definitely "come and got him"!

After our "baby boy's" show, one of the true kings of the broadcast hill, Casey Kasem, took the mic. Casey also began his KRLA stint in 1963 and carried it until '69. In 1970, he developed his *American Top 40* franchise of shows; shows that are *still* being heard around the country in various forms.

Casey's famous voice has been used for countless cartoon characters, too—including forty years of being "Shaggy" on *Scooby-Doo*.

KRLA's Creative Collective (left to right): Dick Moreland, Reb Foster, Casey Kasem, "Emperor" Bob Hudson, Charlie O'Donnell, me, and Bob Eubanks.

As Eleven-Ten became the Los Angeles ratings powerhouse, opportunities outside the studio box were coming to most all of us. I received an offer to host a television game show for NBC called *Quick As A Wink*.

I knew it was destined to be right up there with *What's My Line?* and *To Tell the Truth*! But to jump at this Alex Trebek–like chance for game-show immortality, I had to turn down an offer from Dick Clark to MC a new music show he was cooking up called *Shebang*.

Sorry, Dick...

KMPC
5939 Sunset Boulevard • Los Angeles 28, California • Hollywood 9-5341
50,000 Watts • 710 Kilocycles

DAVE HULL : KR

LA

DEAR DAVE;

CONGRATULATIONS ON YOUR PROPOSED MCA-TV GOODY.."QUICK AS A WINK".

RUMORS ARE ABOUT THAT W. MARTINDALE WILL TRY TO ARRANGE A COMPETING SHOW...."QUICK AS A DAVE."

INCIDENTALLY, I JUST PURCHASED SOME NEW FINS FROM A NEIGHBOR FOR MY 1964 GRAF ZEPPELIN.

CORDIALS,

GARY OWENS

cc; Godzilla.

Dave Hull Will Emcee MCA-TV's 'Quick' Show

Dave Hull, Los Angeles disc jockey, has been signed by MCA-TV as master of ceremonies for a new daytime TV game show, "Quick As A Wink."

The half-hour series, first segment of which will be taped at Universal City Studios on Feb. 26, is planned as a five-day-a-week venture, with Kathleen Nolan and Clu Gulager already set as special guests on the initial segment.

Continued on Page 7)

With *Quick As A Wink*, I felt certain to become a game-show immortal in the flutter of an eyelash!

MCA 'Quick'ens Its Tape Prod'n

Universal City TV is planning another tape series, "Quick As A Wink," to be produced under aegis of MCA-TV as a daytime game show.

KRLA deejay Dave Hull has been signed to emcee, and pilot will be taped at U Feb. 26. Kathleen Nolan and Clu Gulager, both U TV pactees, will guest on pilot.

Casey stepped up to the second-choice table and took the *Shebang* position. He was its host for nearly a decade.

My shrewd television savvy got me to *one* pilot episode of *Quick As A Wink*. Then—in the blink of eye—it was over. Those network eyes closed tight after that!

I did have the privilege of sitting in for Casey twice on *American Top 40* down through the years, however...

JOINING IN with congratulations to Casey Kasem on the first anniversary of "Shebang" are, from l Johnny Hayes, one of the Paris Sisters, Bobby Sherman, Hullabalooer Dave Hull and pretty Donna Lor

Afer turning down down *Shebang,* I at least got to be a guest on the show to celebrate *it's* longevity...Congrats, Casey!

After Casey's shift on KRLA, it was time for our program director, Reb Foster.

More talent.

More creativity.

Reb could speak as his pleasant, charming self out of one side of his mouth, and then turn the other side to the microphone and become the obnoxious and opinionated old lady, "Maude Skidmore."

Listeners would wait every hour for more of her venom about Hollywood, politics, weight loss, and life in general.

Reb would also later emerge as a serious music entrepreneur with a nose for talent. As the sixties moved on, he would own and/or represent some of the biggest acts in the biz.

After Reb was Bob Eubanks. Bob may have been the ultimate impresario of the bunch. He owned several teenage nightclubs—the famous Cinnamon Cinder chain. The clubs even had a hit record made about them, "Cinnamon Cinder" by the Pastel Six.

As a concert promoter, Bob became the man responsible for bringing the Beatles to California. Later, of course, Bob brought his skill and good looks to television, becoming an international star on *The Newlywed Game* and so many other shows.

Then it was my turn from nine to midnight with my nightly *Homework Hotline* antics.

Two different disc jockeys would follow me with their graveyard-shift, insomniac stretches: Arlen Sanders (not to be confused with the Kentucky Chicken Colonel, *Harland* Sanders!) and Bill Slater. Both of these night crawlers were noted for playing an enormous amount of hit music and pretty much keeping their mouths shut.

Last Call

One night, amid this daily celebration of cool creativity, in the middle of my show, amidst all that homework—and fresh from the hamstrung horror of WFLA—I get a call. *Off the air.*

"Dave! *This is Dick Lawrence!* I've got just one phone call! You've got to get me out of here!"

Huh?!

"What?!" I shouted back. "And what do you mean, I've got to get you out of here?! Where's *here*?!"

He was in Southern California.

In San Diego.

In jail.

"I'm not kidding, Dave! I can't handle it in jail."

"What are you in for?"

"DUI!"

Yes, he was a drinker. And, yes, he'd been picked up by the San Diego police.

Dick Lawrence...

Did I have to relive that last day at WFLA again? How he'd berated me in front of all those people at the station?

"No, I can't do that, Dick."

"Why not?! I've *got* to get out of here."

"Call somebody else; I'm not going to help you. I wish you the best of luck."

Click...

That was the last I ever spoke with him. But it wasn't the last I thought about that situation and how it played out. True learning experiences are *good* to hold onto.

But most should never be repeated.

Bigger Than Santa Claus

DAVE HULL FOR ROSE QUEEN!

KRLA: 1963–1969, The Hang-On-Tight Years

My professional life was going great; my personal life needed some dialing in.

My brother and I remained incredibly handsome and suave, still living on the beach. We had, in fact, taken things an upscale-notch higher, moving from Seal Beach to Belmont Shore.

It was there that I did some more of that salt-air thinking and regrouping. I asked Jeanette and five-year-old Mike to come out to Southern California, and I offered to find them an apartment in our area.

Jeanette agreed, and having her close by was just the static-to-clarity I needed to bring thoughts of a home and a family into focus.

For about a year, Jeanette struggled with the annoyance and blinding discomfort of having to go to and from work in the shoreline fog; plus, of course, she had to deal with me. I suppose at times the two seemed pretty similar!

In 1964, we had a quiet wedding in Las Vegas and then moved back to my old comfort zone of Arcadia. We lived in an apartment complex across from the Santa Anita Racetrack while we worked to scrape up enough funds for our first home.

We were still in that apartment when our daughter Lisa was born. Young Mike was totally excited about his new sister arriving home from the hospital—and he wanted to share that excitement!

So...(unbeknownst to us until later)...he pounded on nearly every door in the complex telling all our neighbors that he was getting a new sister and that she was "gonna be an American!"

Sensing their rapt interest, he assured them that he "would come back to tell them more as new information broke!"

I think I may have been having an influence on him...

About eight weeks later, after Lisa was baptized, Mike kept his word. He went another round as town crier.

"My sister *used* to be an American," he told them all, "but now she's a Catholic!"

Dave Hull: Stunt Man

My family was growing and so was my popularity at KRLA. The demands of that popularity were also climbing the charts.

A combination of many things toppled KFWB and put KRLA on top of the Los Angeles market. The personalities of Eleven-Ten were certainly our main draw, but listener interaction was also vital— and fun.

Contests and stunts that kept our audience involved became like family lawn games after a big dinner! And the KRLA listeners were definitely a family.

One contest *literally* kick-started a new part of my radio career. It set me in motion! The Hullabalooer was speeding toward a reputation that would put me in the same danger-league as Evel Knievel, Richard Petty, Roy Rogers, and the Red Baron! I'd race golf carts, crash a hot-air balloon, straddle fierce bronco-bucking burros, and man a float in a major parade!

I was a man on the move!

And it all began with a brand new 1964 Suzuki motorbike!

Now, right around this time, the Beach Boys released their *All Summer Long* album. It featured the tune "Little Honda"—a song that would later become a number nine chart hit for a group called the Hondells.

American kids were getting into the "groovy little motorbikes," so KRLA decided to give some away. Through commercial wrangling, Suzukis became the prize choice.

This was *true* listener interaction because it involved face-to-face meetings—with *me*! And you had to answer your door *in just the right way*. (And these *were* the days when people still opened their doors to a knock!)

I had to ride the Suzuki.

I would ride up to a random home somewhere in Southern California and knock on the door with a tape recorder in hand. Then I'd wait for someone to answer and to *specifically* say to me: "Are you here to give away the Eleven-Ten KRLA Suzuki?"

If they did, the brand new bike was theirs! Of course, I then had to borrow the winner's phone to call the station for a car to pick me up!

It didn't take long for tens of thousands of people all over the Southland to answer their doors to the postman, the gardener, the milkman, or anyone who would just ring the bell, with that KRLA "catch phrase."

For weeks, my brother-in-law, Jack Fraser, and I rode everywhere on twin Suzukis the sponsor had given us to promote the giveaway—*until* we got caught in one of those rare L.A. downpours. Neither those "groovy little motorbikes" nor their operators weather monsoons well.

"First gear, hang on tight…"

This groovy little Suzuki kick-started my career outside the sound booth.

Hull's Kitchen

The KRLA family of fun extended to internal dealings as well.

Our disc jockey staff meetings were held in the "Tap Room" of the Huntington Sheraton Hotel. One morning, after we'd all run up a monster breakfast tab, one of the guys had me paged to the telephone.

"Mr. Dave Hull, telephone please. Mr. Dave Hull..."

I didn't know it, but just as soon as I left, the entire crew ran off—leaving me. *And* the bill.

No one was on the phone that I picked up.

Hmmmm...

I ran through the Tap Room's kitchen, sprinting around cooks and waiters. I leaped out of the back door and headed *my friends* off at the pass. I was standing with my arms folded as they all came around the corner of the building—*laughing*.

The smiles kind of waned as they reached for their wallets. But the "fun" never stopped.

The Great Loud Lemon Hoax

Down the road, as the always-changing face of radio brought Bill McMillan in as our news director, he arrived in a brand new car.

Always fun...

Someone in his department fastened a tiny wind whistle underneath the radiator behind the grill. On the way home, Bill heard it, of course—this horrible high-pitched piercing shriek.

He took the car back to the dealer.

Nothing!

For months, mechanics would road-test the car and come back scratching their heads. McMillan traded in the car not long after.

Junk, Jive, an' Wail

Back on the outside, I was off the soaked Suzuki but about to climb aboard one of the most impressive vehicles to ever represent a major-market, number one, bona fide, class-at-all-costs radio station.

It was the holidays and our gift to our listeners was yet another amazing promotion designed by Dick Moreland.

"Let's enter a 'junky float' in the Santa Claus Lane Parade in downtown Hollywood!" he said.

Great!

Sounds good to me!

Rumor had it that KRLA had laughed off my idea of spending five grand on a "real float," so I got my revenge with a "free" junky float. But in actuality, KRLA commissioned a professional float builder in Pasadena who, over the years, had won several grand prizes and sweepstakes awards in the Rose Parade. Our Junky Float *would* be a real float, topping any of those cheesy, chrysanthemum-shrouded New Year's Day beasts.

During the sixties decade, the Rose Parade had Grand Marshals that included Richard Nixon, Dwight Eisenhower, Arnold Palmer, Bob Hope, and Walt Disney.

Dave Hull the Hullabalooer would be on the Junky Float in the Santa Claus Lane Parade!

Something this big naturally needed planning.

Weeks before the parade-spectacular, we urged listeners to take or send any piece of junk or trash they found around their house to the float builder.

It became an exercise *from the heart*!

Some sent sentimental close-to-home-and-family items, like porch swings, washing machines, and backyard playground equipment, which had to be taken to the builder by truck. Some sent broken blenders and other midsize junk. Other listeners sent smaller, but probably just as meaningful, things.

We got a lot of everything!

Parade day excitement for our float rivaled Walt's opening of the Magic Kingdom. It was a buzz sure to eclipse the upcoming New Year's Eve vigil along Colorado Boulevard for the Tournament of Roses.

Yes!

This was *our* float! With *me*! And tens of thousands of pieces of KRLA fans' junk attached to it!

It was a pilgrimage of art as our Junky Float traveled the six-mile parade route to the thunderous applause of hundreds of thousands!

Nobody trash-talked our Junky Float at the Santa Claus Lane Parade! It wasn't our most sanitary stunt, but we came out smelling like roses!

"LET'S HEAR IT FOR ME!" Dave and his horn are so well known that the float was the most popular one in the whole parade! Dave was touched by the loyalty you all showed him and "loves you all!"

The Hullabalooer gets mobbed! Everyone wanted a personal souvenir of the Santa Claus Lane Parade, and what better souvenir could they ask for than part of Dave's float?

But then the frenzy started.

Teenage girls *swarmed* onto the float, ripping my suit jacket and shirt to shreds!

Some slight discomfort and a small amount of fear began to creep into the festivities.

To make things even *more* pulse-pumping, Jeanette and the kids were watching the whole *mob scene* on TV. But the small-screen Sylvania didn't really give them a good look at me or what was actually happening. They had no idea the extent of things until I arrived home.

I was a mess.

One thing that led to a lot of *genuine* carnage during the rush of fans was that much of the float was constructed with chicken wire. Amidst all of the "adulation," I was getting shredded by the metal. When I came in the front door, my clothes were in tatters and I was covered in blood. I looked like a combination of Freddy the Freeloader and Norman Bates! Jeanette and I just looked at each other.

But despite the chaotic gore, the float was the most popular in the parade! It was much bigger and even more impressive than the one carrying Santa Claus himself!

Our "community involvement" entry would also become the insightful and goofy genesis for the long-running, *still*-running "Doo Dah Parade" launched in Pasadena in the seventies.

After I mopped up the blood, bandaged my lacerations and punctures, and put on clothes that didn't look like shark-sliced fishnets, I realized that the parade had offered one of the most heartwarming shows of fan appreciation I ever received.

The fans had held up signs: "Dave Hull for Rose Queen!"

I may have been a bit unsteady trying to fill the shoes of "Ike" or Bob Hope as Grand Marshal, but I *think* I could have held my own with Martha Sissell or Nancy Davis!

That meant a lot.

Dave is astonished at THIS sign! He wants to give his special thanks to all of you who spent the time making those signs, and also hopes you'll all be there for the parade next year.

Fan Fare

LESSONS FROM THE PORCH PEOPLE

KRLA: 1963–1969, The Surfing-into-the-Sunset Years

The "mobs" of KRLA fans weren't limited to contest crazies, parade screamers, or even Hudson's eccentric "Commandos."

No.

We also had the true *kitchen cabinet*—the mondo-dedicated Porch People!

The station's studios in the carriage house on the grounds of the *very* prestigious Huntington Sheraton Hotel in Pasadena made for a "Drucker's General Store" setting—a literal *porch* where tales were spun and friends made.

Our studio was above the carriage house, in which—going back to the turn of the century—horses were kept. It was an incredibly cool setup. Perfect for the continual "settled in" gathering of the Porch People.

But our little group of rockin' devotees was "concerning" to the people who actually owned portions of the hotel. The Huntington Sheraton sold homes on the grounds, which were serviced by the hotel but were independently owned *by very influential people*. And these well-off people were the ones most concerned about our ability to *control* the Porch People.

I expect some of them may actually have seen the parade.

We told them we could handle any situation. If security was needed, we would take care of it.

Amid conversations and experience-sharing, there was always plenty for the Porch People to see.

WITH THE DAY'S WORK DONE AT ONLY 9 A.M., DAVE BORROWS A BIKE AND BUZZES AROUND THE GROUNDS OF THE HUNTINGTON SHERATON HOTEL.

The kids would wait to see the DJs come in and out. They could get autographs. They could check out the recording stars who would come do guest shots in the studio, answering request lines and doing interviews—big stars of the day like Jan and Dean, and the Righteous Brothers.

No matter what shift I was working, I enjoyed groovin' with the Porch People and gettin' my motor runnin' around our cool studio digs during my off hours.

My Forever-Fans

Amongst any group or circle of friends are always those who become special.

I developed *two* special friendships from that porch. Who these friends were—and *are*—says so much about what KRLA was and how its spirit and positive power still lives.

Mike McKey was a kid, twelve or thirteen, from a wealthy family in the nearby steak-and-sports-car community of San Marino.

But Mike had a problem; a shyness problem. Especially around other teenagers. He lacked some other "coolness" factors as well— Mike would ride his bike to the porch, while other kids cruised up in their cars.

One night when I pulled into the studios and walked by the porch, I noticed a couple of the other teens making fun of him.

I kept thinking about this while I got things together for my show.

I couldn't let it go.

I came back out and said that I need some help inside. I pointed to Mike. *"I need YOU to come in and give me a hand on tonight's show…"* In he came, and he stayed for a good portion of the broadcast.

No one ever made fun of that boy again.

Mike now lives in a home on the sand in Oceanside and he remains my longest fan—since 1964. *And* since '64, we still talk several times a month, and every February 14th, Jeanette receives a Valentine's Day card from Mike.

That is a fan—*that* is the lasting impact of radio as it should be. It's what so many grew up with and learned so much of life from.

Then there was Maureen—I called her "MoMo."

Maureen Moore came in one afternoon to use the restroom—and never left. She would find anything that needed to be done, in any department, just to stay. Later, she volunteered to act as my producer and ended up working with me for years. And MoMo (now Maureen Cameron) *still* calls, asking if there's anything she can do!

My forever-fans helped me both inside and outside the KRLA studio. I cherish them to this day.

Stirrings from Across the Pond

Looking back at some of those stars who passed through that carriage house studio and attracted the Porch People is far more than a simple exercise in the musical Who's Who of the day. In the context of the volcanic sixties, it shows hard debarkation points as to just how radically—and quickly—society was shifting.

Artists like Jan and Dean gave us the healthy innocence of surf and hot rod music with hits like "Surf City," "Honolulu Lulu," and "The Little Old Lady from Pasadena."

The Righteous Brothers topped the charts time and time again with their formula of "blue-eyed soul" and an operatic quality in their smooth voices. They generally wore suits onstage and were inducted into the Rock and Roll Hall of Fame in 2003.

But somewhat quietly, in February of 1963, my soon-to-be-coworker Dick Biondi played a record called "Please Please Me" on WLS in Chicago.

It is considered the first American radio broadcast of the Beatles.

In late '63, both Walter Cronkite (on his news program) and Jack Paar (on his variety/talk show) played film clips of this curious new British band and the fan-fury they were stirring up *across the pond*.

A few quick backbeats later, on February 9, 1964, the Beatles would appear *live* on *The Ed Sullivan Show*. Radio, the music industry, and the world would be changed forever.

And the Hullabalooer right along with it.

When the Reign Comes

BEATLEMANIA BEGINS

KRLA: 1963–1969, The Beginning-of-Something-Else Years

There had never been anything like it.

It seemed that all those fifties pioneers—Elvis, Little Richard, Jerry Lee Lewis, Gene Vincent, Bill Haley, Eddie Cochran, Carl Perkins, and every one of the gospel-to-blues-to-rockabilly-to-rock-'n'-roll ground-shakers—had been reduced to opening-act status.

Not necessarily in terms of *artistry,* of course, but in terms of *impact.*

Beatlemania was a rapid-fire world-scale plague of passion that polarized and pleased—offended and amazed! Parents were *so* confused; the kids were *so* caught up. The girls were all screaming. The boys were all starting bands.

Everyone wanted to be—or *had* to be—a part of this.

The coattails that followed the Beatles were the longest of any act before or since. They created the musical pull of a giant neodymium magnet! John, Paul, George, and Ringo not only did an overnight drum roll into the number one music slot in the world, but they fully and completely changed the entire genre of pop music. *All of it.*

Within their own long-haired electric-guitar-powered world, they generated a nonstop six-stringed army of band after band. But their influence reached into jazz, country, R & B, and every other niche that involved an instrument or a voice and a desire to make *some kind* of music.

And the influence wasn't limited to their raw-harmony sound and their happy-to-sophisticated lyrics and melodies; it included the bohemian freedom and fun of their appearance as well.

"The Fool on the Hill," fancies, *and* fashion...

The Beatles' bohemian influence extended from music to freedom to fashion.

It didn't take long before *legitimate* artists like bossa nova king Sergio Mendez were playing Lennon-McCartney tunes; country-western pickers like Hank Locklin were sharing the same hairstyle as Ringo; and the staid "My Girl"–style of smooth-soul sliders like the Temptations were "psychedelicized" with hard-beat blasts like "Ball of Confusion."

Here in early '64, the Beatles' reign was beginning—their rocking-rocketing rise to overarching omnipotence!

Was it perfect timing? Sure, that was a big part of it. Society was simply ready for this. Universal shock still lingered over the assassination of the President of the United States. The discontent over the escalating Vietnam War—and its debated ultimate purpose—was festering. Both were continent-sized components contributing to a growing social consciousness. And that "social consciousness" developed an appetite for deeper entertainment—or at least entertainment with more punch.

A new, mutinous distrust of authority would also grow, as citizens—especially the draft-age "but we can't vote yet" young—would look to the country's politicians for answers about the war and receive only more questions. *And* induction notices in their mailboxes.

America's brooding and enlightened look at civil rights and the evils of segregation added another explosive element to the break-out mix.

All of that and more would translate into social *change*—the Beatles, their music, and their breakin'-the-rules appearance were certainly representative of *all* that.

And was it talent? Yes! What the "Fab Four" did, along with their acclaimed producer, George Martin, was *elevate* the pop song. Sure, things may have started out with "Please Please Me" and "I Want to Hold Your Hand," but the more-than-three-chords, big-production road through "Eleanor Rigby" and "Sergeant Pepper" to "Michelle," "Yesterday," and "Let It Be" rose like *Lucy in the Sky,* high and far above things like "Norman," "The Wah-Watusi," Pat Boone's "Speedy Gonzales," and other fluff that had charted in the pre-Beatle years.

Deeper entertainment...more punch...

Introducing the Beatles

On March 22, 1963, the Beatles first album, *Please Please Me*, was released in the U.K. on the Parlophone label. Its American equivalent, *Introducing the Beatles* on the Vee-Jay label, hit U.S. stores four months later, minus two cuts: "I Saw Her Standing There" and, ironically, "Please Please Me."

From the beginning, the Beatles reinvented the entire concept of an "album." Each cut was worked into artistry—even the early cover tunes. The old template followed for years by record producers—a hit, the B-side, maybe a second single, and then a bunch of filler—was artistically exposed for the lazy sham that it always was.

Album versions from either side of the Atlantic contained smash after smash that *had* to be played. You don't ignore material like "Love Me Do," "Do You Want to Know a Secret," and the eternally-broadcast "Twist and Shout."

The dying old template was completely buried by the time the *A Hard Day's Night* and *Something New* LPs were released. Classic cuts like "Things We Said Today," "Any Time at All," and "If I Fell" just don't seem to count as *filler. Everything* counted as a hit!

And it was charisma that added gold to the Beatles' crowns. It was four individual pop-hero personalities that eclipsed even the major movie stars of the day with their respective *connections* to the public. Fifty-six-year-old Rex Harrison may have just won the Best Actor Oscar for *My Fair Lady,* but seventy-three million people were watching a young, bright, smiling Paul McCartney look into Ed Sullivan's camera giving them "All My Loving."

The time was right and they had what it takes.

The years of 1963 and 1964 were the starting line for a crazy rock 'n' roll race, and this little four-piece band from Liverpool, England, had its collective feet jammed down hard on the accelerator!

Coconut Oil Confessions

FROM A PRESIDENTIAL APPOINTMENT TO HOG JOWLS

KRLA: 1963–1969, The All-Star-Ascension Years

As long as the Beatles were on top, so was KRLA.
It was a winning combination.

—Bill Earl, *Dream-House*

The Beatles were getting bigger every second, 24/7, *Eight Days a Week*! *(Note my clever insertion of Beatles' song titles throughout!)* but as 1963 ended and '64 began, they still had to deal with *The Long and Winding Road* of a stark social and musical transition period before they hit their artistic and commercial stride.

I actually heard my first Beatles record when I was on WVKO back in '62. "Love Me Do" was already a "modest" hit in England and some copies had found their way, as promos, to some American stations. The DJs at WVKO listened to it, but no one thought it was good enough to play and add to our Tunedex!

But now...

Unlike the guys at WVKO, Dick Moreland and the KRLA staff were waking up to smell the tea and crumpets long before the rest of the L.A. airwave–Yanks when it came to recognizing the Beatles pop-potential. Towards the end of January 1964—before the Beatles had even hit the Ed Sullivan stage—Dick gave me a call.

"Dave!" Dick said, excited and exuberant. "KRLA management has decided that *you* are going to be the president of our Beatles Fan Club—the Beatles Fan Club of Southern California!"

I knew this could turn out to be a serious *Ticket to Ride* in the popularity department—for me, my show, the Beatles, and for KRLA!

And I loved opportunities like this—to be able to get even more involved with the fans. This was something I'd go for *Any Time at All*!

I told Dick that was great, but that I not only wanted to be President—I wanted to be Vice-President, Secretary, Treasurer, *and* Sergeant-at-Arms!

Dick gladly accepted my *acceptance* (but nixed my idea of a formal inauguration in the rose garden of the nearby Huntington Library!).

In February of 1964, KRLA officially became "The Original Beatles Station in Los Angeles"!

The station management not only had insight into the Beatles' potential, but with groups like the Rolling Stones tuning up in the wings, the station could see what the Beatles' *coattails* might bring into this new wave of sound as well. That gave us music momentum; plus we had an energy-young staff. We went right for the ratings throat of the number one—and aging—KFWB.

(Cue a Beatles track...)

Dave: Here's a tune. Paul McCartney and John Lennon wrote this particular recording for ME!

I'm a loser...

Dave: Wait a minute...

I'm a loser...

Dave: This is not right. It's not right!

But I am not what I appear to be.

Dave: Hold on!

(Music continues)

Dave: "I'm a loser"...Hold on—that's the most profound statement I've made all day!

KRLA was also known as "Beatle Radio" and we fielded an all-star on-air lineup: Emperor Bob Hudson in morning drive, Ted Quillin nine a.m. to noon, Casey midday, Reb Foster three to six, Bob Eubanks six to nine, *the Hullabalooer* nine to midnight, Arlen Sanders all night, and Dick Moreland and Charlie O'Donnell on weekends. As the year progressed, we would see Ted and Arlen leave. "Charlie-O" would take Ted's slot, and Bobby Dale—from KFWB and San Francisco's KEWB—would slide into the graveyard shift.

Even championship teams lose players now and then—and after all, this was radio!

In late 1963, my favorite tunes were
Bobby Vinton's "Blue Velvet"
and April Stevens & Nino Tempo's "Deep Purple."

When the Beatles took off,
my favorite hits were all theirs:
"Can't Buy Me Love," "A Hard Day's Night,"
and "I Feel Fine."

I even had the honor of meeting April Stevens—a fav from my "deep purple dreams"— and I didn't have to climb over "sleepy garden walls" to do it!

Spiking the "Punch" at the Dance

Disc jockeys were still working dance and event appearances, too, as entertainment was *deepening,* but on a small scale—like "Oldies But Goodies" *curator* Art Laboe and his traditional dances at the El Monte Legion Stadium.

But now, live music also muscled in with heavier punch.

When most DJs worked a dance, they'd no longer bring just records; they'd bring their "house band." That band would back up a couple of guest artists on *their* hits and then they'd cover many of the other current top tunes.

One of Casey Kasem's house bands was the Ventures—a surf-instrumental band that had the 1960 tidal wave of a hit "Walk, Don't Run." Casey was also close to Eddie Haddad, another L.A. music fixture. Eddie's bunch, the Band Without a Name, was managed by Casey.

The 1960s saw small dances give way to clubs, concerts, and even stadiums!

But it was all changing—and getting big!—so fast!

The small dances were giving way almost completely to the clubs of Hollywood and the Strip—the Whisky a Go Go, Gazzarri's, the Ash Grove, the Troubadour, and so many more.

Then came the famous concerts at the Shrine Auditorium, the Santa Monica Civic, the Forum, and all those "midsized" places—then it was on to the fifty-thousand-seat *stadiums*!

People had always loved live music. But it had never been like this—not on this scale—even with Elvis and some of the other teen idols. Live music, the performers on those stages, and really *each one* of us in any facet of the music biz were going through a transition. We were all just trying to understand what was really happening here and attempting to keep up with the literal day-to-day change! It was a completely unbelievable—and always-exciting—wave of time before things peaked and settled in. And that *settling in* would become a wild kind of normalcy where churning-changes and expanding music-power awareness became the everyday beat of the 1960s.

Better Than Booger—or Worse!

KRLA's "baby boy," Ted Quillin, exited KRLA toward the end of the summer of '64—fired because his show leaned a little too much toward the "blue" side of humor and double entendres. Remember, this was still the early- to mid-sixties. Think back to the TV show *WKRP in Cincinnati*—DJ "Dr." Johnny Fever always talked about being fired from a station for saying "booger" on the air.

He wasn't exaggerating by much!

But Ted Quillin had experienced another "firing" from KRLA, earlier that summer. And I was right in the middle of it!

I was fashionably tanning in front of my cool shoreline pad (which I was still sharing with my brother right before Jeanette became my *Girl* for good), when Gary came running out of the house and across the hot sand to tell me that Reb Foster was on the phone. (Again, for you young folks who can't imagine a non-portable world: *There were no cell phones back then!*)

"Dave!" Reb said. "I need you to take the morning show tomorrow—Quillin's been fired! Dick Moreland finished the show today but it's *yours* tomorrow!"

I was sweaty and wreaking madly from the pungent-punch of Coconut Coppertone Caribbean suntan oil, but I stood, dripped, and listened as Reb explained.

The explanation took a while. By the time Reb was getting to the point, our entire house smelled like a spilled pitcher of piña coladas.

What happened was that Ted had played "The Bird's the Word" by the Rivingtons. After the tune had ended, he'd told our listeners, "That's the Rivingtons doing their bird for you…that beat they've got, it's like hog maws and hog jowls."

Station manager John Barrett went nuts! He had no idea what "hog maws" or "hog jowls" were, or what Quillin's Southern reference to them meant—and anyway, he thought Ted had said *"hog balls"*!

And that was a lot worse than *booger*!

To make this thick Southern lingo-gumbo even more unpalatable, Barrett was convinced that "doing their bird" was somehow down in the jargon gutter with "hog balls." To John, Ted might just as well have played the complete Redd Foxx album, *Racy Tales,* on the air and followed it up with a drunken rendition of *"There once was a woman from Nantucket..."*

Well, I worked just one of Ted's shifts before Don Cooke—one of the station's *actual* owners at the time, along with his brother, future Lakers owner Jack Kent Cooke—set Barrett straight in the Confederate cuisine department and KRLA's "baby boy" was back.

At least for now.

Meanwhile, everything was *Flying* high with the Beatles Fan Club! KRLA printed numbered membership cards, prizes were awarded to members for listening, membership could get you into special events, and we had tons of other promotions.

Within six months, over a half-million club cards were sent out!

It was another winner for Eleven-Ten and another defeat for the tiring ratings champ, KFWB.

KRLA was number one!

The Fifth Beatle

"YOUR MOTHER SHOULD KNOW"

KRLA: 1963–1969, The Spy-Scoop Years

My "office" as President of the Beatles Fan Club actually became more geared toward *espionage* than legislative action. The Beatles generated stories, speculations, new releases, and an entire pop-pipeline of news and gossip—everyone simply *had* to know *Every Little Thing*!

And *I* was the insider! I was the spy! I had my finger on the Liverpudlian pulse!

Rumors were flying *Here, There, and Everywhere* about the Fab Four. And the thing about many of them was—*I'd make them up*, right off the *Tip of My Tongue*. That way, of course, I'd be able to affirmatively, absolutely, and completely dispel them! *I had the truth!*

Ringo is <u>not</u> terminally ill!

John's <u>not</u> really from Mississippi!

George <u>isn't</u> giving up his guitar for the trombone!

Paul <u>does not</u> intend to start dating Ethel Merman!

But along with the on-air *news* about the Beatles, fans wanted *them,* in their pale British flesh, even more. Their music had been heard. Their faces had been seen in those live performances on Sullivan's show and on film on Paar's and Cronkite's. But there had been no real *personal* interchange.

Yet...

My *espionage* was about to pay off.

One night at work, I received an anonymous off-the-air, *off-the-record* phone call.

"John Lennon; his wife, Cindy; George Harrison; and his girlfriend, Patty Boyd, will be arriving at LAX in the morning," a mysterious male voice told me. *"They won't be getting off the plane...but they will be waiting while other passengers get off and new passengers get on board. The flight number, gate arrival, and time is as follows..."*

Wow!

I really had to think about this!

Could this be true, or would I be heading out for a wild *Blackbird* chase that would make me look like a hapless early paparazzi and destroy my solid credibility?!

The next morning, I decided I had to gamble. I couldn't risk missing an opportunity like this. I'd better be there—*with my tape recorder.*

I followed the flight and gate instructions perfectly—like a CIA operative delivering an international ransom.

I found the gate and asked at the airline desk if I could board the plane and talk with a passenger before the flight departed. In those days, long before the tight, shoes-off, ticketed-passengers-only, no-shampoo-in-a-bottle security we have today, a friendly request like that was no problem. In fact, the gal at the desk *knew* what I was there for. *"The Beatles are on board,"* she whispered. *"But you better hurry! The plane will be taking off soon!"*

I ran down the gangway and jumped onto the Boeing 707. Sure enough, the two Beatles were there and I got the first *real* interview—ten minutes with John, George, and their ladies. No one else on the West Coast had yet broadcast their voices in that kind of a format.

But then again, that was fitting—after all I *was* the President!

I never *did* learn who had called me that night.

But there would be many more "scoops."

I was the first West Coast DJ to get the inside scoop on George Harrison (right) and the other Beatles. There would be many more...

Over the years, fans have asked me
which one of the Beatles I liked the best.
It was Paul.
We got along very well, and he was the
most playful with me on the air.

I suppose that's why my all-time favorite
Beatles song is "Yesterday,"
written, produced, and sung by Paul.
It remains my favorite to this day,
along with his 1970 hit
"The Long and Winding Road."

I Want to Tell You

Soon after the on-plane chat, I began corresponding regularly with George Harrison's mother, Louise, in Liverpool.

Don't *Ask Me Why*, but on kind of a hullabalooing whim, I called the Liverpool Overseas Information Operator who provided me with the *home phone number* of George and Louise Harrison! That's how things went back then.

Beyond excited, I hung up and called them immediately. Louise answered the phone—but then politely inquired as to whether I had any idea what time it was there? In fact, I didn't. I had completely forgotten to take into account the eight-hour time "discrepancy" between L.A. and London; it was now after midnight! Oops! But George's mom further surprised me by telling me that she would love to speak with me about "the boys" a little later in the morning.

Wow, again!

More espionage!

I got my universal Greenwich mean time clock in order and called Louise back after midnight *our* time—morning, *their* time. She told me that she would be more than happy to tell me some private *Top Secret Information*, things concerning the boys (I could almost see her British-proper but slightly devilish smile over the phone!). She *suggested* that she could give me the Beatles' addresses, telephone numbers, where they were staying on tours, even their girlfriends' names. None of which would generate many *Words of Love* from *the boys*, especially John and Paul.

The calls continued for over a year, with Louise supplying me with all kinds of inside stuff! She seemed to really enjoy her position as a "mother to a star"; she adored her son and would do anything for him—like helping propel him into one of the most talked-about and popular artists on the planet.

I would also have Louise *Carry That Weight* with rumor control. By now, a lot of rumors *besides mine* were circulating—Louise would be the final word.

I became the on-air direct line to all personal Beatles-biz. Our listeners went nuts and screamed for more!

The Beatles manager, Brian Epstein, kind of screamed, too! Epstein and the Beatles themselves wanted to know just *who* was giving me all of their secret information.

I cannot divulge my source!

I Want to Tell You that I was in a very unique position.

I alone comprised the entirety of the executive branch of the fan club, and I was providing a *Magical Mystery Tour* of secret inside Beatles blabber. For this, I became renowned and known as "the Fifth Beatle"!

A SECRET AGENT trailing a spy? No, just a not-so-secret deejay named Dave Hull broadcasting a report on one of his brushes with a gang of foreign agents known as the Beatles.

Although executive head of the Beatles Fan Club, I engaged mainly in covert ops! My endless espionage earned me the title of the Fifth Beatle.

It was a title I was proud of, but it came with royal responsibility and discretion! I never *did* tell George it was his mother who was the mouth of the "leak"! They were very close and *I* wasn't about to be the one to break the news that his "mum" was a bit of a Merseyside Mata Hari!

The British Are Coming!

THE KRLA BEAT

KRLA: 1963–1969, The Sink-*and*-Swim Years

It was a simple light-cardboard poster. Low-budget and bare-basic compared to today's high-tech multimedia marketing tools. But it was a call to *open* arms that put the lemon and cinnamon on the Chelsea bun for L.A. Beatles fans.

Bob Eubanks was bringing the first Beatles concert to Southern California!

We would finally get the quartet *here* in their lovable "pale British flesh"!

The poster may have been simple, but making this concert a reality was as difficult as flying *Across the Universe* in that little Piper plane I nearly wrecked back in Roswell!

Eubanks had to conjure up more of that L.A.–KRLA radio magic! His abilities were extraordinary, but bringing the biggest act in the world to Los Angeles required him to throw everything into the project, including the kitchen sink—for real! And it was his own kitchen sink! Bob had to mortgage his *home* to make this happen.

The concert also provided a great example of how *some* business people have *no* foresight whatsoever. The first bank Bob went to for a loan to secure the concert called his venture an "entertainment scheme" and his personal outlook "naïve."

Of course, the Beatles had also been rejected by Decca Records when the band was hustling for a recording contract (*"Not to mince words, Mr. Epstein, but we don't like your boys' sound. Groups are out; four-piece groups with guitars particularly are finished...The Beatles have no future in show business."*).

But Bob's hard struggle to bring the Beatles to the Bowl had a very positive flipside—showing how some people have *plenty* of foresight and just how it can pay off. The second bank Bob went to for *Help* wasn't quite of the higher *station* in business that the first one was. But despite the décor of a repossessed leaking motorcycle in their lobby, the bank manager—whose son was a big Beatles fan— went for the deal. The bank had Bob's house and Bob had the Beatles at the Hollywood Bowl!

And, wow, here's a surprise: the concert sold out in about three hours! Well, it wasn't a surprise to Bob, but it *was* a surprise to the Hollywood Bowl. The Bowl had handled Sinatra and every one of the show-biz biggies, and they were *sure* they couldn't—and wouldn't— sell the famous amphitheater's eighteen thousand seats *in one day.*

They were wrong. *Bob* was right.

Bob even tried to set up a second show for the following night, but that idea couldn't *Come Together* because Beatles manager Brian Epstein didn't think his boys could sell out a second show.

And that bank thought *Bob* was naïve!

I may not have mortgaged my house like Bob, to bring the Beatles to So Cal, but I did help get 'em through customs at LAX! (Left to right: Derek Taylor; yours truly—the helpful Hullabalooer; Ringo Starr; and John Lennon.)

I Am the Walrus

The day of the concert predictably involved more than just *Rock and Roll Music*.

The pre-performance press conference, held at Bob's Cinnamon Cinder in North Hollywood, was stressful enough, with its late start and eight hundred people crammed into the four-hundred-or-so-capacity nightclub. But that wasn't all. Later, *some* of us wound up being lifeguards!

And it wasn't at one of our local beaches!

Now, when the world-famous, recognized-everywhere, arched-stage, everybody-who-is-anyone-has-played-there Hollywood Bowl amphitheater was built in 1922, it was the opening overture for a series of never-ending changes in its glamorous superstar face.

One of those manicure-makeovers included the addition of a reflecting pool directly in front of the shell-shaped stage.

The Bowl's famous shell-shaped stage became even *more* famous after the Beatles concert sold out in an unheard-of three hours! (Left to right: Bob Eubanks, me, and Derek Taylor.)

From 1953 until 1972, the soothing ambience of the water glistened and rippled in front of the performances of artists like Leonard Bernstein, Henry Mancini, Sonny and Cher, Otis Redding, Miles Davis—and now, of course, *the Beatles*.

So here it is, August 23, 1964—*our* night at the Bowl—and I'm working on- and offstage with KRLA jock Charlie O'Donnell. Charlie and his venerable voice had rocked the stage with Dick Clark on the original *American Bandstand* shows from Philadelphia.

We were standing to the side of the stage when a young teenage girl apparently wasn't content to *bathe* in the ambience of just listening. No.

Got to Get You into My Life...

And the pool was her perfect waterway shortcut to the band.

But it became an *eerie* canal!

Her bout of Beatlemania (a common malady of the time!) obviously drowned her senses, causing her to forget that *she couldn't swim*!

Man overboard!!!

Charlie and I splashed in like Wally Walrus chasing Woody Woodpecker, and we bailed her out of the Highland Avenue version of *The Octopus's Garden*.

Bob Bats a Thousand

When all was sung and done, Bob didn't exactly make a fortune on the concert (just about a thousand bucks to be sort of exact) but he *was* able to bail out his kitchen sink—and the rest of his house, too! *And* he learned a lot about the concert-promotion end of the music industry.

Bob Eubanks would *Come and Get It* again. He and his growing wisdom and savvy would return the Beatles to the Bowl in August of

1965, *this* time for *two* back-to-back shows. And a year after that, in the summer of '66, he dropped the boys right into the center of the forty-thousand-plus-seat Dodger Stadium.

(Cue Commercial...)

Announcer: Nine days till "B" Day in Los Angeles! Nine days till KRLA brings the Beatles to Dodger Stadium!

Hurry! Time is running out!

Dodger Stadium becomes Beatles Stadium, Sunday night, August 28th. There's still time to get tickets to see the Beatles, but better hurry to a nearby Wallichs Music City store or one of the Mutual Ticket Agencies in Southern California. It's too late now to order your tickets by mail!

See the Beatles! Sunday night, August 28th, 8:00 p.m. at Beatles Stadium!

Warped Wax

The second of the two Hollywood Bowl shows in '65 has long been regarded as one of the Beatles' better live performances, but recordings of all three of their Bowl concerts—in one form or another—eventually supplied material for their 1977 live album, *The Beatles at the Hollywood Bowl.*

Bob Eubank's savvy and foresight was seen again when Capitol Records asked for his permission—as promoter and the guy "in charge" of things—to record the '64 Bowl bash and subsequent performances. His deal was to let them, *but* when and if an album was made, Bob would get to write the liner notes.

Fine...

Years later, producer George Martin jumped into the project. And Martin had the credentials and the skill. He had produced all but one of the Beatles' original albums and is considered one of the greatest record producers of all time. (The guy had thirty number one hits in the U.K. and twenty-three in the U.S.A.!)

So naturally, it is he who wanted to produce this live album. And he, of course, wanted to write the accompanying text.

*Again, fine...*for a price.

The contract from '64 still stood.

George Martin *did* cut a deal and write the liner notes, but the production end proved to be a lot tougher. The album created a nightmare web of work for Martin as he tried to take relatively poor recordings and mold them into release-worthy material. The technical manipulations and gyrations that went into *The Beatles at the Hollywood Bowl* became legend- and lore-filled.

And that wasn't the only Beatles album to be shrouded in strangeness and curiosity!

The Beatles' 1964 maiden musical voyage at the Hollywood Bowl also provided the opportunity for KRLA newsman Jim Steck and I to conduct a series of interviews with John, Paul, George, and Ringo. Those interviews not only made for some great exclusive pieces on KRLA, but they were also the Fab Four fodder for one of the most "interesting" of all the Beatles collector-curious albums, *Hear the Beatles Tell All.*

By November of 1963, Capitol Records was the contractual home for the Beatles. But other than the "She Loves You" single on the Swan label and a couple of other ancient oddities, the Beatles' earliest recordings were on the relatively small Vee-Jay label—and most of the cuts were included on the *Introducing the Beatles* album. But Vee-Jay was really milking the sparse catalog it owned.

The dozen tunes from *Introducing the Beatles* were stretched out into material for such Vee-Jay "compilation" LPs as *Jolly What! The Beatles & Frank Ifield On Stage* (Frank Ifield was an Australian recording artist based in the U.K. This album has an entire legend of its own behind it!); *Songs, Pictures and Stories of the Fabulous Beatles; The Beatles vs. the Four Seasons;* and *The 15 Greatest Songs of the Beatles.*

Hear the Beatles Tell All was intended to be a promotional piece for the rest of the Beatles' 1964 summer tour, but it wound up being a full release in Vee-Jay's Beatles stable in September of that year.

Side One was Jim's interview with John only; on Side Two, *I* interviewed all four of the boys. But in its rush to market the record, Vee-Jay reversed our "roles"—the labels on the first pressings read "Jim Steck Interviews John, Paul, George, Ringo" for Side One, and "Dave Hull Interviews John Lennon" for Side Two. After they caught the error, Vee-Jay requested that all copies of the records be returned—but those are the kinds of twists that make true collectors' items. And it seemed so many things in the LPs of the day were *bent as a nine bob note*—especially when it came to the Beatles!

Another of those freak-misprints on *Hear the Beatles Tell All* happened when whoever was putting together the graphics for the album's jacket became a little confused while listening to my "radio voice."

The collage of graphics on the front featured randomly placed phrases and questions relating to the interviews. One of the blurbs is "GEORGE TALKS ABOUT THE PADDY BOYD."

Huh?

This Beatles album *and* its cover were "bent as a nine bob note"!

You see, in radio you don't pronounce T's. We were taught to pronounce a T like a D. That's considered a "soft approach" to pronunciation of certain letters and sounds; that "softness" prevents an ugly pop in the microphone.

Well, what the graphics guy was *trying* to convey was that I talked with George about his girlfriend, *Patty* Boyd!

Keeping the Beat

And the ripples from the Beatles' first splash at the Bowl were far from over. When Bob Eubanks gambled his home and went high-stakes on the Beatles, he was on his way to winning something not only for himself; he was winning something for all of us in radio and music. What he did went so, so far!

Another double-down effect of that wager was a pioneering experiment in journalism. The *KRLA Beat* put the print media into musical motion, preceding *Tiger Beat* magazine by a full year and *Rolling Stone* magazine by three!

Originally planned as just the program for the Beatle-Bowl concert, the *KRLA Beatle Concert Souvenir Program* name was cut to *KRLA Beat* and the short fold-over became a regularly published *newspaper* that included the KRLA Tunedex, columns by me, Bob, and other Eleven-Ten Men, and the latest news about current bands and artists.

"America's Largest Teen NEWSpaper" was eventually available at music stores everywhere and at our studios. Its weekly must-have acquisition became another regular stop within the rolling and growing music scene in Southern California.

It was now a part of daily life to stay immersed in the music and the personalities and to keep absolutely on top of it all. No one wanted to be the last to know that Gerry and the Pacemakers were releasing a new single or that the Dave Clark Five would be starring in their own movie.

The speed of this race was not *even* about to *Slow Down.*

Scuzzy Scandals

From Stowaways to Skivvies to the Stones

KRLA: 1963–1969, The Pop-Star-Pandemonium Years

All of the interviews, the more-than-legendary Hollywood Bowl performance, the screams from the girls, the start of the *KRLA Beat*—even my plunge into the "moat"—were history-making, for sure. But none of that stuff flirted with, well, a *federal criminal offense*!

One more collateral *situation* played its way out from Bob Eubanks' first Beatle-Bowl. And that situation was the most infamous "stowaway" scandal since 1928!

You see, back in '28 a nineteen-year-old European guy named Clarence Terhune hid himself on board the Graf Zeppelin dirigible; he became the first stowaway to fly across the ocean.

Clarence may have achieved some heights, but *the world hadn't seen nothin' yet!*

Right after the Beatles played their last tune and bounced off the Bowl stage, they headed for Denver and their next gig via a chartered flight from LAX. I had also jetted off to the airport, hoping for a last-minute interview at the bottom of the plane's loading ramp. Jim Steck, of course, was there with me.

"I'm getting on board!" Steck suddenly told me. "I'm going to fly with them to Denver!"

What?!

I quickly tried to explain a couple of things to Jim.

"*First, you're not on the charter flight manifest.*

"*Second, it's against the law to do something like this!*

"*Third, it's a really bad idea!*"

It appeared, however, that my incredible wisdom was about to be ignored.

In fact, Jim didn't give me even one slight, condescending moment where he even *pretended* to mull over what I was saying.

"I'm going!" he said. And up the ramp he ran.

I followed him!

My real purpose was to try and convince Jim of the "bad idea" part of my suggestions! But when the Beatles' security people at the top of the ramp by the plane's door recognized the both of us, they waved us in.

No problem...

Yet.

Please fasten your seat belts...

When we got to Denver, there were, of course, *no* accommodations for us anywhere! And we had only thirteen dollars between us.

Worst of all, our names were *not* on the flight manifest.

And that *legally* classified us as *illegal* stowaways!

When everyone was getting off the plane, the first one to see *me* was Ringo.

Then the Beatles' road manager, Neil Aspinall, spotted us.

Then their press secretary, Derek Taylor.

Ringo seemed pleased. Neil and Derek, not as thrilled.

Derek gathered up his things and took me right to Brian Epstein, who by now was trying to enjoy an unwinding drink in his hotel room. Epstein was the only one who could manipulate the manifest and get us on it before we were *all* in *Misery*.

Brian was even less happy than Neil and Derek at our Clarence Terhune act (although I'm pretty sure he didn't really know much about Clarence—beyond the basics that we *all* certainly know!) but he *did* "fix" the flight manifest.

That perked me up in a hurry!

I figured we were on a roll at that point, so I also asked Brian for front row seats and backstage passes for Jim and me for the performance two nights later at Denver's Red Rocks Amphitheater.

I mean, we were already there and everything.

I don't know just how delighted he was with that, but he *did* give us the all-access.

Now it was time to call our boss at KRLA, John Barrett, and *explain* the whole situation—mainly why we were now 1,013 miles from where we were supposed to be!

Barrett actually took the complex news pretty well—but he was vehement about our possible future in federal custody: "If your names aren't on that manifest, you're *doomed*!" Then he wired us fifty bucks and return plane tickets home.

Pick Your Enemies...

There was another Barrett I had to contend with in Denver—*Rona* Barrett. Rona was no relation to John, but she did have a connection to virtually everyone in show business—mainly because *her* business was *their* business.

Rona Barrett has spent decades as *the* entertainment reporter for publications and television shows such as *Good Morning America* and NBC's *Today* show.

And she recognized *me.*

"Dave, I'm Rona Barrett," she said, introducing herself at the Red Rocks concert. "And I'm going to lose my job."

What?

It was quite an ice-breaker!

"I'm going to lose my job if I don't get an interview with the Beatles," she pleaded. "And you're the only one I know here who can get me in to see them. Can you do that?"

"Rona, let me check," I told her. "I'm not going to say yes or no, but let me go talk to Brian Epstein or Neil Aspinall. If they say yes, then get ready to get in there."

Amidst all the Epstein stress and pressure—which I was probably *somewhat* responsible for—I somehow managed to work it out: Rona Barrett got backstage with the Beatles.

And then she proceeded to trash them in her article.

The headline read: *I Saw the Beatles in Their Underwear.*

Well, of course she did! They were backstage changing and they let her come in, in between shows.

I never forgave her—and the Beatles didn't either!

"Pick your enemies carefully or
you'll never make it in Los Angeles."

—Rona Barrett

Paint It Black...or Blue

Beatles-at-the-Bowl I was epic. But just three months after that, Bob Eubanks was looking for further commercial *Satisfaction* (I know, this is a Stones song, but it does fit perfectly! And there'll be more!), so he brought a very young Mick Jagger and his Rolling Stones to the four-thousand-seat Long Beach Auditorium.

And it was sure different than the Beatles. Eubanks had to *Play with Fire* instead of enjoying *A Taste of Honey*.

"Tell Me, Dave," Bob said. "Would you like to emcee the concert along with Dick Moreland and Charlie O'Donnell?" Well, I wasn't *Sittin' on the Fence* on that one!

"I'd be *Happy* to do it!"

I arrived at the auditorium in my brand new Cadillac—a white Coupe Deville with less than a thousand miles on it. It was a special night, so I had Jeanette, Mike, and my mother with me—all of us sitting tall and proud in that shiny Caddy.

We eased on into the parking lot.

Pop-star pandemonium!

Hundreds of girls made up a sea of feminine fandom that we had to somehow get the car through. And the mascaraed mob was gearing up for a night with a group that was emerging as the "darker, bad-boy side" of what was now officially being called the "British Invasion"— the knees-up parade of English bands sweeping through America on those long coattails of the Beatles.

As we tried to part the skirted sea to slide into our VIP parking area, the girls looked in the car windows and saw me and my family.

And they began jumping!

On the car!

I knew what I had to do! I had to be the brave scout who went for the cavalry! I forced the big door open and made a run for security! You could almost hear the bugles *bugling* as the men with badges came to get my family safely into the concert. The immediate crowd around the car was dispersed as well—but not before making off with one of Mike's shoes during my family's "rescue"!

And not until they had destroyed the car.

They tore it to hell. The top, the hood—they just tore the hell out of it!

We went to the concert in a brand new Cadillac; we limped home in something that *Wild Horses* had run over.

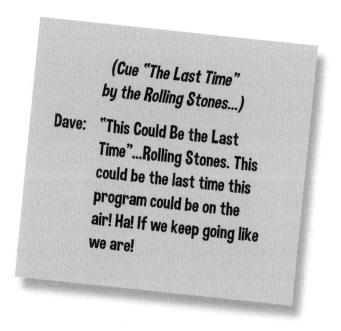

(Cue "The Last Time" by the Rolling Stones...)

Dave: "This Could Be the Last Time"...Rolling Stones. This could be the last time this program could be on the air! Ha! If we keep going like we are!

Neither we—nor our insurance company—had much *Sympathy for Those Devils*! (Though the cops *did* manage to find Mike's shoe!)

But we had work to do! I was the emcee!

The Stones concert wasn't the first— or last time—I was besieged by feminine fandom and pop-star pandemonium!

Once I parked what was left of the car, I went backstage with the Rolling Stones. Even then, the Stones were becoming known for their tireless touring—very little time was set aside for anything but performing and partying.

They definitely hadn't set aside *any* time for hygiene.

SORRY ABOUT THAT, MICK . . . .

The Stones' busy schedule included partying and performing—not much else!

In the dressing room, they'd removed their pants to clean up with a bit of a sponge bath—no time was even *considered* for a full shower.

I noticed that all of their legs were blue. *Levi's denim blue.*

I asked them where they had bought their jeans.

New York...

I looked at their schedule and did some quick calculations. New York had been eighteen days ago. Eighteen days in the same jeans. Eighteen days of a lot of wear, a lot of body heat, and little washing.

The blue dye and that pale U.K. skin were becoming sweat-fused and permanent!

Oh well, *It's Only Rock and Roll...*

And ultimately, that's what *all of this* was all about.

Beatles, Bones, & Boris

As 1964 ended, Saturday nights became especially "interesting" at KRLA. It was like the Beatles meet Frankenstein!

Along with my weekday shifts, I was doing a Saturday night six-to-midnight show—the *Saturday Night Special.* But on Halloween night, management cut the show by three hours and put in a nine-to-midnight spookfest hosted by Bobby "Boris" Pickett, the Karloff-voiced "singer" who had a giant hit in 1962 with "Monster Mash." That Halloween, Bobby opened the creaking door to his full creepy closet of monster voices, noises, clanks, chains, and screams!

From that night on, through the rest of '64, Saturday night was a six-hour bash with me playing mostly Beatles tunes and Bobby Boris rattling bones 'til the witching hour!

And these kinds of chaotic nights wouldn't be the *only* ominous portals opened over the next few years as the 1960s were detonated and defined.

Speaking of creepy chaos...another promo op we KRLA DJs got was to cruise around in the Munster Koach to dig up young viewers for the upcoming TV series! Herman's ride was created by the legendary Los Angeles Kustom Kar King, George Barris. (Left to Right: a macabre me, Herman Munster, Bob Eubanks, and Emperor Bob Hudson.)

Help!

SOUL-SEARCHING IN PARADISE

KRLA: 1963–1969, The Cynicism-in-the-Sun Years

On February 23, 1965, filming began on the Beatles second movie, *Help!*

Their first motion picture, 1964's *A Hard Day's Night* had been an absolute smash, coming in at number nine in the top ten for that year—just behind flicks like *Mary Poppins* and *Viva Las Vegas* (and soundly vaporizing *Santa Claus Conquers the Martians*). *TIME* magazine rated *A Hard Day's Night* as one of the best "All-*TIME* 100 Movies." The black-and-white documentary-style work is credited with having influenced 1960s spy films, *The Monkees* television show, and pop music videos. It is considered the first feature film that could later be characterized as a "mockumentary."

Help! would follow *A Hard Day's Night* in success and impact, but with a bigger budget that allowed it to be filmed in color and on location in places like the Austrian Alps and the Bahamas.

The higher profile big-time, big-screen look of *Help!* was not the *only* change *Twist(ing) and Shout(ing)* within the *evolving* world of the Beatles.

In September of 1964, Derek Taylor had resigned both as the group's press agent and as Brian Epstein's personal assistant. The split was ugly and followed a heated battle between Epstein and the always intense and edgy Taylor.

But Taylor remained in the music game. In 1965, he and his family immigrated to America. Taylor had gotten to know Bob Eubanks pretty well during the bringing-the-Beatles-to-the-Bowl ordeal, so when Derek returned to "the colonies," Bob hired him into the music management firm he now owned, Prestige Publicity.

Ironically, Derek's first job was to sign and handle the all-American band, Paul Revere and the Raiders.

Kicks just keep gettin' harder to find...

Taylor's second official act was to go with *me* to Paradise Island in the Bahamas to interview his former employers and to report on the filming of *Help!* for KRLA and Prestige.

It was an awkward situation for Derek to say the least. In his book *As Time Goes By: Living in the Sixties,* that *edgy* cynicism is loud and clear as he bitterly describes the meeting with his old friends:

> *We arrived in Nassau to find the Beatles just leaving for dinner in town. They were less than glad to see me, old pal in radio drag with a tape recorder over my shoulders.*
>
> *"This is Derek Taylor, reporting from the Bahamas. I have with me Ringo Starr of the Beatles. Hi, Ringo. Nice to see you again."*
>
> *"Hi, Derek. Nice to see you again. What are you doing with a microphone under my famed nose?"*
>
> *What indeed?*

DEREK TAYLOR AND THE HULLABALOOER step off a sleek jet after an exciting trip to the Bahamas for visits with the **BEATLES**.

Derek may have suffered from some personal displacement and "identity loss," but emotional wrenching aside, for three weeks we all lived in Paradise—an island that lived up to its name—with a suite of rooms that adjoined. Derek and I were in one room, Brian Epstein in his own, John and Paul in theirs, and George and Ringo in the last.

The things I learned...

The boys were becoming *different*.

A Taste of Duck Soup

We were primarily there to cover the making of a seminal rock 'n' roll movie. But if contemplative observations and personal peering into souls came along with that, well, then, *Bob's your uncle!*

The basic premise of *Help!* was that the four Beatles were being pursued by an Eastern cult because Ringo was in possession of a "sacrificial ring."

Okay... (You could taste a large ladling of the Marx Brothers' *Duck Soup* here.)

One scene had Ringo being splotched with red paint in front of a giant idol. As the action played out and the filming went on and on, the rest of us sat in the sand and talked about hundreds of subjects—all the things that were going through the boys' minds.

Contemplative observations and personal peering into souls...

That sort of ramble was a big part of the "life-examination" factor that helped define the 1960s. *Everyone* began to *think* about *everything*.

It could be seen—and heard—in the huge difference between Beatles starting-line works like "I Saw Her Standing There" and the much higher-octane tunes from the new *Help!* Soundtrack, such as "You've Got to Hide Your Love Away" and "Yesterday." The *real* strangeness of "Lucy in the Sky" hadn't floated down quite yet, but the times were indeed a-changin'.

Life Through *George-Colored* Glasses

One day when I was setting up to interview George Harrison, I laid my *rather expensive* sunglasses down on a beach blanket. He arrived and we began talking—*rambling*—about his finding a small dog on the island and spending hours walking with him.

After a while, George looked down at my glasses and said, "So, that's where I put them."

I informed him that the glasses were mine and that I had just laid them down. He told me I was wrong and that they were *his*. I really thought it was odd, but I didn't dispute it because I wanted to cut through some of the ramble and get the interview done.

So George took *my* glasses and wore them throughout the entire filming.

But I got the interview and many more.

HULL, TAYLOR VISITING SCENE OF BEATLE MOVIE

(KRLA's Dave Hull and Derek Taylor are on Nassau, guests of the Beatles during filming of their second movie. Their reports and interviews are being broadcast daily over KRLA.)

by Dave Hull

Hi, Hullabalooers!

Right now Derek and I are relaxing beside the pool here at the beautiful Balmoral Country Club after our first get-together with out hosts — four fellows named George, John, Paul and Ringo.

You probably never heard of them, but they're singers. Also movie actors. Their group is called . . . let's see, is it the Bugs? No, that doesn't sound right. Maybe they're the Insects. No, that's not right either. Surely I haven't forgotten.

Here it is . . . I wrote it down so I wouldn't f o r g e t. THE BEATLES! Isn't that a funny name? They couldn't amount to much with a name like that.

They're nice boys, though.

Seriously, it was a great thrill seeing them again after their visits to Los Angeles last summer.

They said to tell all of you hello and that they were looking forward to their next trip to Southern California Aug. 29 and 30. They regard last year's performance at the Hollywood Bowl as the highlight of their tour.

Derek and I saw them for only a few minutes today between scenes for their movie. We have a longer meeting scheduled tomorrow, and at that time we'll start asking them the questions many of you sent in to us before we left KRLA.

It was like old home week when they saw Derek. He had been their long-time press officer before leaving the group to move to Los Angeles, and Paul said things didn't seem the same without him.

Congratulates Ringo

I congratulated Ringo on his marriage and didn't have the nerve to tell him what a lot of you said about that!

Neither Maureen nor John's wife, Cynthia, came with them to Nasau and they're razzing Ringo about the nightly calls he makes to her in England. He's been away from her for more than a week now . . . almost half their married life.

Everything is so British here in the Bahamas. It's a British possession, you know, and I feel a little out of place. But Derek feels right at home. In fact, I may have to tie him up to get him back to KRLA.

Beatle Answers

In next week's issue of the Beat we'll have transcripts with our interviews with the Beatles, including their answers to some of the questions you have been asking . . . such as how the other boys are reacting to Ringo's mariage . . . what effect they think it will have on their popularity . . . any possible wedding plans for the two bachelors — Paul and George — plus more information about the movie and what they are doing in it. We will also have more pictures of the boys here in Nasau.

The interviews I got were continuous and so varied—John complaining about the humidity on the island and having to get up so early "just to sit around watching Ringo being filmed"; Paul relating humorous stories about his recent trip to Tunisia; Ringo dispelling rumors that he'd been hurt while diving off a boat during filming.

The lengths of the interviews would vary, depending on the questions and just how complex the boys wanted their answers to be. But mostly the interviews were existential examples of that never-ending let's-interact-with-our-fellow-man part of the sixties' loose-landscape.

As one Beatle would leave, another would sit down in the island sand to record.

Here Comes the Sun...

I'd send the tapes by air express directly to KRLA, where the engineering staff would edit them into separate lengths. The cuts would be played over and over again on the air, from morning until midnight; and then the crew would receive and edit more for the next day.

Nobody seemed to mind if they heard the same interview several times over, constantly reflecting about what the Beatles had said. It was the sixties.

Everyone thinking—and talking—about everything...

And there was that change in *the boys.*

And the reasons for it.

The subject of drugs not only *crept* into later conversations about that thinking-talking period in the Bahamas—it did a reverse back somersault right into the deep end of things...

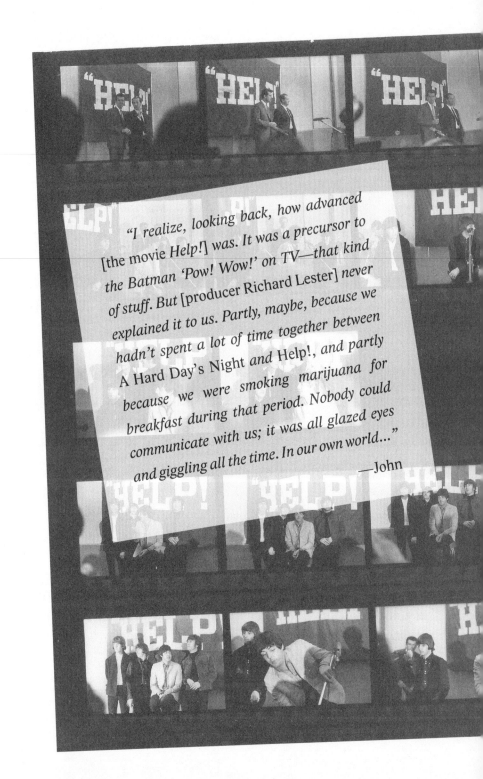

"I realize, looking back, how advanced [the movie Help!] was. It was a precursor to the Batman 'Pow! Wow!' on TV—that kind of stuff. But [producer Richard Lester] never explained it to us. Partly, maybe, because we hadn't spent a lot of time together between A Hard Day's Night and Help!, and partly because we were smoking marijuana for breakfast during that period. Nobody could communicate with us; it was all glazed eyes and giggling all the time. In our own world..."

—John

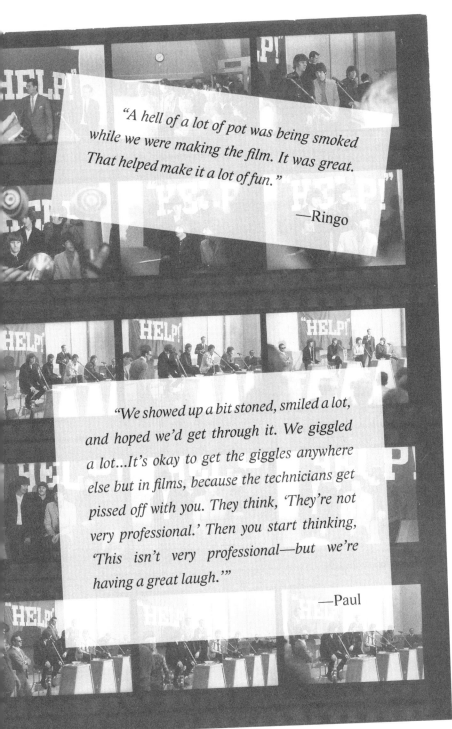

"A hell of a lot of pot was being smoked while we were making the film. It was great. That helped make it a lot of fun."

—Ringo

"We showed up a bit stoned, smiled a lot, and hoped we'd get through it. We giggled a lot...It's okay to get the giggles anywhere else but in films, because the technicians get pissed off with you. They think, 'They're not very professional.' Then you start thinking, 'This isn't very professional—but we're having a great laugh.'"

—Paul

Years later in 2007, Apple Records in England called me requesting permission to release those "on the sand" interviews I conducted back in '65. Those interviews—and in particular, the sunglasses-*less* chats I had with George—were to be used in conjunction with the re-release of *Help!* that year on DVD.

But there was more to that phone call from the U.K. than simple business. It was interesting how those sunglasses—now representative of the *haze* of the time—had come back to haunt, and to unearth even more paradoxical ghouls of the sixties.

The project's lead producer, Joana Human, told me she had listened carefully to the tapes (including the discussion about the shades) and informed me that she was *convinced* George knew that the glasses were mine. He *knew* he hadn't left them on the blanket, and she was certain that he really liked their looks and wanted them for himself.

There were apparently many faces and fronts to the *Revolution*.

At that point in 1965, the entire decade had become a witching hour of its own.

I released the interviews to Apple, and I was paid well for what I had done—and that was as it should be. True musical history was recorded on that tiny Atlantic island. Those interviews were genuine relics of an entertainment era and of four personalities whose essence will never be seen again.

It's Hell to Be Hull

THE PRICE—AND PERKS—OF FAME

KRLA: 1963–1969, The Fiasco-Flavored Fan-Club Years

*"A sign of celebrity is that his name
is often worth more than his services."*

—Daniel J. Boorstin

At the other stations I worked for, I became a public figure of sorts, but at KRLA—and as I assumed the role of the Fifth Beatle—I became...well...*famous.* (This is not self-serving; it's just a fact!)

Dear Miss Stavers,
    The number one disk jockey in the world is DAVE HULL of Station KRLA. He calls himself the "Hulla-balloo-er" and collects horns. Every teenager in California loves him.
                                Chris Huizinga
Anaheim, Calif.

People knew me; and that's a sensitive thing that must be dealt with by people who are *known*.

It was one thing when I was twitching noses and rubbing furry elbows with the jackrabbits in Roswell, or doing remotes in Dayton, wedged between refrigerators and sectional sofas—it was quite another to be the top disc jockey in the top market in America during the most high-profile music and social-power period in this country's history!

That kind of "celebrity" means many things—some good, some not so much.

That kind of celebrity means that your name and your family and your personal life are all thrown into the middle of that race right along with you. Sometimes you get to share victory laps, and other times the whole thing becomes a destruction derby! And the folks close to you, riding shotgun or sitting in the back seat, are not immune from the carnage.

A Scuzzy Smash!

We were living in Arcadia as the KRLA years became the skyrocket they exploded into. My wife, Jeanette, took care of my mail.

One week in 1964, during the early Beatles era, we had ten *thousand* letters come in! We had cardboard boxes *full* of mail. Jeanette divided them into separate categories so that we could answer them by topic!

Even today, with a big TV star, 7,500 to 10,000 letters is a lot. And this was 1964!

I may have been just a little ol' radio personality in L.A., but I *was* known!

Ten thousand letters in a single week was huge—especially in 1964!

My first taste of *personal* interaction with the people "out there"—the people beyond that microphone—came in late 1964 when I had just received the largest share of ratings in the history of Los Angeles radio.

Suzie Cappetta was a fifteen-year-old girl from the South Bay area of Southern California. She and her brother Mike called me one night during my show.

"We have a song about you and we'd like to sing it on the air."

Hmmmm...this could lead to almost anything.

Echoes of Ted Quillin's "hog balls" situation were still rolling around in my head!

"Well," I said, "I want to hear it first."

A few days later, their mother brought Suzie, Michael, and their other brother Robert—along with their cousins, Gale and Paula Chodkowski—up to the KRLA studios. It was out on the station's famous porch that I heard "Dave Hull The Hullabalooer" for the first time.

I thought, *Hey, that's pretty good!*

I had Mom and the kids taken upstairs to our production studio, where the engineer made an acetate disc recording of it. And I played it on the air that night!

As I went to introduce the record, I realized that the only ID I had for the group was the Cappettas—not much of a reach-out-and-grab-you band name there. So instead I said, "Here is 'The Scuzzy, No Good, Beat-Up, Bad Guys'!"

I actually used that word "scuzzy" a lot—I was known for it. "Scuzzy" was endearing, universal, and meant more than one thing; kind of like *aloha* in Hawaiian. But mainly "scuzzy" was reserved for someone or something out of the norm—and that's exactly what the sixties and the people and the music then was all about!

The group's name was later shortened to the Scuzzies—and it stuck!

The Scuzzies were a family affair!

The Everly Brothers' road manager, Don Wayne, *just so happened* to be listening to the station when we aired the song. He called and asked me how he could contact the kids to record the song professionally.

It was more of that radio magic of *being in the right place at the right time.*

Wayne obviously had pull. Together with Bob Field, a friend of his and owner of California Recording Studios (CRS Records), they got one of Bob Eubanks' Cinnamon Cinder house bands, the Vibrants, and recorded the song.

CRS may have stood for California Recording Studios, but Don said, "I'm going to put it on the CRS label. It'll stand for 'Crummy Rotten Sounds.'"

"Perfect!" I told him.

Within six weeks, "Dave Hull The Hullabalooer" by the Scuzzies was ranked in the top ten at the all-powerful Wallichs Music City stores throughout the Southland and on the Top 40 Tunedex at the station.

The Wallichs Music City store at Hollywood's Sunset and Vine since 1940 was an especially important place to have your record displayed and sold. Wallichs took up almost an entire city block of Tinseltown, with full-wall plate-glass windows and preview listening booths throughout. It was record-store state-of-the-1964-art. And "Dave Hull The Hullabalooer" was there!

The Scuzzies really *were* much more than some kids having a little idle fun. Suzie Cappetta along with her brothers and cousins were also known as the Cappetta Kids.

And they definitely had talent.

As a trio, Suzie and her two brothers went on to perform in Southern California and in Las Vegas into the 1990s.

In 2007, Suzie succumbed to cancer and heart failure at the age of fifty-eight. Suzie was a huge part of my success and she left an amazing legacy. She created a unique bit of pop culture and *art*: a hit record about a guy who *plays* records.

And maybe just a little bit more...

"*Someday when we're old and gray,*
And all our days are dull,
We'll look back in memory,
To those carefree days with Dave Hull…"

That Scrumptious Scuzzy Flavor

Those "carefree days" were about to turn *very cold*—but in a good way! And the strong "Scuzzies" influence would add to the chill!

Baskin-Robbins Ice Cream was among those with *interest* in my name. They came to the station and met with Dick Moreland and me, looking for an endorsement.

I was sure it would be just like Bob Hope and Buick, Dinah Shore and Chevy—or (for those of you born after Truman left office) Michael Jordan and Nike!

Yes, it would be just like that!

Well, almost...

"We want Dave Hull to promote Baskin-Robbins," they said.

"Okay, name an ice cream after him," Dick Moreland countered.

"You mean something like *Hullabalooer Huckleberry*?" they asked.

"No," Moreland said. "He's always using that word 'scuzzy'—and now he has that hit record. Make it Scuzzy—*'Scuzzy Ice Cream'*!"

They seemed confused, but they wanted the deal.

"Well," said one of their reps, "what kind of *flavor* should it be?"

"Throw *everything* in it," I said.

So they did.

Each KRLA DJ was allowed to choose an ingredient. It turned into a great promotion whereby customers tried to guess what was in it. The whole thing was a jumble of green and red, which made for a hideous color display in the stores' freezer cases—kind of like when Ford made fuchsia-painted Escorts. It had cherries and stuff; it was a real mess.

And it was the awful-est *tasting* ice cream. But it sold like crazy!

Within two weeks after its release, Scuzzy Ice Cream led the chain in sales!

And Moreland was right: I *did* have a hit record with the Scuzzies. And now Baskin-Robbins was featuring me with a hit *flavor*—what more could a disc jockey want?!

The sunny, funny, fuzzy, scuzzy Hullabalooer...

TASTING SCUZZIES at Baskin-Robbins, while Scuzzy fans join in awe, Dave Hull enjoys the sweetest recognition ever won by a personality of his fame and status.

(Cue Jingle...)

K-R-L-A Number One Most Requested Song!

Dave: Our request lines have been buzzin' for this one. Most requested tune this hour. Number One!

(Cue "Fortune Teller" by the Rolling Stones...)

*...We're happy as we can be
And I get my fortune told for free...*

Dave: Had a whole host of requests for that one! That's for Nick Maswell of Anaheim, where it's 80 degrees, and Billy Smith of Downey, where it's 87 degrees. And the Hullabalooer here, where it's now 48 degrees, 'cause I'm air-conditioned!

EXCLUSIVE INTERVIEW WITH CALIFORNIA'S #1 DISC-JOCKEY

DAVE HULL

INSIDE RADIO by DAVE LOEVNER

The Dave Hull Fan Club

But what a disc jockey could *want* has nothing really to do with what he often *gets* as the everyday beat goes on.

And that provides so much of the fun!

Right on the *"fancy words"* heels of the Scuzzies, a local high school journalism student from Temple City named Linda Thor found another creative road into my life of hullabaloo.

Linda was a very, very bright girl. She was *so* bright, it was scary—I mean she was very sweet, but very...well...*bright!* And she was a total fan.

She wanted to start a fan club for me. However, I was skeptical of the idea. Fan clubs tend to have enthusiastic roots in the genes of impulse buying—which means they generally have a big up, a quick down, and a short life span.

I didn't want her to go to a lot of work and trouble for nothing.

But I didn't know Linda and her organizational resolve! It didn't take me long to discover that Linda had a certain *something*—something extremely competitive and long-term.

Linda did it right. She set up monthly meetings, produced a professional-looking monthly newsletter, formed dozens of fan club chapters throughout the state, and wrote articles about me that nobody else had printed *anywhere*. She came up with clever promotions, created ideas for events, and held stunts between club chapters that encouraged competition in getting new members. Plus, she would later rally the tear-filled troops when I was fired from KRLA. She was a Jill-of-all-trades when it came to the finer points of being a true *fanatic*!

Linda's dedication and talented work lasted through my entire six years at KRLA.

I had no idea of Linda Thor's organizational resolve and dedication!

Dave Hull
International Fan Club
634 Sefton Ave., Monterey, Park, Calif.

Vol. 4 No. 1 　　　DAVE MAKES THE WORLD A HULL LOT BETTER 　　　Jan. 1967

HAPPY NEW YEAR

DAVE-1967!

One of the best things to ever happen to me and the Dave Hull Fan Club happened one year ago this month.

It was in January of 1966 that Linda Thor was asked by me to take over the administration of the fan club.

It was a year ago that Linda obtained Kim Sudol, Jan Jackson, and Marcia Levine to serve with her; and what a job they've done!

Under Linda's direction, our fan club bulletin has had a great facelifting from a mimeographed sheet to a professionally printed newspaper.

The club's finances have been taken out of the red, Chapter Presidents have been given greater responsibilities, and membership has doubled all in the space of one year.

And what about me during this past year? I've continued to be the same bungling boob I've always been. But I'm making a few New Years resolutions to hopefully pull myself out of this chaotic condition.

Dave looks forward to 1967.

First of all, I resolve to better my last years scoring mark with the KRLApes basketball team, which means now all I need is to make four points a game.

Secondly, I resolve to never leave my horn at home for another Beatles concert simply because it doesn't look as if there is going to be another Beatles concert.

And finally, I resolve to apologize to Dick Biondi for making all those wisecracks about his looks, and I will, just as soon as I can get up enough nerve to look him in the face.------------------------------------DAVE

Join the Dave Hull
International Fan Club
Send $1.00 for one year to:　DAVE HULL
634 sefton, mon...
Monthly Bulletins,...

NAME _____

ADDRESS_____

ZIP _____

DAVE HULL FAN CLUB

Our Leader
KRLA

Name_____

Address_____
is a member in good standing and a confirmed
HULLABALOOER

She did the fan club right!

The club even held some of their meetings at our house. We had rooms full of precious teenage girls—only fourteen, fifteen, sixteen. They loved the Beatles, they loved the radio station, and they worked very hard. But, again, those were simpler times—'64, '65, '66, '67. Things were different. Parents letting their daughters head off to the house of a disc jockey?!

It was a different time back then, with teenage girls visiting a DJ's home! (Left to right: Marcia Levine, Jan Jackson, Me-me-me, and Linda Thor.)

But it *was* different then. And I took pride in being well-respected. I didn't do any of the stuff that B. Mitch Reed wound up doing and saying on FM. I wasn't Howard Stern; I never got into that. I didn't have to. If you can make people laugh *naturally,* you don't have to step over the line.

(Cue commercial...)

Hi-ho-hey-hey
Chew your little troubles away
With Wrigley's Spearmint Gum!

(Cue "The Jerk" by the Larks...)

Girl, hey what's that you're doin'?
Girl, girl, what's that you're doin'?

...Do the jerk, with soul now, girl
Do the jerk, A-hey!

Dave: I have a fan club out in Monterey Park. It's headed by Linda Thor, Kim Sudol, Jan Jackson, and Marcia Levine, and they called and wanted me to play
that one...
for me!
Huh-huh!
That's real
confidence,
girls!

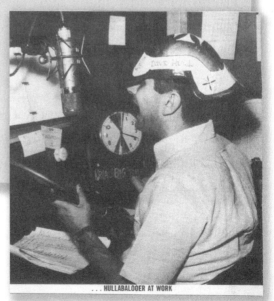

. . . HULLABALOOER AT WORK

Linda indeed had that certain something—she is now the chancellor of one of the largest community college districts in California.

Some Serious Business

> *"A celebrity is one who is known to many persons he is glad he doesn't know."*
>
> —Lord Byron

I used to have to take a roundabout route home from the station because I was always being followed by the girls and other fans. I could see 'em back there in my rearview mirror—two or three carloads.

I would speed up.

They would speed up.

I don't remember the name of the street I took that went through San Marino. It wasn't the main drag, Huntington Drive, and it wasn't Foothill—*hmmm...it was someplace in between.* But one thing about it, when you got to the signal, it was always green for you. And if you turned a sharp left and hit the sensor, it would turn the signal light red for *them.* So I'd head for the open road while they were stuck at the light! I learned that trick pretty early on.

Then things turned ugly. The *sunny, funny* "tumultuous uproar" of hullabaloo got dark and frightening. One of those folks who *knew* me began to send letters to my home. This wasn't a few carloads of kids whooping and hollering; this was a head-on hurdle that would be tough to get over.

The letters appeared to be *threats.*

They included pictures of me getting into my car, and of me headed home.

And pictures of all Jeanette's and my children.

And a page from *The Rise and the Fall of the Third Reich* about mass execution.

This was serious.

We called the local Arcadia police. They advised us to report this to the FBI because of the tie-in to KRLA—*a federally licensed station.*

The entire thing became like a movie—but without the fun of escapism. The FBI agent arrived and reality really hit. This certainly wasn't *The Untouchables.* This was so terribly true and it was all about *us.* My entire family was a part of this out-of-control ride.

So much, though, still defied reality. We *had* to be in a movie. The FBI agent arrived—impeccably dressed, Elliot Ness-style—and showed his credentials.

He was all-business.

The situation was one of the few in my life that was completely humorless.

He was, too.

He took down the information and said, "We'll get back to you. We *will* investigate this."

About a week later, he called.

"We know who it is," he said.

He came back to the house and explained what had transpired.

Since technically we had not *actually* been threatened, they weren't able to arrest the guy.

But...

They had *explained* to him that *If anything happens to the Hull family, anything at all—if they fall down and break a leg or get a runny nose or anything—you'll be the first one we come after!*

"He understands the gravity of what he's done, Mr. Hull," the agent told me.

I'll bet he did.

The whole thing scared the bejesus out of us, but we never had a threatening letter again—from this guy or anybody else.

And the FBI never told us who he was.

Dave Hull's Hullabaloo

As we bounced back from our Dirty Harry/Scorpio moment, my name was about to jump from a hot 45 and cool ice cream flavor to melting in with the rest of the music media mogul entrepreneurs of KRLA in their big-time ventures.

Reb Foster and Bob Eubanks had their nightclubs. Casey was building an entertainment empire. *I* was commercially viable as well.

And those people I was *known* by knew *that*, too!

In late 1965, a few months after Derek Taylor and I returned from the Bahamas, I was approached by a "well-financed" company that wanted to totally remodel the old Moulin Rouge nightclub on the Sunset Strip.

And rename it "Dave Hull's Hullabaloo."

I was listening.

They had already begun to lock in acts for the club—and they were top-of-the-chart artists: Sonny and Cher; the Beach Boys; the Righteous Brothers; Jan and Dean; the Doors; Peter, Paul and Mary; the Byrds; Johnny Rivers; the Turtles; Steppenwolf; and so many more.

It was in 1965 that the release of "Yesterday" brought harmony to my heart, but that year I also really liked Sonny and Cher's "I Got You, Babe" and the Byrds' "Mr. Tambourine Man" and "Turn! Turn! Turn!"— all three became #1.

The company proposing this full-scale haven for heightened hullabaloo sure looked like it had it all together—this seemed almost too good to be true!

"It's bad luck to take advice from a crazy person."

—Herb Tarlek, salesman,

WKRP in Cincinnati

But I was sold.

We made a deal.

And it happened. Dave Hull's Hullabaloo was "Hollywood's largest teenage nightclub"!

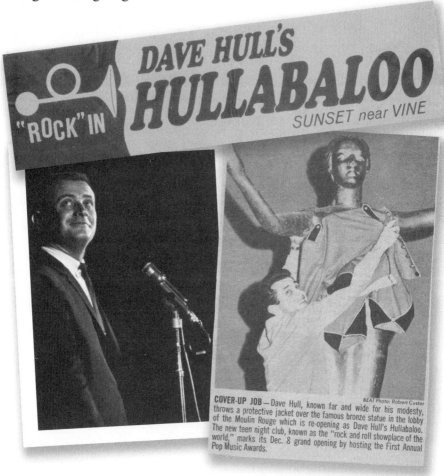

COVER-UP JOB—Dave Hull, known far and wide for his modesty, throws a protective jacket over the famous bronze statue in the lobby of the Moulin Rouge which is re-opening as Dave Hull's Hullabaloo. The new teen night club, known as the "rock and roll showplace of the world," marks its Dec. 8 grand opening by hosting the First Annual Pop Music Awards.

The elegance and dignity of the Moulin Rouge changed when they handed *me* the keys! I had found another home for my hullabaloo!

My hometown excitedly promoted the new Hollywood club created in my honor.

Furry Hats and Spinning Stages

Every club needed a great warm-'em-up and bring-'em-in house band, so we found one that added some hullabaloo of their own. We signed the Palace Guard—a band whose musical talent may just have been overshadowed by their outfits!

They wore these belted-up, bright-and-brassy matching military uniforms—yes, very *palace guardy*—and lots of times they wore these big Brit furry Beefeater hats! They were just the musical thing for

Dave Hull's Hullabaloo!

But the band could play, too. Pre-Hullabaloo, the band had been called Don Grady and the Palace Guard, featuring the actor who would go on to fame as Robbie Douglas on television's *My Three Sons.*

Emitt Rhodes was with them, too. Emmitt later joined the sorta-kinda successful band, the Merry-Go-Round (we all remember "Lovely Woman," don't we?), and would become a popular solo artist as well.

The Guard had some chops; that's for sure. And they released a couple of singles and an album.

The Palace Guard—and all the acts—appeared on a 360-degree revolving stage that dated back to the building's original days as the famed and ornate Earl Carroll Theatre (owned by and named for the famous Broadway impresario) in the 1930s. As one group finished, the stage would turn, the back curtain would open, and the audience would see the next emerging act. After the rear curtain closed, the preceding group would exit.

It was an incredibly storied and cool venue, and we had a *very hip* music-menu that featured stuff like "Bono Bubble-Up," "Billy Joe Royal Jell-O," a "Byrd Dog," "Scuzzy Fuzzy Fries," and naturally, a "Beatle Burger"!

Teenagers and even older audiences went nuts.

Part of the deal was that I would appear onstage nightly to introduce the major acts—ostensibly for free, but within our initial agreement I was to be paid $65,000. You could buy a lot of Scuzzy Fuzzy Fries in the mid-sixties for sixty-five grand, considering that the average national price for a house ranged from $13,600 to $21,500, a new car would run you about $3,000, and gas to put in *that* was just thirty-one cents a gallon!

What a great deal!

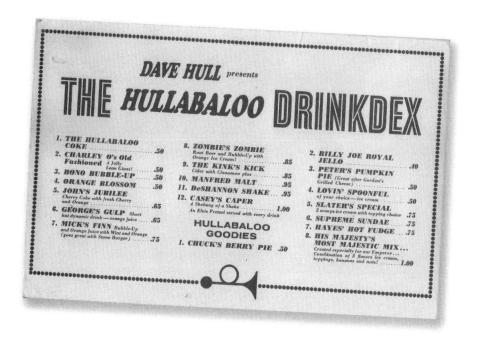

A Scuzzy Fuzzy Fiasco

fi·as·co [fee-as-koh], noun
a complete and ignominious failure.

Within days after the opening of the club, the mustard came off the Byrd Dog in a very big and messy way. The guy who really was *the company* that set all of this up, *sued himself,* and a receiver was placed in the club to take all the money as it came in—and award it back to the guy!

It was twisted legalese and backdoor bamboozling that was messier than a truckload of spilled "Jan and Dean's Favorite Beans."

My sixty-five Gs, my name, and the entire future of Dave Hull's Hullabaloo seemed to be spinning to the rear, just like the club's stage!

This slick self-suing swindler's massive manipulation of legal loopholes and license eventually led to a California state law that prevented complex cheating *creativity* like this in the future. For *now,* however, I was getting screwed out of my money; my name was being dragged through the Billy Joe Royal Jell-O; and the artists were coming to *me* for their pay!

They had gotten wind of the *problem* (the receiver at the door was a pretty big hint) and they all wanted cash up front before they went onstage!

(Cue Pacific Finance commercial...)

If you have bills to pay, and it's cash you need today,
first of all, call Pacific Finaaaaannce!
If your bills make you worry, and you want help in a hurry,
first of all, call Pacific Finaaaaannce!

DAVE HULL'S HULLABALOO
The Rock 'n Roll Showplace of the World!

ADMIT ONE   **$350**

6230 Sunset Blvd.   Good for all regular performances Wednesday
Hollywood   through Saturday, 7:30 P.M. to 12 Midnight;
Phone: 466-8581   Sunday, 2:00 P.M. to 12:00 Midnight

It really was one of those rapid-fire gut-checks, like a plane crash—one minute you're soaring and sure; a second later you're nose-first into deep muck.

We took the guy to court, of course—and, *of course,* it took three years of hassle to settle everything. We spent thousands in attorney fees to get what was rightfully owed to us in the first place.

But during those three years, the club did continue to run, bringing just an insane amount of rock 'n' roll talent to the Sunset Strip! That made it so much sadder when the court case ended, the club closed its doors, and the last Bono Bubble-Up was eventually poured.

Dave Hull's Hullabaloo became the Aquarius Theatre. The landmark building at least kept Hollywood hoopla alive as it presented the stage productions of *Hair, Jesus Christ Superstar,* and the July 21, 1969, hurricane-force performance of Jim Morrison and the Doors.

Hospital Hullabaloo

Those three years of legal spinning were taking their toll on my health. I'm surprised I didn't wind up with some sort of stress-court-lawsuit-induced aneurism. But I did develop a bad kidney infection that landed me scuzzy-side-up in the hospital.

My little *sterile vacation* was announced on KRLA—along with comments I had made to one of the jocks about how terrible the food in the hospital was!

Well, the guys from the Palace Guard heard it. And they set out to save me!

They put together a huge cheeseburger with all the trimmings—it was a behemoth version of their namesake "Grand Guard Burger" served at the club. They also brought along a grocery-size bag of fries (I don't remember if they were Scuzzy Fuzzy Fries or the more deluxe "Freddy's Fries," named after Freddy and the Dreamers!), and a large Coke.

It wasn't exactly an official dinner made up of the closely regulated return-to-health ingredients of hospital food. In fact, the mere presence of this monster-meal within the hallowed halls of medicine set off alarms everywhere! At the first whiff of the onions and grease, sensitive monitors began to flat-line and beep-wail throughout the entire building!

The boffo-burger, fries, and Coke contraband—*and* the delivery of this kingly feast by six rock 'n' rollers dressed in formal British palace guard uniforms—caused some concern with hospital security.

Sorry boys, this is as far as you go...

Now, I've got to tell you, the crazy band circus that went on in *A Hard Day's Night* and on *The Monkees* television show was actually pretty accurate. There's something about the camaraderie that comes with music—simply playing it and really *feeling it,* joined together with art-at-all-costs like-minds.

The Palace Guard fit that mold. That was pretty obvious as all six of them dangled from the hospital's fire escape—in their outfits—climbing up to my room to smuggle in the banned-band burger.

It was delicious!

And they had to go back down the same way they came in; they couldn't risk getting caught using the elevator!

> *"You oughta get a haircut—*
> *they won't let you in Disneyland."*
>
> —Micky Dolenz, *The Monkees*

DAVE HULL IS CAUGHT TRYING TO "BORROW" A UNIFORM.

Hullabaloo and hijinks were the name of the game with the Palace Guard!

Monkees, Swine, Crabs, & Me!

Speaking of the Monkees, one of the *happier* times where my name was elevated to astounding heights outside of radio was when I was asked to be in an episode of their show.

By this time, Bob Eubanks, Wink Martindale, Casey Kasem, Sam Riddle, Charlie O'Donnell, and others were all taking their talent from microphones to the camera in big ways.

Me, too—and on TV, *The Monkees* was about as big as it could get!

Now, the show's producers may not have said, *"I'm a Believer"* when it came to their endorsement of my potential for superstardom on TV—but they did think enough of my acting talent to cast me in a *Monkees* episode called "Your Friendly Neighborhood Kidnappers," airing for the first time on October 3, 1966.

The plot was *heavy*.

And complex.

You'd need to pay attention!

The Monkees decided to enter an amateur night band contest, pitted against several different groups—all *far less* talented than they!

Certainly!

But one band was named the Four Swine—yep, you guessed it, *the bad guys*! And they knew they couldn't win with the Monkees involved. So they decided they would have Micky, Mike, Peter, and Davy kidnapped, and then release them the day *after* the contest!

(Are you following this okay?)

I played the MC of the amateur night program.

The plot gets tense and cliff-hanging as the Monkees escape their kidnappers just in the nick of time to make their scheduled appearance at the contest!

Wow!

But the ending had a twist; a surprise finale that was right up there with Charlton Heston looking at the Statue of Liberty at the climax of *Planet of the Apes*.

The winner of the contest wasn't the Four Swine *or* the Monkees! No!

It was Larry Crabtree and the Three Crabs!

Our heroes were devastated, but *I* got to monkey around on one of the most swingin' music shows of all time!

When the credits rolled, it was *groovy*—and maybe even *scuzzy*—to see my name up there with the Monkees, especially after all my time with the Beatles. It really brought things full circle.

Without the Beatles, there would have been no Monkees—and *none* of so much more.

In 1966, besides my current Beatles favorite, "We Can Work It Out," I liked the Monkees' biggest song hit of the year, "I'm a Believer."

And I loved the all-time classic #1 hits "Cherish" by the Association; the Beach Boys' "Good Vibrations"; and the timeless "When a Man Loves a Woman" by Percy Sledge.

Me? Unknown?!

L-R: Dennis Wilson, Phil Everly, unknown, Brian Wilson, Don Everly and unknown

Beach Boys Concert (originally issued as Capitol KAO-2198, October 1964, ***) was not only the Beach Boys' first #1 album, but also the first "live" album to top the charts, where it was one of the biggest selling albums during the 1964 Christmas season. It is raucous, energetic, often clumsy; for some it may be downright embarrasing, as many shows from that period were, at least to ears raised on contemporary "live" recordings. But as a documentation of the time and for sheer fun, it is a hard set to beat (and is, arguably, their first "party" album).

The release of *Pet Sounds* brought a small flood of reviews and articles on Brian Wil-

tially acoustic, the lineup consisting of strummed guitars, some often hilarious bongos, and near accappella vocals throughout. And noise; never forget the noise: laughing girls, pouring drinks, munched chips...

There is a real sense of iconoclasm in the selection of material and the performances each is rendered. While several party songs receive obvious treatment, interspersed are some rather serious songs that receive the *same* type of interpretation, including a hilarious pseudo-folkie arrangement of "You've Got To Hide Your Love Away," a real folk protest, "The Times They Are A-

I was so excited to meet the Beach Boys, who played one of my fav hits! But apparently this photographer was less enthused—I guess he never voted for me for most handsome DJ!

The entertainment world beyond that microphone may have produced ups and downs for me—from fan clubs to television appearances, stalkers to lawsuits—but ultimately it was all tied into an era that made such an historical impact.

I'm proud, happy, and fortunate to have been a part of this era from the very beginning—and to have been able to see a legacy formed. A legacy that has, well, a taste of *immortality* attached to it. And that's the greatest thing in the world that can be associated with somebody's name.

It's even tastier than ice cream!

A Time for Cryin'

"DO YOU WANT TO KNOW A SECRET?"

KRLA: 1963–1969, The B-Side-Myself Years

KRLA was now number one.

KFWB was on the radio ropes.

But in April of 1965, 930 KHz on the Los Angeles area AM radio band became "93-KHJ." With its new programming consultant, Bill Drake, and his bullet-train "Boss Radio" format, KHJ was re-tuning car buttons and transistor dials all over the Southland. Drake, along with business partner Gene Chenault, would renovate and rock Top 40 radio.

KHJ's DJ lineup included "Boss Jocks" Gary Mack, Roger Christian, Sam Riddle (all three, ex-KRLA DJs), and future heavyweights Dave Diamond and the "Real Don Steele." KHJ was definitely out for broadcast blood.

But I was still on top, *With a Little Help from My Friends*—one in particular! I *still* had Beatles releases before anyone! Including "Boss Radio"!

My "procurement" of advance copies was a huge part of that ongoing *clandestine espionage* that surrounded my position as fan club prez and the Fifth Beatle.

From the first *Hippy Hippy Shake* of the Beatles' recording career, new 45s and complete studio LPs came fast. And because Beatles LPs shattered that mold of one hit backed by a bunch of filler, every new album meant about a dozen more legitimate *hits* that needed to be played.

And I played them.

And I was always first!

My "in" was a pressman who worked at the Capitol Records manufacturing plant in Glendale. He saw to it that I got all of the Beatle releases well in advance of the other DJs and stations in town—apparently because he liked *me* and what KRLA was doing.

It really was a James Bond–ish scenario—Goldfinger with gold records.

And I never did meet my ethereal *Nowhere Man* in person.

Never.

But I would talk to him on the phone. And he'd give me The Word: *"You'll get the copies...it'll be done!"*

Don't Let Me Down...

After each call, I always had the desire for a martini— *shaken, not stirred.*

"The name's Hull. Dave Hull."

I *did* know my Mr. X's name, however—a name he asked me to keep under wraps because he knew exposure would mean being fired.

So I have *never* identified him, even to this day!

I just *Let It Be*...

I may have lacked the Aston Martin and Walther PPK automatic, but throughout 1966 and into early '67, I was definitely Agent 007 of Eleven-Ten, providing the secret shadows for the delivery of advance release after advance release of Beatles booty.

(Cue "Steal Away" by Jimmy Hughes)

Dave: Steal Away...That does not mean grab everything in sight! Ha, ha! It means steal away from your home, you see...

KHJ was certainly becoming a powerhouse, but *we* were still number one. *That* was what drove them to do what a two-year-old *Bad Boy* will do when he wants what he can't have: *I'm Gonna Sit Right Down and Cry*...

Boss Radio was going crazy at our advance Beatles scoops! The grooved vinyl was about to hit the turntabled fan!

The brass at KHJ went directly to Capitol Records and sobbed, "Dave Hull has got to be stopped!"—*Cry Baby Cry*!—"And we must have an affidavit from you people—since it's *your* material—that *all* the radio stations will get the same song at the same time!"

The Real Don Steele *really* wanted the songs first before *anyone*. I wasn't on the air until nine p.m., so that meant Steele, in his afternoon spot, could now have a new song before *me*!

No.

You Can't Do That!

So I moved to afternoons and went head-to-head with him. That put us in better shape, but this infamous "cry baby incident" led to even more tears than I could imagine.

KHJ had actually gone to court and gotten cease-and-desists and writs and *habeas corpuses* and *corpus delectis* and all sorts of other stuff in Latin that boiled down to my being cut off from my musical mole at Capitol.

I object!

I objected to being forced into *Fixing a Hole* in the Beatles black-market underground pipeline. Especially when that pipeline led directly to *me*!

"I'm not going to roll over like this," I told John Barrett.

I held up my latest Capitol contraband: a brand new copy of the never-before-heard single of "Strawberry Fields Forever" backed with "Penny Lane"! (Beatles producer George Martin would eventually say that he believed "the pairing of 'Penny Lane' with 'Strawberry Fields Forever' resulted in probably the greatest single ever released by the group.")

"I'm going to play it!"

"We have these orders here from the court, Dave!" said John. "You play it, and I'll fire you!"

Well, I had a decision to make, didn't I?

Yes.

I played the record.

Both sides.

I played "Strawberry Fields Forever" and then I played "Penny Lane."

"Now give us a call and tell us which one you like better!" I told the listeners.

John did lead vocals on "Strawberry Fields"; it was Paul up front on "Penny Lane"—and I had *my* neck stuck out on both.

"Penny Lane" won hands down on the phone voting.

By 1967, my favorite song was a split between "Penny Lane" by the Beatles and the Turtles' hit "Happy Together." Both became #1.

A Less-Than-Model Employee

On the B-side of that scenario, I was about to experience a *thumbs down* in management's voting for me!

Reb Foster called me the next day. "John Barrett's not happy with you."

"Not happy" became *really, really, really vehemently out-of-our-minds angry!*

The next day—night, really; *Saturday* night—a huge party was being held at the mansion of Capitol Records executive Alan Livingston, *the* guy who had signed the Beatles in 1963. This tasty Hollywood soiree was for British model, singer, all-around socialite, and must-know personality "Twiggy." While England's Jean Shrimpton is considered the world's first real *supermodel*, Lesley "Twiggy" Lawson was the five-foot-six, hundred-ten-pound heir-apparent.

She was important.

And she was British.

Also attending her party would be other hip-society biggies like Sonny and Cher and maybe even Ringo and George.

I told Dick Moreland that it would be better for me to go to this wingding than to be on the air that Saturday. He agreed.

But he sort of forgot to tell John Barrett or Reb Foster about our plan so that they could get a fill-in for me. When my Saturday night showtime rolled around—*and I didn't*—as far as that pair was concerned, I was AWOL. *On top of* my insubordinate Beatles preview-play!

They launched an all-out investigation.

It was like searching for a fugitive on *Dragnet*.

They called around.

They found out I was at the party.

Then they kept calling the mansion and calling the mansion to try to reach me, but no one was answering—not even the butler! There was a party going on!

(And again, kids, *there were no cell phones!*)

Even though I wound up the subject of an all-points-bulletin, it was always good PR for me to go and hobnob with the stars.

My biggest hob and knob of an impression was made with Cher! After the party someone asked her what she thought of me.

Maybe it was my debonair crew cut...

Maybe my suave horn-rimmed glasses...

She told them I reminded her of a shoe salesman.

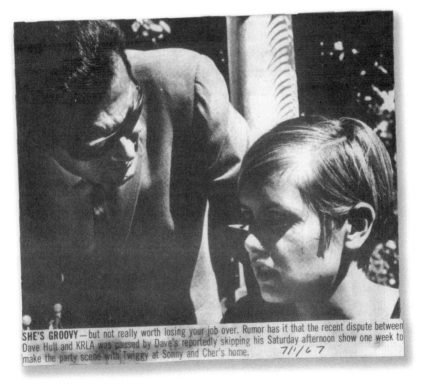

SHE'S GROOVY — but not really worth losing your job over. Rumor has it that the recent dispute between Dave Hull and KRLA was caused by Dave's reportedly skipping his Saturday afternoon show one week to make the party scene with Twiggy at Sonny and Cher's home.   7/1/67

My attendance of British-model Twiggy's party instead of my KRLA shift made the Hollywood gossip columns—though their facts weren't exactly spot on. (While Cher did "notice" me at the party, it *wasn't* at her and Sonny's pad!)

(Don't) Cry for Me, Pasadena

On Monday I arrived at the KRLA studios and they let me go. Just like that.

"You're making a big mistake here," I said.

Besides the Twiggy party mess-misunderstanding, the legal pressure from KHJ had been heating up.

"I want to be able to demonstrate to the court that we have taken definitive action about your employment, Dave!" John said.

But then he took me aside. "Look, just take a vacation for a few days, until we work this out."

We Can Work It Out...

I did and *they* did; but the "working things out" took eleven days.

Eleven days was too much for the fans—and here's where those *additional tears* that stemmed back to the cry babies at KHJ began to fall!

Now, the sixties was host to a lot of "love-ins"—events of varying shapes and sizes that revolved (oftentimes in the *physical* form of dervish dances and spinning mind trips!) around music, protests against society's ills, and just groovin' together as a group. Well, when my fans heard that I'd been fired, *they* got together for a "cry-in"!

I'll Cry Instead...

My fans vowed to stay on the KRLA porch and weep until the Hullabalooer returned to the air!

Even local television news covered the "cry-in"!

DAVE HULL

International
Fan Club

634 Sefton Avenue   Monterey Park, Calif. 91754

PRESIDENT
LINDA THOR

WHAT CAN <u>YOU</u> DO??

<u>JOIN THE "CRY-IN"</u>   We will meet at KRLA* to protest the firing
of Dave and to ask KRLA to take him back. Bring signs to
carry and a handerchief to cry. "CRY-INS" will be held
this Thurdays, Friday, and Saturday (and through next
week if necessary) from 3:00 to 6:00.

<u>PETITIONS</u>   Start petitions circulating among your friends and
bring or mail them to KRLA* as soon as complete.

<u>LETTERS</u>   Get your letters in immediately to station manager,
John Barrett, KRLA*. Tell them <u>exactly</u> how you feel without Dave.

<u>TELEPHONE</u>   Use your request lines to verbally protest. Many
fans are simply saying, "I have only one request---bring
back Dave Hull!"

<u>SPREAD THE WORD</u>   Tell your friends, enlist their help, and
bring them to the "cry-in".

<u>VERY IMPORTANT</u>   We do not want to do anything improper or
illegal. Be polite, co-operative, but firm. We want
Dave to be proud of us. Act like ladies and gentlemen
at all times.

WE ARE COUNTING ON <u>YOU</u>!!

SEE YOU THERE!

*KRLA is located   Huntington Sheraton
                                          . Busses stop at the

TURNED ON TEARS—Disc jockey Dave Hull is gone (not far) but not forgotten as his fans stage a "cry-in" at door of Pasadena radio station KRLA. With onions supplied by the station, the teen-agers mustered a few tears, but giggles and fun prevented the gloom from getting completely out of hand. Hull, KRLA said, was fired for failing to appear for his show. —Staff photo by Larry Crockel 5/5/67 Independent

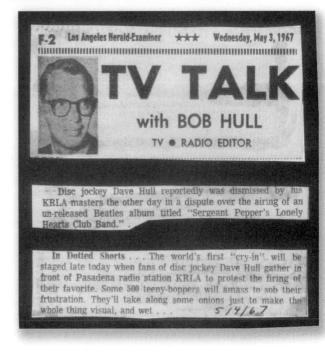

F-2   Los Angeles Herald-Examiner   ★★★   Wednesday, May 3, 1967

TV TALK
with BOB HULL
TV ● RADIO EDITOR

Disc jockey Dave Hull reportedly was dismissed by his KRLA masters the other day in a dispute over the airing of an un-released Beatles album titled "Sergeant Pepper's Lonely Hearts Club Band."

In Dotted Shorts . . . The world's first "cry-in" will be staged late today when fans of disc jockey Dave Hull gather in front of Pasadena radio station KRLA to protest the firing of their favorite. Some 500 teeny-boppers will amass to sob their frustration. They'll take along some onions just to make the whole thing visual, and wet . . . 5/4/67

'WORLD'S FIRST CRY-IN — KRLA station manager John R. Barrett was the target of the world's first "Cry In," a demonstration by 500 youthful fans in protest of the dismissal of popular disc jockey Dave Hull Hull was removed from his daily program on the station but was restored to his show after his attorney asked that he be granted an unconditional release or be returned to the air. 6/3/67

The populace rose up (and then sat down and cried!) in response to my firing dictate by KRLA's programming king, John Barrett. The weapons of choice were painted signs and potent onions.

On Page One of the June 1967 edition of the Dave Hull International Fan Club newsletter—right below the monthly subhead that read, *DAVE MAKES THE WORLD A HULL LOT BETTER*—I issued a heartfelt thanks to the fans:

> The month of May has to go down as the most "exciting" month in my radio career to say the least.
>
> As most of you know, I was "off the air" at KRLA for a period of eleven days last month following a disagreement with the station's management.
>
> The controversy began with an argument over the playing of [cuts from] the new Beatles album and my failure to show up for my Saturday radio show. Instead of working I decided to attend a Beverly Hills party for Twiggy.
>
> I would really like to tell you exactly what was said between us in the negotiations and meetings during my eleven day absence but since the boss reads these fan club newspapers too, a man could get fired for an article like that.
>
> But now that I'm back with KRLA and time has mellowed the whole situation, the management of the station and I are actually getting along better than ever before; and for this I want to thank you.
>
> For without your support I'm sure the station's management would never have

been willing to listen to my position in our later discussions.

I also want to thank Baxter Ward and ABC Television for their excellent coverage of Linda Thor's "cry-in" demonstration which I thought was very cute.

It's true that literally thousands of you telephoned the studios and wrote stacks of mail daily and some of you took the time to personally come down to the station to tell the boss exactly what you really thought of me.

And even though thousands of you expressed your opinions about me, they still hired me back.

(Cue Hamm's Beer commercial)

From the land of sky blue waters...
(echo, echo)...

(Cue "Wheels" by the String-A-Longs)

Dave: You're stringing along with the Hullabalooer...I promise not to tell anybody.

Fan Club Flashbacks

by Linda Thor

I was turning fourteen years old when the Beatles arrived in the United States. That event defined my generation and to a large extent my life. A huge Beatlemaniac, I, of course, was attracted to Dave Hull, the Fifth Beatle. I founded the Dave Hull Fan Club.

I have many great memories of the fan club. We established chapters throughout Southern California. Members competed to earn points by requesting the song "Dave Hull The Hullabalooer" or writing letters to KRLA management praising Dave. When Dave got fired, we staged a "cry-in" that generated media coverage and helped achieve his reinstatement. We made a home movie, a melodrama titled *The Hull Story* which we showed at chapter meetings.

When our high school classes were over, the chapter officers and I would drive to the KRLA studios in Pasadena and watch Dave on the air. And we met many stars who came to see Dave to promote their records, such as the Mamas & the Papas, Crystal Gayle, and Ian Whitcomb. Most memorable is that Dave arranged for fan club vice president Kim Sudol and me to receive invitations to the press conference held in conjunction with the first Beatles concert at the Hollywood Bowl. Prints of photos taken that day were later sold to fan club members as a fundraising activity for the club.

Dave used to talk about me and the other fan club officers on the air. Amazingly, some of those comments still exist in "air checks" today and delight my adult children—as well as colleagues who know me only as a veteran community college administrator.

Yet as I reflect back on my twenty-five years as a community college chief executive officer, I know that my early leadership skills were developed by heading up the Dave Hull Fan Club. As fan club president, I learned to communicate, to promote, to advocate, to organize, and to raise funds. And I had a great time doing it!

Dave and me on the "set" of *The Hull Story*!

Thanks for the memories, Dave Hull!

Linda M. Thor, Ed.D.
Chancellor, Foothill–De Anza
Community College District

Turn! Turn! Turn!

FROM HOUSE BANDS TO HORNS

KRLA: 1963–1969, The Coattails-of-the-Comet Years

The Beatles' coattails were now like the bright wake-tail of a comet, extending around the globe. Their aura had become the blazing *Magic Carpet Ride* (Yes! A Steppenwolf tune!) for not only the entire British Invasion—from the Stones to the Animals to the Kinks to The Who to the Zombies and beyond—but for us *Yanks* as well.

We had our own in-house "invasion" right here in the U.S.A., especially in Los Angeles. L.A. began competing with the San Francisco Bay Area for a claim to America's biggest bands.

And it was a battle! The Bay Area would turn the volume up with artists like the Jefferson Airplane, Janis Joplin, and the Grateful Dead; Los Angeles would counter with Sunset Strip superstars like the Doors, the Byrds, and the Mamas & the Papas.

All "those boys who were starting bands" back in '63 and '64 were coming of age; and each new monster act and gold record chart-buster was adding more curves, straightaways, and speed to this race!

"Beatles, Beatles, Beatles. We ate, drank, and slept Beatles 24/7. Everyone I knew was caught up in the scene. After seeing A Hard Day's Night, *I knew that I had to be in a rock band. I used to listen to the album tracks over and over while playing my bongos with a pair of sticks that my mother had gotten me. I learned bass drum high-hat patterns from Ringo."*

—Terry Rae, drummer for the Palace Guard,
interviewed by 60sgaragebands.com

The entire music scene was now becoming about all-sensory entertainment—not just *listening*.

And all of us at KRLA were right in the heart of it, in one way or another.

the Standells

Boys in Boston had also started bands; but apparently Beantown's Standells didn't like my sound as well as I liked theirs! (I think they were ready to pour *Dirty Water* into my horn!)

Even though the old-school/memories-of-El-Monte kinds of dances had become pretty much just that—*memories*—DJs were still making appearances with their "house bands."

I had been working with Thee Midnighters since 1965, and they had developed into a stand-out band in their own brass-percussive right. They were one of the first Chicano bands to come out of East L.A.—the culture-rich *barrio*. With horns, percussion, keyboards, and all the rest, they were an incredible group.

My own house band, Thee Midnighters, has a still-standing legacy of Latino-influenced R&B!

They had a string of big hits: 1965's "Whittier Boulevard," the follow-up "Land of a Thousand Dances," and other true classics.

But it was interesting: although still so steeped in their Chicano roots, as the sixties moved on, even *they* began to grow their hair and get "the look."

Those Big Ben–sized coattails of the Beatles transcended and influenced so many things!

I liked Thee Midnighters—they were nice young kids. And they liked me. And they always showed up! They would work right up until you said those magic last-dance words: "That's it, you can go home!"

We paid them a hundred and seventy-five dollars for four hours, and they worked hard, earning every played-for penny!

Let's take a trip down *Whittier Boulevard...*

And after decades and decades of those last dances, Thee Midnighters are still around! And their original hits remain as obligatory dedication tunes on any true low-ridin' oldies show.

Revelaire Revelations

But those "last dances" were fading like summer teen-love in September—the clubs and the concerts were really taking over the live music scene.

And again, *we were all so involved!*

Reb Foster, as KRLA's program director, was my boss. He was also a mega-entertainment entrepreneur when it came to managing bands and working them into that all-encompassing "scene."

Reb owned a club in Redondo Beach called the Revelaire—and like I keep saying, things were changing fast!

The house band at the Revelaire was a surf-pop six-piece called the Crossfires. Their locally produced 45 of "One Potato Two Potato" on the "Lucky" Token Records label wasn't exactly burning up the charts. Actually, it was a very cold spud!

So, like everyone else, they grabbed onto those Beatles/Brit-Invasion coattails. At Reb's suggestion, the Crossfires changed their name to the Turtles, grew their hair, signed a contract with a then-unknown record label called White Whale, and recorded a tune by a guy from Minnesota who was getting a lot of quick notoriety as a songwriter-musician—Bob Dylan. "It Ain't Me Babe" soon hit the top five for the Turtles, Reb, and White Whale Records.

The Turtles' first out-of-the-shell concert appearance was at the Rose Bowl, opening for Herman's Hermits!

One week you were local; the next you had hair, a new name, and a world tour.

That's just how it all worked then!

The Turtles followed up "It Ain't Me Babe" with the million-selling "Happy Together," followed by "She'd Rather Be With Me," and more.

But something new was always tuning up for Reb Foster.

One day Reb came to me and said, "I'm going to sell the Turtles!"

I told Reb that this band was a big moneymaker—maybe he should think twice!

Nope.

"I'm going to start a new group called Steppenwolf," he told me.

"Born to Be Wild," "Magic Carpet Ride," "Sookie Sookie," "The Pusher," the soundtrack to *Easy Rider*...

Well, *that* worked!

A while later, he said to me, "I'm going to sell Steppenwolf!"

I told him that he'd finally gone NUTS!

First the Turtles...

...then Steppenwolf!

"I've got a new group," he said.

Again.

"Three Dog Night!"

Reb had the knack—he gave *Joy to the World* (Hey, I'm pretty good at this!) through all of his bands. He was doing what we were all doing, really—our staff was continually involved with things that no one else would or could do. It wasn't because we *planned* it that way; it's just that we *did* it that way. And that's what made it so magical in the Dream-House.

Bob Eubanks, of course, owned the successful Cinnamon Cinder teenage nightclubs along with his concert promotions. Besides the Beatles and the Rolling Stones, he also produced one of the first concerts by that "Dylan guy from Minnesota"—also at the Hollywood Bowl. His artist representation and interaction ranged from classic acts like the Righteous Brothers and the Beach Boys to "U.S.A. Invasion" stars like the Byrds, Paul Revere and the Raiders, and the Beau Brummels.

In 1968, I found myself moving to some new artists for hits.

I was a big fan of Herb Alpert's "This Guy's in Love with You," "Mrs. Robinson" by Simon & Garfunkel, and a hit by a new group, the Lemon Pipers, "Green Tambourine."

And from left field, Richard Harris's "MacArthur Park"!

Casey's Folly

The "transition" had long ago leveled out into that "everyday beat of the 1960s" but a steady percussion of bands continued to line up to get into the race. And as these *Sunshine Supermen* burst out of garages and rehearsal studios, they all needed someplace to be heard.

There was still a little "old school" left, and I had one last dance left in *me*.

Casey Kasem asked me to host a show for him in Redondo Beach at a rec center. He had been getting busier and busier with his television appearances, and a throwback dance at a rec center just wasn't high on his priority list anymore.

I asked him how much it paid.

"You get half the door," he said. "Whatever they take in, you get half.

The rec center gigs were winding down, but I always had a little bit of "old school" in me!

"But if *they* don't make anything," he added matter-of-factly, "*you* don't make anything."

I asked him about the band.

"Yep, there's a band," he assured me. "And they want to work the whole show."

Okay...so, who's the band?

"It's a new group," he told me. "The Chicago Transit Authority."

Thinking about the money-pie, I asked him how many guys were in the group.

He finally got excited. "They've got horns, they've got drums! Oh man, they've got saxes and trombones and trumpets, and oh man, they'll knock the place down!"

Oh God! I thought. *This "half the door" thing will go out the window in a hurry!* I figured a band the size of the Lichtenstein Polka Army was going to want the entire gate!

"Two hundred and fifty bucks," Casey told me. "They want two-fifty."

Two-fifty?

Cool.

Okay.

I'll write them a check...

And I did—before they even started the show.

The place was packed, the door was big, and the band—this Chicago Transit Authority—wouldn't get off the stage once they got going!

All for two hundred and fifty bucks!

They thought they'd landed in heaven with this crowd and their response.

Now, all of these guys were going to make, what—fifteen or twenty dollars once everything was split up? And I kept asking them if they wanted me to do something.

Anything?

"No, man, everything is cool," they just kept saying—and playing.

I was a muted lump on a horn-sectioned log—and I made eighteen hundred bucks!

It was the first show the Chicago Transit Authority—known soon after as just *Chicago*—ever worked on the West Coast.

And it was the last event that Casey ever let me host for him!

Chicago graduated from the rec centers, of course, and hammered into the race at top speed—releasing close to forty albums over the next five decades.

We were *all* in this at full throttle.

We all figured *I'll Follow the Sun* with the Beatles, cruise down *Route 66* with the Rolling Stones, and find some answers *Blowin' in the Wind* as we got into Dylan's lyrical poetry through Reb's Turtles and Bob's Byrds. We would *Turn! Turn! Turn!* the world of music into a true universe of its own; taking it *Eight Miles High*—a hell of a lot higher than Elvis and his pompadoured pioneers could ever *Imagine*.

It was all too beautiful!

"You've Lost That Lovin' Feelin'"

THE BATTLE-AXE BIRTHDAY AND OTHER MISTAKES

KRLA: 1963–1969, The I-Never-Did-Grow-My-Hair Years

Most people's image of the most popular disc jockey in Los Angeles would be a cliché-croaking clod with the depth of a saucer and the intellect of a mongoloid mosquito.

In reality, the persona is bogus. First of all, Dave Hull lives in Arcadia, which isn't exactly a hipster's haven. Secondly, the popular KRLA platter-planner is a dedicated family man, clean cut and serious.

—Tom Livingston,
Arcadia Tribune, September 3, 1967

Behind the mad-machinations of "public figures" and "celebrity" are people—people with private lives *inside* that may not be exactly what you see on that you-always-have-to-be-"on" *outside.*

You've got stuff going on at *work* and stuff going on at *home,* and they're different. Sure, *everyone* has that, but when your *work* is the entertainment-fishbowl that has so many flies on the wall and eyes in the shadows, those two facets of life become more like parallel worlds than a simple separation. They can be totally different universes!

The newspaper reporter was right: I lived in Arcadia, in the Highland Oaks section. My house wasn't in the 90210, it wasn't in the Hollywood Hills, it wasn't gated, and it wasn't on an island.

It was in a sleepy little vortex of calmness nestled in the San Gabriel Mountains foothills.

The land where Arcadia lies was purchased in 1875 by Elias J. "Lucky" Baldwin. When ol' Lucky first saw the area, he is quoted as exclaiming, "By gads! This is paradise."

But a very *sedate* paradise.

Even Arcadia High School is, well, *sedate.*

Unlike my own Alhambra High School, which featured as graduates car-racing legend Mickey Thomson and super-model Cheryl Tiegs—and of course, me!—a recent search at a "Famous People Born in (insert name of place here)" website led to the following results for Arcadia's homegrown high school:

> *Arcadia High School*
> *There is no description for Arcadia High School*
> *There are 0 famous people who studied here*
> *No results have been found.*

(The site seems to have missed one, however: Debra Turner-Logan, the actress who played little Marta von Trapp in *The Sound of Music,* long before she was *Sixteen Going on Seventeen*!)

But *we* liked it—"we" being me; my wife, Jeanette; and our kids, Lisa, Mike, Brian, Mark, and Clark.

We had thirty-one hundred square feet of house, along with land and dogs and kids! It was a perfect and pretty normal life!

I enjoyed a (mostly!) normal life in the sedate paradise of my family's Arcadia home.

Hull wrapped himself in the Beatles Union Jack and became "The Fifth Beatle" to Los Angeles listeners. However Hull did not go whole hog and grow a Beatle haircut. During the summer of 1964, Hull kept his neat crew cut, and even though he was a Beatle buff during his nighttime show, he was actually a very conservative guy during his home life.

—Bill Earl, *Dream-House*

Dave Hull—Serious, Dedicated . . .

THE HULLABALOOER IS ALL BUSINESS as he intently questions Beatle Manager Brian Epstein (left) verifying a point with KRLA Teen Topper Vaughn Filkins as he pursues an answer.

And even though we—especially *me*—were trying to exist as a family while I bounced between those parallel worlds, I *would* cross over from time to time.

I'd bring the goofy husband thing into the entertainment world, and vice-versa.

The next week I flew to the Bahamas with Dave Hull, the squarest disc jockey at KRLA, an amiable shorthair who believed that Medicare had to be the worst thing to happen to America since the New Deal.

—Derek Taylor,
As Time Goes By: Living in the Sixties

HE TURNS ON THE CHARM when the ladies are around — but they don't seem to complain.

And that was fine.

That was me.

Having a fair amount of *hullabaloo* in both worlds made me who I am.

But I was always doing something wrong!

Okay, it wasn't exactly *wrong* wrong; it was just *hullabaloo!*

The Perfect Chord

Jeanette and I were celebrating our anniversary—it was our eighth or ninth.

"Are you going to play me a song today for our special day?" she asked sweetly.

"Of course I will, dear," I said with equal sweetness and complete and unequivocal love! "It's our anniversary!"

I was in my afternoon time slot, three to six.

I went on the air.

She sat home and listened.

And listened.

And listened.

3:00.

4:00.

5:00.

5:30.

5:45.

Finally she called the hotline.

Some of her morning sweetness had soured.

"You haven't played a song for our anniversary, and you promised you would!"

"Hon," I said, retaining *my* sweetness. "I'm so sorry. My head has been on other things. The next record, it's for you and me!"

By now it's nearing six o'clock, so no time to pick out the perfect tune; I have to go with the last cued-up 45. I announce for all to hear:

> *"I've been saving this moment all day."*
> *(Nice recovery, right?)*

"It's my wife's and my anniversary. This next record is for her!"

Hit it!

"You never close your eyes anymore..."

Yup. That's right. "You've Lost That Loving Feeling" by the Righteous Brothers spun through the airwaves.

A perfect anniversary? *No results have been found...*

Going Medieval

Then there was Jeanette's *birthday*.

Now, I knew she wanted something for over the fireplace; something "regal" like crossed swords. You know, *medieval*. Okay! Perfect! It was her birthday and I came up with what I knew was the ideal gift. Something personal and something she truly wanted!

I got her an antique battle-axe—*and* a mace!

It did get quite a response...

"You gave me a battle-axe?!"

I knew that she was in awe. She really couldn't believe it.

Then I realized that *she really couldn't believe it!*

But it was a genuinely beautiful and warm interaction in the long run. By Christmas, the Yule fire would burn bright beneath the mantle, crowned by Jeanette's always-in-season battle-axe and mace.

Holiday Hijinks

But Christmases were memorable even without the feudal weaponry.

They were an important part of that in-family hullabaloo.

One holiday season I was putting up our Christmas lights on the roof when I lost my balance and fell off—waving and thrashing as I headed for the ground!

"Mom," one of my boys told Jeanette, fairly nonchalantly, "Dad just went flying past the window."

"...a dedicated family man, clean cut and serious..."

Another Christmas *interaction* with a noble "service employee" reminded me of my phone call to the "long-distance information operator" in Memphis.

The whole family was piled into the car and we decided to swing through the drive-up window at a fast food joint.

"Hi...may I help you?"

"Yes!" I asserted into the crackly speaker.

Now, it *was* the holiday season and I was definitely in the spirit! The lilting strains of "The Twelve Days of Christmas" were running through my head!

So I prepared a song:

"Ahem. *We'll have...seven hamburgers, six french fries, five Coca Colas, four chocolate sundaes, three onion rings, two 7-ups, and one l-e-m-m-m-m-o-n-n-n pie!*"

I was delighted!

But the ever-crackly crackly speaker fell silent.

The kids, however, were loving my performance!

Then the silence was broken...

"Sir..." The woman on the other end sounded...strained. *"May I help you...?"*

So I sang it again, with an even more festive tone than before!

Again, this was followed by a one-two punch of pure delight on *our* end—and silence on hers.

Finally... *"MAY I HAVE YOUR ORDER PLEASE?!"*

I figured third time's the charm!

Nope.

"Please move to the next window!"

The kids were so pleased. Jeanette was rolling her eyes, though—sort of like when I had the hands full of mud-and-money in Columbus!

Just after Christmas, I looked out the window on a very early morning to see my driveway completely covered in what appeared to be the entire of the Oregon coast-of-pines!

I had to be on the air by 5:30 a.m.—that meant I had to be up by 4:00 and on the road soon after.

What I saw out of that window was an organic, green version of "TP-ing" a house! Hundreds of "used" Christmas trees had been piled on our circular driveway!

The car wasn't coming out of the garage through *that* forest, so I needed help from the boys.

I woke everyone up!

"I'll pay each of you five bucks if you'll get up, get dressed, and haul all those trees up the street and *re*-pile them in front of the local "bully's" house.

We *knew* who did this!

It didn't take long. We all made an assembly line that would have made Santa and his elves proud! I made it to my show on time, and the guy up the street had to have wondered how an entire dead Ponderosa pine stand could have moved that quickly!

A Very Brady...uh, Hull Life

This next part is delicate! Kids. Children. When they enter into the discussion, it's like that frightening scene you've suffered through in so many sitcoms and in real life—the doting grandmother asks her friends if they'd like to see some pictures of her grandchildren. They naturally and politely say yes, and then she unravels an accordion-file of photos that would rival the archives of *LIFE* magazine!

But our kids—and the *hullabaloo* surrounding all of our interactions—is important! It's me! And like the drive-through-window Christmas song, a lot of it is just plain funny!

To start with, we were just one warm body short of the Brady Bunch. And like that brood, we were—as modern sociologists like to refer to it—a "blended family" (although many times I figured a *real* blender was used when this mix was whipped up!).

Mike was Jeanette's from her first marriage; Mark and Clark were mine from *mine*. Together, Jeanette and I had Lisa and Brian.

(Cue the theme song: "Here's the story of a lovely lady...")

If this *had* been *The Brady Bunch,* I think the majority of episodes would have been about Brian:

"Brian's New Little Brother"

It was already the six of us when I received custody of my eight-year-old, Clark. Brian was about three.

Clark arrived with all his bags and Brian came to the door. He'd been primed that he was going to "get a new brother."

They met.

Brian just looked at him for quite a while.

"You know," Brian finally said, "you were really *big* when you were born!"

(Cue laughter; Alice smiles knowingly and rolls her eyes!)

"Brian's Full House"

A few weeks after Clark moved in, when he was all set up and attending school in Arcadia, he brought a friend home.

Again, we saw that *inquisitive* look from Brian.

He sized up Clark's friend.

"Are you going to live here too?!" he asked.

(The rest of the family exchange looks, smiling behind coy hands-over-their-mouths!)

"Brian's First Confession"

As Brian got older, he was on track to receive his First Communion in our church. But before that, of course, is that dreaded *First Confession*!

Jeanette and I drove him to the church.

He went inside.

He entered the confessional.

Bless me Father, for I have sinned. This is my first confession...

When Brian came back out to the car, he had his hand in his mouth and it was hard to understand him. But we caught that he was saying that he believed he had just received the "weirdest penance anyone ever got"!

Now, he had been through the classes and expected the standard "ten Hail Marys and ten Our Fathers, etc." but this one wasn't in the workbook.

Jeanette and I looked at one another, knowing that he had been alone in there with the priest. So we asked him, calmly—trying not to be dramatic or alarming—"Brian, now we know that you've been taught to *never* talk about what you and the priest discussed; *however,* in this case, we'd really like you to tell us what transpired so that we can better understand this *weird* penance the priest asked you to do."

"Well," Brian said, sounding like Demosthenes with a mouth full of marbles, "I went inside and knelt down. I said my 'Bless me, Father' and I started to tell him my sins..."

As we probed around, we figured out that Brian wasn't aware that there was another person on the *other side* of the priest, in the *other side* of the confessional. He didn't know it was a "two-seater"!

He'd started to talk while the priest was still conferring with the repentant soul in the other hot-seat. So the good Father had told Brian, "Hold your tongue, my son."

Which Brian did.

Literally.

(Still in the parking lot, Mom and Dad fight back laughter, trying to gather their composure before pulling away.

Fade to commercial...then back for the heartfelt, lesson-learning tagline at the climax of the show.)

As we were readying to take off, we saw the priest headed toward the car.

We could only imagine what he must have been thinking as Brian mumbled and choked through his first confession. *Poor child...what a terrible impediment...*

However, a little heavenly wisdom had brought forth some realization.

"I am very sorry about what happened," the priest told us. "I will *never* use those words in a confessional again!"

(Knowing smiles all the way around...audience laughter...fade to end.)

Of course, not every episode would have featured Brian. Our daughter was very Marcia-like as she matured into a young lady!

"Lisa Makes the Pros!"

The kids were *all* growing up. The boys were excelling in sports, and Lisa became a cheerleader and a song-leader.

And, of course, her brothers made fun of her! I guess to them, pom-poms and human pyramids didn't compare with helmets and end-around-runs through a stormy sea of linebackers!

But the pom-poms in *Lisa's* arsenal were power-packed. After she graduated from Cal State Northridge—where she reigned as both "Miss Panorama City" and "Miss Northridge" in two separate Miss California pageants—she became a cheerleader for the Los Angeles Rams, three years in a row!

Those "goofy boys" never made fun of her again. She was the only one in the family to get us to the "pros," and the boys were forced to *plead* with her to leave Rams tickets for them at will-call.

(The boys all look at each other sheepishly, roll their eyes with a wry smile, and shake their heads, now older and wiser!)

Cheerleader: Arcadia High School graduate Lisa Hull was named recently to the Los Angeles Rams cheerleading squad. Hull, who now resides in the San Fernando Valley, is an editorial associate for Teen Magazine.

Arcadia High graduate joins Rams cheerleaders

By Richard Horrmann
Staff Writer

Like many high school athletes who dream of some day playing pro ball, those who stand on the sidelines and cheer them on may also have dreams of going on to the big teams. Lisa Hull was no exception.

"I knew at that time that it was something I wanted to do. I did also know I wanted to go to college, get a degree and have a career," said the 1983 Arcadia High graduate.

Not knowing whom to contact or what to do to become a professional cheerleader, the former high school junior varsity pepster, varsity songleader and Orchesis dance team member temporarily set aside one of her dreams in order to attend college.

Now at age 24, with a journalism degree and secure career, Hull's aspiration to become a Rams cheerleader is about to be realized.

Hull, an editorial associate for Teen Magazine, was recently one of 36 women out of 250 contestants chosen to represent the Los Angeles team for the upcoming season.

"I wanted it so bad that it became something I had to work on day and night," said Hull, who endured two weeks of grueling interviews and routines during the tryouts. While the mental stress created by the contest was almost as difficult as the physical challenge, she said her toughest critic was herself.

"You have to believe you have to deserve to be on the squad, but yet
See CHEER / 6

My talented daughter, Lisa, had the last laugh over her brothers when she became the only one in the family to tackle the pros!

"Lisa's Dating Game"

Lisa was becoming a beautiful young woman.

A cheerleader.

A song-leader.

After school, the phone would start ringing and the boys would show up at the door.

Something had to be done. It was time to discuss "dating" with our daughter *and* when it should begin. Dad would handle this one.

Lisa wasn't at all happy when I decided on the chronological dictate of sixteen!

She accepted it, but it was a tough "holding pattern." When she finally reached our predetermined dating age, I added a further fatherly, Mike Brady-esque addendum—I told her I wanted to *meet* the boys before they went out.

Our oldest son, Mike, who loved his sister dearly ever since running through our old apartment complex announcing her birth, became interested in the plan as well.

By now he was coaching football at the high school, and he knew the boys there better than anyone. The word about Lisa's father's interview-discussion system became *the* topic of conversation around school.

One boy who seemed to be in perfect accord with the policy asked Lisa for a date.

She graciously accepted.

He told her he would pick her up twenty minutes early for his "meeting with Dad."

No.

Lisa told him that he didn't *really* understand the concept—it wasn't that easy.

There was *protocol*.

It would be necessary, she explained, for him to call and set up an evening when the two could meet a few days *before* the date. Then, and only then, would any subsequent contact be arranged, allowed, and/or sanctioned!

Well, this news spread even faster around the school than the original proclamation!

But it was fair, since *every* boy went through the same process—there was *no* discrimination!

(Fade to Dad looking very wise, arm around his daughter, and her looking up at him lovingly!)

Okay, the Brady Bunch also had a dog, named "Tiger." Even *he* had some episodes written for him—like the nail-biter, *"Tiger! Tiger!"* where Tiger runs away and fathers a litter of puppies!

Likewise, we had *our* share of adventures with "Recruit."

"Recruit: Lost and Found!"

My family has had a number of pedigreed German shepherds—mainly for the children's protection. Recruit was one of the best, with grand champions in his blood line. He'd lie down anywhere and watch the kids for hours.

I'd heard more than once that my show was going to the dogs, but at home
it was true! Over the years, we shared a lot of love with these best friends.

Our home in Arcadia was located up in the highlands near Wilderness Park. Coyotes would approach the back yard, where the children were playing, and Recruit would go nuts, chasing them off the property and back up where they came from.

But then he disappeared.

It was heartbreaking!

"Recruit! Recruit!"

He had been gone for days. We checked first with the Wilderness Park rangers, then the Humane Society, then animal shelters, and then the local animal hospitals.

Nothing.

But a little while later, a Caltrans highway worker was clearing some roadside brush. She mentioned to another shovel-wielding coworker that she had a peculiar feeling they were being watched. He searched around and spotted Recruit's head peering out of the ivy at them along the side of the road!

Recruit had gotten himself caught in a coyote trap. Evidently, someone had found him in the trap and freed him, but most of his right front paw was missing. They had put him in a box and for some reason had set him by the side of the road.

The workers called the California Highway Patrol who in turn notified us, after getting our info off of Recruit's tag.

The officer told me of the dog's condition and advised us to "put him to sleep."

That wouldn't happen on *The Brady Bunch,* and it certainly wasn't going to happen amidst *my* family's hullabaloo!

"No!" I told the officer. "Please take him to the Arcadia Animal Hospital immediately and we'll pay whatever is necessary!"

The officer did just that. I called and informed the hospital staff that our dog was on the way and needed surgery, *now*!

Veterinarians worked over the course of a year to salvage Recruit's injured paw. But they finally told us that it was no use—he would lose his right front leg entirely.

This experience helped our kids to grow up, in a poignant way.

Together, we found out the name and address of the Caltrans worker and mailed her a nice cash- and love-filled reward. And it now became *the kids'* responsibility to watch out for Recruit, as our "best friend" adjusted to his new situation, using his left front leg as a tripod. Even with just three legs, he would *still* charge the coyotes whenever he smelled or saw them nearby!

(Fade to a family portrait with the dog out in front; and at least one of the boys holding up "horn fingers" over another brother's head!)

One other Recruit episode would be written into our family playlist. It was an episode that involved Recruit and *me*—much like the Brady's "Father of the Year," where Dad learns as much as the kids!

"Love Thy Neighbor"

One Sunday morning, I was relaxing and reading the paper when a knock came at the front door. It was the woman from across the street yelling that our dog was in their yard attacking their cat.

I told her that she must be mistaken and pointed to Recruit, flopped asleep by the back door.

"No!" she screamed. "Not *that* one! It's that other dog of yours!"

Well, our son Mike had left his Doberman mix with us for the weekend (Recruit loved him and they'd play and play together). But evidently "Thurman" had jumped the fence and was indeed in the neighbor's yard.

I rushed outside to find our neighbor's husband whacking Mike's dog with a broom in the middle of Highland Oaks Drive.

It was a very dramatic scene!

I told him that if he laid another hand on Thurman, it would probably be his last!

"You keep your dog off my property!" he shouted.

"Well," I shouted back, "you keep *your* dog off of *my* property, too!"

Things quieted down for a minute.

"I don't own a dog..." he said.

"Then what do you call that?" I said, pointing to his wife!

(Groans and "uh-oh's" from the audience. And maybe one of those long, drawn-out "wahhhh-wahhhh" whines from a muted trumpet!)

This would not turn out to be one of my *finer* moments. Our families never spoke to one another again, and within a year those neighbors moved away!

(Fade to Dad looking each family member in the eye, as one by one, everyone shakes their head and leaves; until he's left alone, head down, kicking at rocks, contemplating the error of his ways!)

Bottom line: I was always doing something wrong!
Wahhhh-wahhhh...

All Things Must Pass

LOCKING UP THE DREAM-HOUSE

KRLA: 1963–1969, The End

The Beatles movie *Help!* had its "royal première" on Thursday, July 29, 1965, at the London Pavilion, Piccadilly Circus, London.

When I finally saw it, I couldn't help but think of my time on location with the boys and those *changes* I had started to feel and see.

On March 4, 1966, eight months after the release of *Help!*, a quote from John Lennon was printed in an interview by a reporter-friend of his, Maureen Cleave, in the *London Evening Standard:*

"Christianity will go. It will vanish and shrink. I needn't argue with that; I'm right and I will be proved right. We're more popular than Jesus now; I don't know which will go first—rock 'n' roll or Christianity. Jesus was all right but his disciples were thick and ordinary. It's them twisting it that ruins it for me."

What Lennon's motivation was for saying it—and what he allegedly *really meant*—was explained many different times in many different ways. I understood that. I knew he was "studying religion" at the time and so much of what was being said by so many different personalities was so "far out"—*at the time.*

But for me, a simple Catholic boy from Alhambra, John bringing Christ into all of this was too much. Especially in that manner. Within days, I quietly began backing off from promoting them as I had in the past.

In England, John's comments went pretty much unnoticed—simply a part of the entire interview; just more now-common ramblings of the 1960s.

But about five months later, on July 29—exactly one year after the premiere of *Help!*—an American teen magazine, *Datebook,* reprinted the quote out of context and used it as part of a cover story: "The Ten Adults You Dig/Hate The Most."

It brought down a shower of fire and brimstone! A plague was set loose upon the land! Radio stations in the South banned Beatles music! Rallies were held where Beatles records were broken, burned, and buried!

In June of 1966, just before this lynch-Lennon fever erupted, the infamous "Beatles butcher cover" had been released—and then quickly recalled. As the first cover for the *Yesterday and Today* album, that little "work of art" featuring John, Paul, George, and Ringo sitting amongst gory meat and dismembered dolls had already stirred up plenty of *bloody* controversy!

Now this!

The blush-innocence of "Love Me Do" and pictures of the boys in suits and ties had long ago gone the way of 78s and "mono" LPs.

The future was paradoxically swinging toward the darkness of things like the Doors' prophetic 1967 dirge, "The End."

It was also in 1967 that Brian Epstein died of a drug overdose.

This controversial "butcher cover," along with John's comments about Jesus, signaled the Beatles' loss of innocence and the beginning of the end of my association with them.

Run for Your Lives, the News Is Falling!

"The End," Lennon, Epstein, drugs: So much of where we were as a nation was getting more intense, more complex, more frighteningly interesting, and more *activist*. A few years before, you wouldn't see the bright eyes and open ears of the younger generation sponging up on news programs. Beaver Cleaver didn't include *Meet the Press* or *Huntley-Brinkley* on his mandatory viewing schedule.

Budget referendums and Adlai Stevenson speeches just weren't teen fodder.

But now...

Now the news was different. The Vietnam War was on everyone's mind. And it was the lead-in to every media report. The *new* news of the 1960s editorialized the war and exploded the real and perceived problems with modern American society. Dry reporting crumbled into dust; attacks on the establishment—like John Lennon's—became the center-punch of current events.

KRLA's news department was anchored by Richard Beebe and Lew Irwin—Richard having come to Eleven-Ten in 1959, Lew in '64. And both were extra sharp in that "center-punch" stance. As the sixties and its intensity rolled on, they would form a "troupe"—a biting satirical bunch called The Credibility Gap. Along with Harry Shearer, David L. Lander, and Michael McKean, Beebe and Irwin's troupe made albums—and a difference in how people looked at and absorbed the news. (Shearer and McKean, of course, would go on to "form" the eighties-defining mock-metal megagroup Spinal Tap; and McKean with Lander became the greasy duo, "Lenny and Squiggy," on TV's *Laverne & Shirley*.)

But there was still the daily news to report at KRLA.

Sort of.

It was definitely *new* news.

Beebe was a graduate of the Pasadena Playhouse. During the fifties, many actors and actresses from Hollywood and New York went there to hone their skills. And Richard Beebe had skills.

Richard would "play" the roles of principals in interviews and reports. But the listeners didn't know it was him! The spins and humor were brilliant. He was a genius.

Harry Shearer was now involved at the station, and he and Beebe would write these wacky "news" pieces, and then they'd go upstairs into our production studio at KRLA and quickly record them. When they were done, they'd call me on the intercom and say, "Go outside— we're going to drop the tape down!"

And down it would come—BOOM!—and we'd put it in the newsroom and play it over the air. Beebe and his boys fed a lot of the sixties' hunger for news, and ultimately vital information. Their broadcasts were politically potent and socially steaming.

The news was different...

RADIO ANNOUNCER [Beebe]: *Hemingway once defined courage as 'Grace under pressure,' but this wasn't grace under pressure—it was Mary Lou under water! Without thinking for a moment of his own personal safety, Senator Kennedy panicked. Suddenly, he remembered what his father once said years ago...*

JOSEPH P. KENNEDY [David Lander in an echo chamber]: *Teddy! Bring me my pills! And while you're at it, always remember: If you're ever trapped under water in a car with a girl, make sure both of you get out alive, or else some politically ambitious judge could write an inquest report that could make you look baaaaad!*

RADIO ANNOUNCER [Beebe]: *Those words ringing in his ears, the senator filled those massive Kennedy lungs with air and dove repeatedly into the murky waters!*

—The Credibility Gap

Hard Act to Follow

In July of 1966, the first bricks in the Dream-House unofficially began to crumble when Emperor Bob Hudson had a falling out— *a physical falling out*—with KRLA's general manager, John Barrett.

Barrett called him in to discipline him about his playing of Hudson's own single, "I'm Normal"—a parody of the current novelty hit "They're Coming to Take Me Away Ha-Haaa!"

Bob had been told specifically not to do it.

But *no one,* of course, orders around royalty.

When the management serf confronted His Highness, Hudson picked Barrett up, slammed him up against the wall, and said, "Don't you *ever* call me down here for something as idiotic as this. I am The Emperor."

He was beginning to believe he was.

"Get off the freeways, peasants! His Highness is coming..."

John fired him at once. "Don't ever step foot on this property again!" he told him.

Then Barrett called me.

He told me the whole story—about how Hudson had "abused" him. And then he said, "I want you to take mornings."

"No, John, I don't want to," I said. "I've got the biggest numbers in the afternoon."

I was just kicking the butt of the Real Don Steele at KHJ. I was just tearing him up.

"If you won't take it, then what am I going to do about mornings?" John pleaded.

"If you're a smart man," I told him, "you'll go back to Bob Hudson and tell him you made an awful mistake and that you want him back on the air tomorrow."

"I can't do that, Dave," he said. "He *physically* pushed me up against the wall!" And then he told me, "If you don't take the slot, I'm forced to hire Charlie O'Donnell."

Now, I have always loved Charlie O'Donnell and I admired his talent, but filling the gilded boots of The Emperor was going to be beyond tough. Hudson was the personality universally credited for "building KRLA into number one."

No one could do it.

"If you don't get Bob back," I countered, "we will lose all of our morning ratings to KHJ and Robert W. Morgan! We'll lose it all! So get on the phone!"

"I simply cannot do it," he said, ending the conversation.

He hired Charlie O'Donnell.

"Charlie will last one year, and that's all," I told John after receiving the news.

Within days, Emperor Bob Hudson was hired by KBLA and placed in his same familiar six-to-nine a.m. slot.

It made morning drive interesting—and congested.

Down the dial from Hudson at AM 1500, Charlie-O was now one of the Eleven-Ten Men.

And Morgan was ruling at 93-KHJ.

One year later, almost to the day, John Barrett tells me, "I'm letting Charlie go. Will you *now* take the mornings?"

This time I said yes.

I wouldn't even think about following the act of Bob Hudson in the mornings, but I'd follow Charlie O'Donnell.

You have to look at the people listening; you have to think of them. To follow Emperor Hudson would have killed me. But following Charlie O'Donnell, who was not doing well, *that* was an inspiration.

Pick a Car, Any Car...

The card shuffle of personalities was constant and fast. Sometimes it was like watching a super-sleight-of-hand magician pull aces out of shirt cuffs and coins out of ears. You'd try to stay on top of it, but before you knew it, the deck was shuffled again and your lucky card could wind up on the top, the bottom, or in the pocket of the guy at the next table, along with two doves and a four-foot Chinese fan. And this was true for fast shuffles from within and *without* of a station.

The biggest influence from *without* was KHJ, of course. The Bill Drake Top 40 twister was sucking up ratings and personalities—and it was chasing me!

The first time they called me, I politely declined. I was loyal to KRLA, of course, but I *did* have further incentive: John Barrett gave me a ten-grand *re-signing* bonus!

Then Drake and KHJ came calling again.

I told Barrett.

His reaction was to ask me a question: "What kind of car do you want to drive, Dave?"

"I wouldn't mind having a new Cadillac," I replied nonchalantly.

"Go down to Symes Cadillac," he said. "Tell them what you want, and we'll pay for it—cash."

I used John's personal office phone to turn down KHJ *again*.

"If you don't accept this offer, Hull," Drake told me, "you'll never get another opportunity from me!"

No problem...

But I've often thought about what might have happened had I gone over to KHJ in its heyday; I wonder how long I would have lasted under micromanager-supremo Bill Drake.

But John Barrett—well, John always gave me all these perks. I wasn't going anywhere.

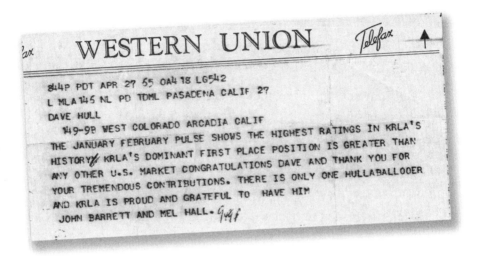

With all the perks and appreciation that John Barrett gave me, I wasn't (willingly) going anywhere!

FM Turns Up the Volume

While KHJ might have been reshaping AM Top 40, the FM band had opened wide in L.A.—KMET and KPPC were rolling in hipness and stereo sound.

Up until now, AM had been King. The technology of Amplitude Modulation was simpler than that of Frequency Modulated broadcasts and easier to engineer into receivers. AM signals had extraordinary range and the whole package had a lot of seniority, having been around since 1906.

Every car radio was AM. (And tape players—four-track, eight-track, or cassette—were still in the same fantasy class as iPods and No Smoking signs in bars.)

And those car radios meant something!

Every kid had—or wanted—a car. It was a rumbling rite of passage, and they wanted their music turned up loud to supplement the sheer coolness of cruising.

But that oddball Frequency Modulated FM band, developed by a guy named Edwin Howard Armstrong back in the 1930s, sounded better in terms of audio output, because it is not susceptible to atmospheric and electrical interference like AM is. And FM could transmit *stereo*. Your favorite band or artist could sound like they were right there in your back seat with you and your gal.

And suddenly, in ever-industrial ever-progressing America, FM technology was becoming easier and cheaper for modern receivers to handle.

At home—out of the car—FM presented a whole new world of sound. Music was deep, rich, and a lot more real on home *components*. And a few programming trailblazers like Tom Donahue and L.A. AM radio deserter and rogue B. Mitchell Reed caught on quickly to that kind of aesthetic power.

What was once the limited snoozy path of classical music and other "stuff the kids hated," FM radio now was the "free form" forum for all those fresh-out-of-the-garage musicians and bands that needed "someplace to be heard."

With FM you could take things to a completely new level of musical depth, too. You could put on your headphones and "dream... right between the sound machine," as John Kay and Steppenwolf would tell us, and expand your mind with Country Joe whispering *"LSD"* quietly in one speaker while music filled the other.

Psychedelic!

KFWB waved their white AM flag on March 11th of '68 and went all-news, sensing the end of music and the rise of talk on the KHz side of the dial.

KHJ had become the AM leader as KRLA began to tread water on that wave of change. We went to automation at Eleven-Ten to try and buck KHJ's tide of more-music-less-talk.

Of course, what that translated into was less *interaction* between DJs and listeners.

It was man versus machine.

By the spring of '68, every shift except for morning and afternoon drive time and three to seven p.m. on Sundays was automated on KRLA.

The machines were winning.

During this time is also when the final issues of the *KRLA Beat* went to press.

In the very first issue of the *KRLA Beat,* my column told the readers and listeners that *"the pictures inside were taken by KRLA, and are so exclusive that they are printed in disappearing ink! You won't see them anywhere else..."*

Well, those "exclusive" pics weren't the only things disappearing with time.

But I did have one more, *one more* last dance left in me. In November of 1968, I did a special for the station with me interviewing George Harrison. George gave his cut-by-cut commentary about the new double Beatles album that became known as the "White Album."

For me and for KRLA, it marked the end of Beatlemania. It was my last project associated with the Beatles, and my last extra-feature hullabaloo for the station.

My "White Album" special with George Harrison marked the end of Beatlemania both for KRLA and for me. From left to right: Reb Foster, Program Director Doug Cox, Dick Moreland, George Harrison, me, and DJ Roy Elwell.

January 3, 1969: Off the Air

With Lennon, Jesus, on-air automation, FM and FM's expansion of the artist pool, "Top 40" really becoming top *everything* in the way of music variations—so much was over.

So much had changed.

In late 1968, Doug Cox had come into KRLA as the new program director and erstwhile savior of a fading, mechanized, sterile radio station.

On January 1, 1969, my contract with KRLA was up. And Cox was doing some heavy cleaning in the Dream-House—attempting personality transfusions and keeping-up-with-the-times CPR on a broadcast cadaver.

By Friday, January 3rd, I still had not been offered a new contract. After that Friday show, I was summoned into Cox's office and let go.

Fired.

Replaced.

*Dis*placed.

A sacrifice to a hungry god of change that no one knew how to satisfyingly appease.

AM radio still had plenty of listeners and a place in the world of entertainment, but that hungry, snorting god scared a lot of people.

I was still in the six-to-ten a.m. slot, going head-to-head with Robert W. Morgan—from *number one* KHJ.

I was gone on a Friday and on the following Tuesday, the periodic ratings for Los Angeles radio were released:

I got a 12.3. Robert W. had a 10.7.

I had beaten him like one of Ringo's snares. But I was now at home and Morgan was still *on the air.*

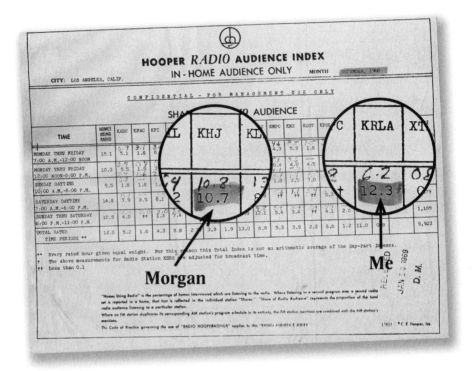

See! I beat Morgan. See?! Not that I'm holding onto this or anything...

Cox put William F. Williams in my shift. Williams had been with KRLA for a short time in another time slot.

In morning drive, he lasted about as long as Arthur "Big Guy" Carlson's helicopter-drop turkeys on *WKRP in Cincinnati.*

Just a few months later, in the fall of '69, Doug Cox himself would be gone.

One Simple Theory (Reprise)

In 1970, George Harrison released his solo album and title song "All Things Must Pass."

The Beatles had broken up.

But George's tune was optimistic about change, and it also echoed the now tried-and-true Dave Hull's One Simple Theory: *Take whatever is thrown at you and make the most of it!*

I had definitely done that!

The 1960s were "thrown" at all of us—some parts gently lobbed with a velvet glove, others hurled with a greasy catapult!

But I took it all—the good and the not-so-good—and at least made it fun! From the espionage-scoops on Beatles records, to helping create and expand the concept of big-venue "concerts" as opposed to just small-club "performances" (even though I had to do things like swim a moat, watch my new car get crushed, and catch an ever-haunting glimpse of Mick Jagger's blue legs!), to releasing my own personal album of private Beatles interviews and conversations, to my stowaway run to Denver, to my *insider trading* with Mrs. Louise Harrison, to my three-week *fact-finding* mission to the Bahamas; to wading into the newsprint sea of the most widely read teen newspaper of the time, the *KRLA Beat.*

And most of all, to a close and unique association with *the* most influential rock 'n' roll performers in the history of music—an association that propelled radio station KRLA to the greatest heights in California broadcast history.

And it all worked!

It worked so well for the millions of fans who listened and cared about KRLA radio–1110 and its air personalities during those wild years.

My fan club president, Linda Thor, was certainly one of those millions—one of the absolute most important! She, too, was watching the ink disappear. In a letter to a fan club member, Linda captures the emotions that so many of us were feeling as we realized that "all things must pass":

DAVE HULL International Fan Club

634 Sefton Avenue   Monterey Park, Calif. 91754

PRESIDENT
LINDA THOR

February 17, 1965

Dear Kathy,

...I was always disgusted with fan clubs that abruptly stop, so we have been preparing people for the end gradually...It breaks my heart to give up the fan club as I have enjoyed it more than anything I have ever done and, of course, I adore Dave.

It's difficult for me to talk about giving up the club and I find it hard to put my thoughts into words, but I hope you understand how I feel.

Yours,

Linda

We do, Linda.

We do.

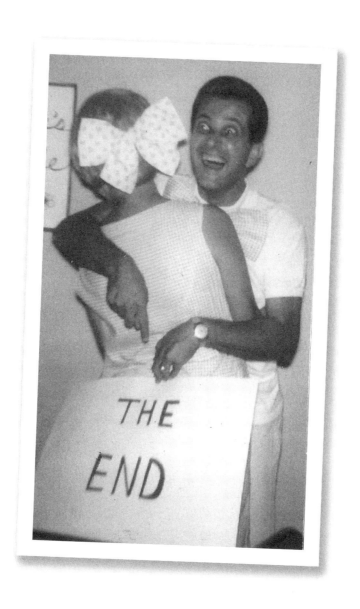

Voodoo and Baseball Don't Mix

"SPRING" TRAINING, HULLABALOOER-STYLE

KFI: 1969–1971

"KFI, Los Angeles, Earle C. Anthony, Incorporated"

This vintage ID is still used at KFI, 640 AM in Los Angeles. It's a retro-reverential station call—complete with scratches, pops, and somewhat less than state-of-the-art audio. And it should be. KFI goes back a long way and its history is important. Today, KFI reels in ratings with its local and syndicated talk format, always at or near the top of the listenership charts in America's second largest market—and that includes both the AM and FM side of the dial.

The station fired up in 1922 in Earle C. Anthony's garage, reaching listeners over a fifty-watt transmitter made from a crank telephone. The station's *format* consisted mostly of ol' Earle yelling into a carbon microphone in his garage: *"Can you hear me?!"*

If this bit of broadcast magic was working, a family member in the house would answer back with the non-creative but to the point: *"Yes, I can hear you!"*

And KFI's operating frequency was not necessarily 640 kHz in those days; it was pretty much *any* frequency Earle could get the transmitter to operate on.

KFI took a Super Eight step forward when on-air operations were moved to the top of Earle's Packard automobile dealership, with a broadcast schedule that filled up a full four and a half hours a day.

By the time World War II exploded, KFI was getting bigger—nearly Packard Clipper–size—and was now an NBC affiliate. The reassuring "fireside chats" of FDR could often be heard on the now-permanent 640 frequency.

The "FI" in KFI stands for "Farmer's Information." On winter evenings between 1924 and well into the late 1970s, KFI would broadcast frost reports, advising citrus farmers when to turn on wind machines or light smudge pots to keep their orange and lemon groves cozy and warm.

With its ties to NBC, KFI would air events like the 1927 Rose Bowl game and performances by Jack Benny, Burns and Allen, Fred Allen, Eddie Cantor, Rudy Vallee, and other acts associated with the Keith-Albee-Orpheum (KAO, later to become RKO) vaudeville circuit. RKO was owned by RCA, which owned NBC. See, even in those days you saw an alphabet soup of who-owns-who in the entertainment world!

Eventually, technology advanced beyond Earle's crank, allowing KFI to kick its power up to 50,000 clear-channel watts. You could hear it on the Moon and into galaxies far, far away. In fact, from what I understand, until Pluto was downgraded—its planetary status revoked and its inhabitants cast into a depressive funk—the Plutonians were still talking about that wacky '27 Rose Bowl game between 'Bama and Stanford ending in a 7-7 tie!

And they knew all the words to Rudy Vallee's "Life Is Just a Bowl of Cherries."

KFI's sheer, terrifying, 'round-the-universe power helped define the term "50,000-watt blowtorch"!

I would be joining that history-heavy, interplanetarily-enjoyed, farm-informing, fireside-chatting influential mix; but I didn't know it quite yet.

First, of course, I had to get over the shock of being ousted from KRLA.

It wasn't easy.

Again, so much was so different back then—especially for fans of local radio. It wasn't a world of computers or the Internet or "social media," where every second of every day you know exactly where your fav personalities are and where they're going (and when they're trimming their nose hair or engaging in other forms of personal hygiene). You couldn't follow the performers you loved most around their studios or movie sets or even their houses with high-def "web cams" and watch them itch, scratch, grunt, groan, tie shoes, and pick their ears with a key.

Nope.

Back then, when a radio personality—especially a local one—was axed from a station, he was gone. Vanished and banished. Oh, a blurb *may* have appeared in the Entertainment section of the regional paper, but more often than not, the part of your day and all the good times you'd shared with him were simply no longer there. A frantic call to the station might get the switchboard operator telling you that "So-and-so has decided to pursue new avenues in his career...thank you." *Click.*

That was that.

Later on down the road, you might be traveling through Bismarck, North Dakota, or the Moose River area near Jackman, Maine, and *Surprise!* You'd hear your old friend still spinning the wax.

Or you might never hear from him again.

Not even a formal or loving good-bye.

> *"Baby, if you've ever wondered,*
> *Wondered whatever became of me,*
> *I'm living on the air in Cincinnati,*
> *Cincinnati, WKRP..."*

I, however, was lucky, fortunate, and blessed.

I would get to remain in the area; the place where I was born and raised. Where I became the Fifth Beatle and stirred up enough of a hullabaloo that I didn't ever have to go back to keeping jackrabbits awake in the middle of the night in a space-alien-infested desert!

But like I said, I didn't know it yet!

Elvis Calling!

Speaking of aliens...as my career continued, I would continue to deal with a lot of supernatural surprises and odd things and people.

In fact, after the King of Rock and Roll died in 1977, I would wind up receiving phone calls from Elvis himself (channeled heavenly through Jim Roope), calling straight from The Mansion Over the Hilltop!

By then, I was BACK at KRLA (we'll get to that later!!); but as I look back on these phone calls, I can see how they had bearing on the rest of my career. So I thought it appropriate to include some conversations I had with the King as I continue the story of my radio life...

Elvis: Hello, baby!

Dave: Oh, hi...Ladies and gentlemen, guess what?
That's Elvis! The voice of Elvis from heaven!
We feel so much better—it's humanizing to know
that you're okay up there, Elvis.

Elvis: Everything's fine up here, baby—everything's just
wonderful. I'm on cloud nine, so to speak.
No pun intended, baby.

Thank you, thank you very much...

The Colorful Carousel of KFI

When I dragged myself home from my last KRLA "meeting"
with Doug Cox, I naturally had to tell Jeanette.

What?!

Then we both needed time to let the news settle in and the shock
wear off.

And really, I don't know if that kind of shock ever really, totally,
one hundred percent wears off. The KRLA years had been far more
than a job—for me and for the fans. This kind of "breakup" is right
up there with your best friend moving to someplace that grows corn,

seeing your favorite president ousted after just one term, or having your first pet goldfish die when you're four.

It's traumatic!

Anyway, we started to breathe deeply and soon realized that above and below 1110 kHz were a lot of other radio stations. Here. *In Los Angeles!* Unlike my first limping attempts to jump into L.A. radio, this time I marched boldly up to one of the biggies. Well, I didn't *exactly* march; I called. I phoned the KFI program director, David Moorhead (a man who would go on to help manage "underground" FM station KMET for a decade).

It just so happened that Moorhead was reading an advance copy of the Hooper rating book showing how I had sunk Robert W. Morgan.

The right place at the right time...

He asked me right then and there if I would take KFI's Sunday evenings, beginning *that* weekend.

I was fired from KRLA on a Friday and back on the air just over a week later on KFI.

Great!

But...

There I was again, on my second L.A. station, working Sunday nights from six to midnight.

But that obscure little corner of dark weekend exile didn't last long. KFI was building itself into a new music station featuring a light-adult-hits format, and they wanted a more contemporary staff. Plus, they were still a full-service NBC station with all the big network shows, advertisers, and pull.

Within a few weeks, I was offered mid-afternoons, Monday through Friday, preceding Dave Garroway's show. Dave was a media pioneer. Not only was he the founding host of NBC-TV's *Today* show from 1952 to 1961, but before getting in front of the camera he was also "the nation's best radio personality" as voted by his peers in the 1948, '49, and '51 *Billboard* magazine polls.

Jay Lawrence ("Uncle Jaybird," left) was another personality who rounded out the talented colorful carousel of KFI!

So here I am, with my new show just ahead of Dave Garroway *and* just ahead of KFI's new all-night personality, a giant radio name with an equally giant reputation in New York and San Francisco: Al "Jazzbo" Collins.

Jazzbo was bona fide radio-royalty—easily one of the most "interesting" disc jockeys ever, with extra eclecticism à la Emperor Hudson. Al Collins' fans titled him a "hipster saint," a "jazz icon," and "a radio legend on both coasts"! He would bring the listener into strange places like his "mushroom-encrusted, burger-aplenty Purple Grotto"!

Al was also the one to popularize the term "convoy" in the CB lingo of coast-to-coast eighteen-wheelers. Even with his bohemian base, Collins could get real blue-collar. With KFI's nighttime nationwide reach, Jazzbo developed a line of diesel-driving disciples, who called in from truck stops everywhere. Jazzbo became their interstate intermediary, conveying messages to and from the drivers' families.

I was feeling quite eccentrically comfortable as I turned 'round on the colorful carousel that was KFI.

From the classy and historical dignity of Garroway to the beatnik vibe of Collins, I decided I could stretch out a little; I'd be creative and "fashion-forward."

And I'd *start* with Jazzbo.

And his wild wardrobe.

Al Collins' work (and/or formal) wear—day and night—consisted of his signature trademark jumpsuits created for him by his wife.

I had a great idea! And it was even slightly *scuzzy*!

I got listeners everywhere along KFI's intergalactic signal range to rip off those "Do Not Remove Under Penalty of Law" tags found on furniture, mattresses, and pillows and stuff and send them into the station!

The "great" part of my great idea was to have Jazzbo's wife make him a jumpsuit out of the tags!

I really was kind of an early Michael Kors, long before ol' MK ever sent a tall, skinny girl down the runway in his groovy upscale garb.

Within days, the KFI mailbox was overflowing with thousands of the "outlaw" tags. We didn't actually get any from the Moon or Pluto, but we did get some from as far away as the United Kingdom and Finland.

When Jazzbo's wife finished her *couture de label* creation and Al hit the red carpet (well, KFI's studio, anyway) he acknowledged that while the new jumpsuit was a "bit scratchy," overall he was darn proud of his new duds! They would look perfect as he descended into the Purple Grotto for his show, and the shiny slickness of the tags would be practical if any ketchup oozed out of his Purple Grotto Burgers and onto his *bodice*.

So my first KFI stunt was a runway runaway, in terms of that always-lusted-after listener interaction. And as far as we knew, no one was ever arrested, indicted, imprisoned, or in any other way forced to suffer under any "penalties of law" for their label-cutting crimes!

Hulloween!

Okay, Dave Garroway was still broadcasting in his ever-sharp bow ties and thick, studious spectacles; I had spiffed up Jazzbo with the new tags-up jumpsuit; and now it was October.

Time for Halloween.

Time for something innovatingly eerie.

Now, KFI had access to a nearby auditorium, and that gave me yet another *great idea*!

Today's Halloween all-night horror movies and the midnight madnesses of *The Rocky Horror Picture Show*—none of that ghoulishness had really grabbed the throats of the macabre set yet.

Yet...

"Let's set up the auditorium and show spooky movies all night on Halloween and invite all the listeners," I told management. "It'll be a great promotion!"

"Hmmm, you think that'll work?" they asked.

"It will if we make it simple," I told them. "We'll have listeners send in a self-addressed, stamped *large* envelope, and we'll send them back a *mask*. That will be their admission ticket!"

"A mask? What kind of mask?" The staff now looked a tad concerned.

"A mask of *me*! A hideous-Hull mask!" This idea was really heating up now. "It'll be *Hull*oween!"

Hundreds of listeners wrote in, got their masks, and showed up in all sorts of weird costumes—but all with the same freaky face.

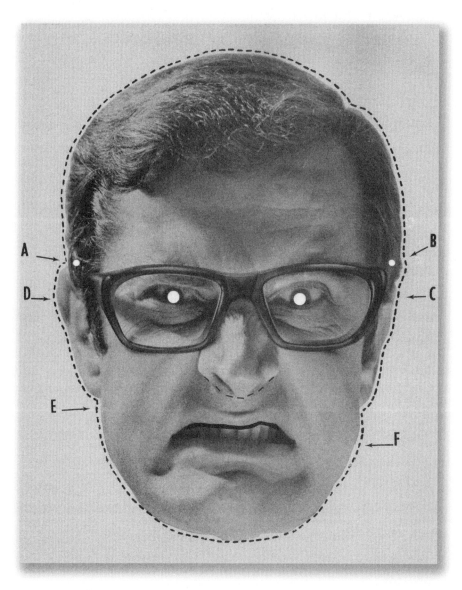

The movies we showed were scary, but the most disturbing thing was looking out at the audience from the stage. Standing there facing them all, I could see nothing but hundreds of hideous *me's* looking back!

KFI●640

This is an authentic scarey-looking Dave Hull Hulloween Mask*.
Accept no substitutes. When this mask is attached to your head,
or someone else's head, it will admit you, or someone else, to a
good old-fashioned spooky Hulloween evening at KFI Radio.
Just some of the horrifying things planned include a movie whose
title we are not allowed to publish (we don't want to scare you

unti
stai
Da
gue
you
Yo
to
A
y

KFI●640

SECRET HULLOWEEN INSTRUCTIONS FOR YOUR PERSONAL DAVE HULL MASK

1. Bravely face the mask. Stick a piece of string or rubber band through the punched hole marked "A". Going in an easterly direction, thread the string or rubber band through the punched hole marked "B". If you are left handed, reverse this procedure.

2. Look at the hole marked "C". Look up at the ceiling, you've spent too much time staring at the scarey looking thing. When you've recovered your composure, look at the hole labeled "D". Hold the mask up to your face. Your left eye should see through the hole marked "C"and your right eye through the hole marked "D". If this does not happen, check the position of your eyes...to far apart...to close together...one on top of the other...try step 2 from the beginning again.

3. Medical research, under clinical conditions, has ascertained that even scarey looking people must breath. Therefore, with a knife, slice along the line under the nose marked "E".

4. Finally, in order for you to scream, cut along the mouth line marked "F".

5. Cut along the dotted line surrounding the entire funny looking mask being careful not to look at the mask too long.

6. Place the mask in front of your face, put the string around your head and look in the mirror. Now say, "AAAAAHHHHHHHHHH!"

(It is important that you place the mask in front of your face and not on the back of your head. If it is not in this position our ushers will become confused and think you are walking out upon your arrival.)

It was like being in a fun-house mirror maze, where all the warped glass was shattered and reflected back in multi-monstrosity, like what you might see through a mutant fly's eyes!

Happy Hulloween!

328 • Dave Hull

Elvis: I was just thinking, maybe someone down there oughta do an investigation.

Dave: Oh, wow. You think I oughta do it for you? What do you need?

Elvis: Well, you know, you could spearhead that for me, baby. I know you used to be a private eye, didn't ya? In between radio jobs, you've done just about everything, I think!

Dave: Ha ha! My whole thick file must be up there! Yes, I have, Elvis—what is it you want me to investigate?

Elvis: Has anyone ever determined why I'm the only guy ON EARTH who's buried in his own backyard?!

Parker & Hull in the Lineup

My mattress-tag jumpsuits and masks and Jazzbo's hipster-cat ways were creating a fun vibe, but I was finding out that deep down, the button-down world of NBC affiliation really spelled N-O H-U-M-O-R throughout the rest of the daily schedule. I also found out that Dave Garroway's bow ties were spinning every time he heard my horns honk and all the rest of my hullabaloo as he readied for his show. A horn-blowing nutcase doesn't quite jell with the horn-rimmed humorlessness of staid and serious broadcasting.

In management's words: "Something must be done."

And what was done would prove to be yet another of those magic radio hat tricks. They moved me to a slot *after* Garroway, before and after Dodger baseball.

The colorful carousel of KFI was *really* predominately blue at the time—Los Angeles Dodgers blue.

In 1958, the "Bronx Bombers" shocked the sports world by moving to the left coast! Two years later, KFI became the flagship station for L.A.'s newest team—and for the golden Hall-of-Fame, Emmy-winning voice of the Dodgers' play-by-play man, Vin Scully. Along with his longtime partner, Jerry Doggett, "Vinny" traveled west with the "trolley dodgers" and became yet another part of the greatness that was KFI.

KFI became sports-synonymous with the Dodgers.

One morning, the station's sports director, Chuck Benedict, called and asked me if I wanted to join him for lunch and a day game at Dodger Stadium (Dodger owner Walter O'Malley took very good care of everyone who was part of the extended Dodgers *family*).

Sure!

I got to meet a lot of the players in the locker room, in the clubhouse, and behind the scenes—it was terrific! One guy in particular really impressed me. He was humble, intelligent, humorous, and good-looking. It was the Dodgers' young first baseman, Wes Parker—a Gold Glove superstar.

Wes is an intelligent, classy guy. His father became a multimillionaire through his mega-company, Parker Manufacturing (how many of you are jotting down notes in this book with a Parker pen?!). Wes went to the finest schools. His mother was the heir to the Joslyn Foundation. Wes had a lot of good stuff in his background! He was nothing like some of the sappy, look-at-me types in pro sports.

I told Wes he was a rarity as far as I was concerned, and I'd like to have him come down to the station after a game when he was able.

And he did.

The original plan was for us to go on the air together and take a few phone calls. But we were having so much fun that first night, we never did get around to taking calls.

The show quickly evolved into "Parker & Hull" (I started calling it "Parker & Hull" right away; I'm just not the kind of guy who likes to say "Here I am!" so it's always the other person first) and after just a few months, the popularity of our combination made for a great double play!

Baseball "Boog Alou"

This would prove to be only the *first* swing at a grand slam in the ratings department!

Now, with Wes's honesty and personality, and with the station's hyperdrive power and coverage, things began to really happen. First,

KFI offered to extend my contract if I agreed to stay in the time slot that surrounded Dodger baseball.

Yes!

Parker & Hull became a full entertainment and sports show with listeners calling in (finally!) and asking personal and professional questions of Wes and about the fun and excitement of Dodger baseball in general.

Even the great Vin Scully would call in.

Naturally, the show featured a lot of *nearly*-award-winning wit.

"Groaners" were born on the Parker & Hull Show, advancing comedy 50,000 watts and many light-years ahead of what it once was (at least I *think* that's what they must have been saying on Pluto).

One night, a listener sent me a very corny joke about a professional athlete. I read it on the air and you could almost see flowers wilting, eyes rolling, and even skunks holding their noses! I called it a "groaner."

Now that I think about it, radio really pioneered something else: the idea of something "going viral" (again, long before computers and the Internet). Our vehicle for spreading words, emotions, fun, and interest was centered in the human ear and things going out over the airwaves.

Groaners went viral.

Within a few days of their initial laff-riot and cultural impact, KFI began receiving hundreds of letters marked, yes, "Groaners."

The mailroom was kind of an isolated cave when it came to being in touch with what went on 24/7 in—and out—of the fertile minds of the KFI personalities.

Groaners...

Stacks and stacks of 'em...

The mail clerk calls up the PD. "What is all this groaner stuff?"

"Hmmm...It's gotta be Hull," Moorhead told him. "Just jam all that stuff into *his* box!"

And they did.

This was highbrow humor at its best...

"And now we have a Groaner from Bob, a listener in Downey, California...'If Boog Powell was a member of the Alou family...he'd be Boog Alou!'"

Long before the Internet, our Groaners went viral with Dodger fans!

Nebuchadnezzar's Barbecue

Parker & Hull was batting a thousand, so Fred Claire, the Dodgers' director of publicity, suggested to Walter and his son, Peter,

O'Malley that the club consider inviting me to spring training at Dodger Town in Vero Beach, Florida—with all expenses paid in full.

He thought it a good idea that I watch the afternoon or evening spring training games and then go on the air with Wes and talk about it all—pump up interest in the upcoming season.

I thought it was an incredibly ground-breaking, highly insightful, and in-every-way-superb idea, too.

Especially the "all expenses paid" part.

The O'Malleys agreed.

Perfect!

But we would be adding a third voice and personality to the show: the voice and personality of the manager of the Dodgers' Triple-A farm club, the Spokane Indians. The Indians' manager's name was Tommy Lasorda. In 1970, Tommy and his Indians won 94 of 146 games and swept Hawaii's Islanders in the Pacific Coast League playoffs.

And Tommy Lasorda has never *not* been a character!

Parker & Hull got funnier by the day with Tommy added to our batting lineup. He was a winning baseball manager and a hilarious addition to the show. But he was also my Vero Beach roommate—and *that* was something completely different.

I love Tommy. But if you value any sort of independence in your life, you probably don't want to be Tommy Lasorda's roommate. He is, after all, the greatest *manager* of all time! *"You're going to do this and then after you finish that, you're going to do this and this and this. And then that."*

Actually, some of the management staff tried to give me a head's up: "You're going to room with Lasorda, and he's going to give you well, *suggestions*. And we're paying for it, so just do as you're told."

I figured, *No problem.*

On my first day, I arrived in the late afternoon and got into the room just as Tommy was putting away his bags.

"Who are *you*?" he asked.

I told him.

"Okay...but there are a few things that need to be done."

Suggestions...this...that...

Tommy was a devout Catholic. Excellent. I am, too. But Tommy insisted that we both attend Mass *every morning*. Every *early* morning. Mass began at 7:30 a.m. and we would be there.

We would be there.

And *my* mornings began even earlier because I was the one who had to shower, shave, and dress first. The man destined to become one of the greatest professional sports team managers of all time was definitely in charge here in our hotel room, too.

The very first morning, however, our game plan took a hit; we had to overcome an early error.

I got out of the shower and Tommy told me that our ride wasn't going to be able to make it; he ordered me downstairs to look for any available vehicle that could take us to church. He was very managerial and game-sure of himself: *"You will find someone..."*

I ran down the stairs, still wet. The first person I ran into (yes, I *really* ran into him!) was the postman delivering early mail to all the players and coaches.

You WILL find someone...

I confronted this loyal and hard-working government employee, a servant of the people.

And he looked at me.

He could see that I was wet and desperate.

That created an awkward dynamic, but he stayed attentive.

Now, I knew that this man dealt with "snow and rain and heat and gloom of night" on a daily basis, but this—like rooming with Tommy—was different.

I explained as calmly as I could that the driver for our ride to church had overslept and that Tommy Lasorda, manager of the Spokane Indians, the top farm club of the Los Angeles Dodgers, (and *I*) needed to get to church.

I asked him if he knew where the Catholic church was. He looked nervous, but told me he indeed knew where this house of worship was—he delivered mail there.

Yes.

Of course.

This was divine intervention!

I was even more emphatic as I got to the point. *And* I was beginning to dry off a bit.

"You are the person *God* has chosen to help us this morning!" I told him.

Whether touched from the hand of the Lord, inspired by my plea, or a combination of both, the postman faced this challenge as stoically as Shadrach, Meshach, and Abednego facing down Nebuchadnezzar's barbecue!

By the time Lasorda came downstairs, the postal truck was all warmed up and ready to go.

We got to Mass just as the bells were ringing and the priest was coming to the altar. As we settled into a pew, Tommy leaned over to me and whispered, "See, I told you so. I knew you'd find someone..."

Deus gubernat navem...

As if on the wings of angels, the mail truck driver waited for Mass to finish and delivered us up unto ere we came—right back to the Dodgers hotel and camp.

Dave: You know, Elvis, a lot of people write me letters and they phone me; they want me to ask questions of you. One woman asked me: What does God think when people fall asleep in church, Elvis?

Elvis: Well, I'll tell you this, baby. As big and as important as he is—I mean, I know how I'd react if somebody found me boring! He came in a room the other day, he was trying to boost the mood a little bit here, and He told the organist to play "Won't You Come Home, Bill Bailey"!

Spring Training Takes On a Hull New Meaning

Since we were staying in camp for weeks, I had some time to come up with another great idea: Spring training!

Spring training?

Spring training!

I urged listeners to send in a spring of any size—anything from one of those little ones wrapped around the bottom of your pen refill to a part of the suspension of a Mack truck. Anything they might have lying around. Just as long as they included self-addressed return packaging.

These springs, I explained, would be professionally "trained" for the season ahead and then returned to their owners at the "home team" in those envelopes and boxes. We printed an official reassuring postcard to insert with each spring:

> *"The enclosed spring is now fully trained—*
> *have a great season!"*
>
> *—Parker & Hull*

Thousands of springs of all shapes and sizes arrived at the station from all over Southern California. No one actually sent in anything from a Mack, but a full front end car spring assembly *was* delivered in a crate by truck.

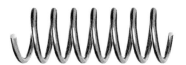

Sticking It to Pete Rose

After seeing the plundered Studebaker suspension arrive, Wes Parker thought I'd gone mad.

But we weren't finished yet.

With the season coming up and the Pete Rose–powered Cincinnati Reds recognized as the heavyweights in the league, Parker & Hull swung into yet another listener urging.

This time we fell back onto a tried and true manipulation of the universe—a sharp tactic that has been here in the United States since at least the 1700s and is maybe ten thousand years old in general—voodoo!

It was time for some ground-ball gris-gris!

With all of their springs trained, we now asked the KFI audience to send in pins and needles—again, of any size—so we could stick them into our life-sized Pete Rose voodoo doll, which we'd had professionally designed and constructed at Madame Tussauds Wax Museum in Hollywood.

We were again "viral" before viral.

Pins and needles of every size possible shot into that mailroom, where by now, the workers in that cave were getting used to all of our hullabaloo (well, sort of...). And many listeners apparently believed, *The bigger the pin, the better the anti-Pete-Rose-base-hitting power*; so the mailroom began sorting through large hat pins, oversized knitting needles, and even a fencing foil (which we ran straight through Paraffin Pete's heart!).

In a pointed twist on the old "Porch People" thing back at KRLA, we'd invite listeners to come to the station to help pierce Pete with the powerful points!

Wes Parker, who is variously described as handsome, tall, trim, wealthy, single, intelligent, a debonair dresser, an expert bridge player and the finest Dodger first baseman since Gil Hodges left, has taken on a new career—he is a radio commentator from 8 to midnight on station KFI in Los Angeles, the Dodgers' schedule permitting. His contract calls for him to be on the air on Monday nights when possible, but he often appears during the week as well—"If the Dodgers win," says Dave Hull, who conducts the show, "he'll stop in." Parker just talks "a little bit about baseball," he says, "but mostly about music, bridge, and items of interest out of the news. I don't think I'd ever want to do play-by-play sports." But lately there has been a decline in the cultural level of his program. "A few nights ago we asked people to send in straight pins to stick in a Cincinnati doll," says Hull. "It looked like the only way we could catch Cincinnati. We've got about a thousand now, but we'll soon have 50,000."

—Sports Illustrated, 1970

Just before a Dodgers-Reds home stand in '70, when the Reds were running away with the pennant race, we had a truck pick up the by-now heavy-as-heck voodoo doll and take it to the stadium where it was placed directly in front of the Cincinnati dugout.

Ge-Rouge!

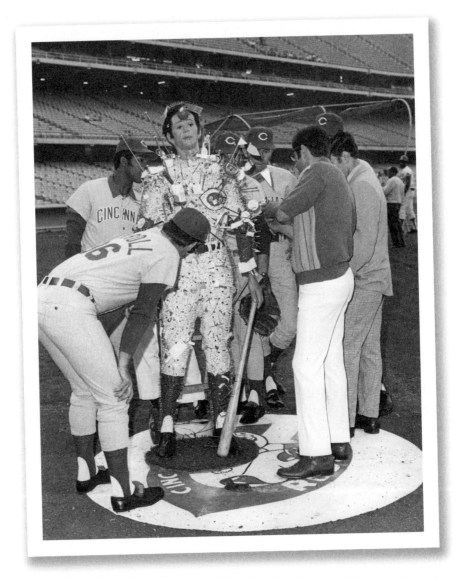

Right before the Dodgers' home stand against the Reds, we place our pierced Pete Rose (created at Madame Tussauds) right in front of Cincinnati's dugout.

But like innocent teenagers playing with a Ouija board who wind up conjuring Beelzebub's spawn or the ghost of Attila the Hun or something equally evil, we did run into a few pseudo-supernatural stumbles.

The Latin-American Dodgers and Reds players from Puerto Rico, the Dominican Republic, and other Caribbean countries wouldn't get anywhere near the doll. Some were from villages that very much believed in the curses of voodoo. There was no humor in this devil! They would turn away, refusing the slightest glance in the direction of the hideous totem!

Our curse must have lacked *La Flambeau,* though; the 1970 Cincinnati Reds won the National League West title with a record of 102-60, 14½ games ahead of the runner-up Dodgers. The Reds then went on to defeat the Pittsburgh Pirates in three straight games in the National League Championship Series to win their first National League pennant since 1961. But they did lose the World Series to the Baltimore Orioles in five games.

Pete must have put a hex on my voo doo vex! 'Cause the 1970 Dodgers got stomped by Cincy's Redlegs.

And Pete still hasn't been allowed into the Hall of Fame. (Wow, I really do hope our doll had nothing to do with that!)

Fore-Sight and Swinging Snakes

One of the serious sides of Parker & Hull was our teaming up with the 1965 Rookie of the Year and longtime Dodgers second baseman, Jim Lefebvre. Jimmy convinced Wes and me to join him in forming a speaker's bureau called Athletes for Youth—a non-profit organization of Dodgers stars who would travel throughout Southern California addressing middle school and high school students on the value of remaining drug-free.

Fred Claire was again instrumental, using his Dodgers publicity office to promote the cause to Southland schools.

Within three years, Jimmy, Wes, and I would be joined by superstars Don Sutton, Claude Osteen, and Lasorda, swinging around the Southland speaking to nearly forty-five thousand students at various schools about refraining from illegal drugs.

And I came up with another great idea!

It was one that would certainly further our cause.

I looked around and saw all these professional athletes and actors appearing in celebrity golf tournaments. So...I decided it was time for Parker & Hull to play in our own tournament, to benefit Athletes for Youth.

My first thought was to reserve the entire Riviera Country Club. But then I realized that I didn't really *play* golf...so I decided to adjust to a different level.

November 15, 1969. The "First Annual KFI 640 Miniature Golf Classic" got underway. It wasn't exactly a multi-team, star-studded pro-am or anything like that. Nope. This was just Wes and me, locked in a mano-a-mano, hole-by-hole, spinning-windmill-by-swinging-snake battle against one another.

And the KFI fans were our very supportive "gallery."

Hundreds of fairway aficionados turned out, along with a lot of other Dodgers players, to, well, essentially laugh at us both.

Guess who won hands down?

Driving with a putter, Dave Hull stunned the spectators with his ineptness. Challenger, Wes Parker, registers typical crowd reaction at right of picture. The ball was found behind the fence at rear of picture.

"Keep your eye on the Hull," was the chant of the crowd. Dave did everything to distract Wes Parker's concentration. National League "Rookie of the Year," Ted Sizemore plots with Wes on a critical hole. The young lady at the left is viewing Dave Hull for the first time.

Pretty Helen Letchworth, held Wes Parker's scoreboard assisted by Dodgers Claude Osteen and Don Sutton. A limping iguana held Dave's board. Seconds after this picture was taken, Dave Hull lost the lead and soundly lost the match. We just put this picture in to make Dave feel good.

Dave: Is it a sin to play golf on Sunday, Elvis?

Elvis: Well, Dave, the way you play golf, you betcha!

(Actually, with a little more practice—*and ability*—I might have been more competitive against Wes. It was that darned dangling snake that did me in!)

Welcome Back and Good-Bye

One night at an away game in Chicago, Wes was hit with appendicitis and was rushed to surgery for an emergency appendectomy. Right off the bat, I began requesting listeners to send in their baseball cards to be put on a huge "Welcome Back Wes" sign, which I planned to hang at Dodger Stadium the night of Wes's return.

Thousands of collector cards were sent in for the sign. To our fans, the cards weren't worth nearly as much as the show of support for Wes.

The sign was hung and pictures of it made national headlines.

The sign is still in Wes's possession; in his garage, of course. That thing was maybe twenty feet long by six feet high! More like a Foster & Kleiser billboard than a party banner.

Wes was indeed welcomed back, and he went on to spend his entire American baseball career with the Dodgers—from 1964 through 1972. (He did play one season in Japan in 1974, as did Jim Lefebvre).

Other things were heading for the last out, too.

KFI's extra-inning association with the team would come to an end in 1973 when Cox Broadcasting (no relation to my doomed KRLA PD Doug Cox), headquartered in Atlanta, purchased KFI for $15 million, the highest amount ever paid for a radio station at the time.

Along with the sale, a new management team would arrive.

These new programming wizards decided that all away games in the East beginning after 4:00 p.m. L.A. time should be *pre-recorded* and broadcast at the regular Dodger home-game time of 7:00 p.m.

Reeeally?

Hmmm...

This was like cooking your breakfast and letting it just sit on the kitchen counter for a while. You know it's there. You can smell the bacon and the coffee from the other room, but you're not going to dig in and try to savor it until it's cold and stale.

By the time the game aired, the bacon would be shriveling and the coffee would be lukewarm at best.

Presenting this concept to the O'Malley family brought an immediate response—the Dodgers soon had a new flagship station: KABC, 790 AM.

Constant changes are a big part of radio that doesn't change...

But *I* didn't remain in the batting lineup of the Dodgers' family of blue quite as long as Wes or KFI did.

My bottom of the ninth came up in 1971. Just before KFI's big 1972 fiftieth anniversary celebration, I said good-bye to AM 640. With the always-rolling changes, another more-ethereal endless-loop saying in the radio world comes to mind: *Job security in broadcast radio is akin to riding a soap bubble—at some point, your ride is going to burst.*

In 1971, my three-year contract with KFI was up—and the soon-to-be-changed management didn't renew it. My bubble didn't really burst, though; this time it just kind of floated me into a different format. One that produced an entirely new kind of hullabaloo!

Dave Hull and His Flying Emotions

By Wes Parker

"As long as you get hired
one more time than you get fired, you're okay."

—Wes Parker

In 1969, the baseball season had just started when Chuck Benedict brought Dave into the clubhouse before a day game. That was my first chance to meet him. And we hit it off immediately. I loved his personality; he was very jovial, happy, with great sense of humor. Just a very engaging human being.

A lot of ball players are kind of emotionally reluctant—I guess that's the best way of putting it—because they have to be so controlled when they're playing games. They have to keep their emotions "structured"; whereas Dave was in a business where he could allow his emotions to fly. And he was like that in person, too! That was my attraction to him.

One of the best examples of Dave and his flying emotions was the Pete Rose voodoo doll. He'd stick pins into a different part of it on every show, like the arm or the shoulder or the leg or whatever. *Stop the Reds!*

But it didn't work!

What did work, though, was our Athletes for Youth program. Dave wanted to be a part of it, and Jimmy Lefebvre and I wanted him to be; he was our master of ceremonies, opening and closing all of our talks to the kids about staying off drugs.

Let me just tell you about Dave: First of all, I consider him the finest, best disc jockey who ever lived—bar none. I've never heard anyone funnier, more engaging, or just more fun to listen to. And I wasn't the only one. My God, he was huge in this city.

And he was always the same person. That's the other thing I loved about him. He didn't change at all from when he was in front of the mic to *not* being in front of the mic. He was exactly the same.

And personally he was a riot, a joy to be around. Giving and humble, considerate of me and my teammates...the way he enjoyed our company made him a spectacular friend. I loved him for it then and I love him for it today.

Of course, we may never forgive him for the Groaners:

> *"If an Irish cow was mauled by a tiger,*
> *would it be a Claude Osteen?"*

That's one of my favorites! And people would cringe— *"Awwww."* And *we* would go, *"Ohhhh"*—like that. And we had a Groaner for every player's name on the team.

We may have been groaning, but Dave's humor was really clean, like Jack Benny's. Jack Benny is a classic, and so is Dave. He never used swear words—ever. Of course, he couldn't on the radio, but that was never an issue with him anyway; he always found another way to do it. He was so inventive.

And he'll tell you how often he got fired because of his particular type of humor. Many of the station owners he worked for couldn't handle it. Some just didn't get it; they didn't understand it.

I used to say, "Dave, as long as you get hired one more time than you get fired, you're okay."

As far as KFI went, I became pretty well-known as part of his show. And, yes, he called it Parker & Hull. He could have called it the Hull & Parker Show, but no, it was the Parker & Hull Show. And every time I was on the air with him, he'd put himself in the background and let me have center stage. He was unbelievable in the way he shared his time and celebrity.

And I never expected any kind of compensation other than another fun time with Dave and the fans. But Dave talked to the KFI bosses and said, "Look, Wes is really good and other stations want him!" This was not true, of course; but then he told them, "You better start paying this guy or we're going to lose him!"

So they started paying me five grand a year to be on his show!

He loved that little economic victory; he was so funny about it. "Hey, you're in the system!" he'd say. "Once you're in the system, those checks just keep popping out, man! Nothing can stop those checks now! They're just going to keep coming every two weeks!" It was hilarious.

Dave really took care of me like an older brother.

One of the most perfect examples was that "Welcome Home Wes" sign. He had all his listeners send in their baseball cards—but they had to be Dodger cards; no other team. And he and Jeanette personally put them on the sign.

Well, the sign was just plastered over with cards of Dodger players from the forties, fifties, and sixties, including one of Babe Ruth as a Dodger coach, which was extremely valuable. But Dave put paste on the back of it and stuck it onto this thing. That ruined the card's collector value of course, but the sign had far more value as a whole to the fans who were a part of it.

And he and Jeanette stayed up the whole night the night before my return, finishing that sign! He didn't have to do that. He's an off-the-charts friend.

And the fun we had!

Like that crazy miniature golf "tournament" for Athletes for Youth. He may not have taken over the Riviera, but he *did* get a miniature golf course up in the Valley to close just for us, and a lot of people came out to watch. Yes, it was just like the U.S. Open! And Don Sutton and Claude Osteen were the rules committee. We competed in a pro-style, full thirty-six-hole, putter-powered showdown, and people just loved it.

We also did a show together out of Universal Studios.

We were doing a lot of things together, not just on the air but off the air, at his home, and at Dodger Stadium. We really became like brothers.

I had a girlfriend at the time named Susan who had ascended to the Miss America throne before I met her. After the original Miss America became Miss Universe, Susan was handed the crown; but she turned it down the next day because of a boyfriend. It's a little politically complex, but the bottom line is that Susan had been Miss America for one day.

Anyway, she was a huge fan of Dave's and we used to go over to his house all the time. Like on Sunday evenings, we'd go play Monopoly. Then we'd go swimming in his pool, and he and Jeanette would cook dinner for us.

As always, Dave had a great idea based on these casual evenings. Our Monopoly Sundays became a *contest*! The contest was supposed to be between just Dave and me, but through some serious Park Place and Boardwalk financial wrangling, Jeanette won!

And that became a running gag forever.

And talk about running, I know Dave has talked about when he was on that parade float for KRLA—but he might not have told you *everything*...

During the parade, of course, people weren't allowed right out there on Colorado Boulevard. But what Dave would do is, when the police turned their backs, he would signal the crowd. He'd wave them on: "C'mon, C'mon!" So they'd start across Colorado, and then the police would corral them and take them back.

When the police were looking at Dave, he'd turn into Mr. Rules-'n'-Regulations; he'd tell the crowd, "Oh no, no, no, don't come out, don't come out! You mustn't break the law!"

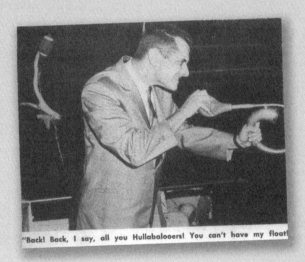

"Back! Back, I say, all you Hullabalooers! You can't have my float!"

But the minute the police turned their backs on him again, he'd wave them *on* again!

But that's his humor—that's Dave Hull right there.

He was always bending the rules *just a bit*; always right on the edge.

And always fun!

Dial-a-Dave

"DAVID, IT'S TIME FOR YOU TO CONFESS"

KGBS: 1971–1973

History is always important in radio.

It means something.

It reminds you of just how far this medium goes back. Prehistoric "electric" names like Tesla, Marconi, and Thomas Edison were integral echoes in the early sounds and development of radio. This form of communication goes back just about as far as Alley Oop banging on a rock with a club in his cave.

I left the back-to-1923 legacy of Earle C. Anthony and KFI and wound up in the back-to-1927 heritage of George B. Storer and KGBS. Anthony and Storer are two radio pioneers who should never be forgotten! Even way back in the twenties, George B. could see the value in radio and its influence in advertising. He bought some spots on Toledo, Ohio's WTAL to pump up his Speedene brand gas stations, and the campaign was so successful for his business that he bought the radio station! And it was just the first of many. Storer Communications grew to be a broadcast giant in radio, television, and cable.

So KGBS had an innovative creator with airwave insight, and by the early seventies, its evolution was major-market solid with an on-air staff that was building a broadcast house unlike any I had ever worked in.

But it would take another of those right-place-at-the-right-time twists to unlock *this* door.

That twist came when my old KRLA buddy, Emperor Bob Hudson, told KGBS Program Director Ron Martin that I was, well, *unemployed.*

Hudson was now the morning man at KGBS.

The twist tightened when Martin gave thought to adjusting the lineup.

The afternoon man was Ron Landry—a veteran jock from Boston and from markets in Virginia and Connecticut. Like Hudson and me, Ron had gotten his radio start in the military.

Landry was considered by fans and PDs a "master of character voices." One of the most famous on-air quotes attributed to Ron was: "A man is only as old as a woman he feels."

Hmmm...

Martin's mind was working.

We'll hire Hull. We'll team up Landry with Hudson in morning drive and slide Hull into the afternoon slot, right after Bill Ballance.

It was not only the perfect shift in personnel, it was also the cross-fade catalyst for a whole new kind of comedy-and-talk radio.

A personality-powerful broadcast staff was always the mainline to success, but the way that *this* bunch of guys operated demonstrated real latter-day pioneering. No longer was this all about playing music, with varying degrees of hands-on promotion out in the field with your fans. Here and now, it was virtually *constant* interaction with the fans—whether it was just talking, or joking, or doing bits, or ringing up the kind of call-in fun I had tasted with *Homework Hotline* and then really *savored* with Wes on KFI.

KGBS mornings now began with the *team* of Hudson & Landry; their wild brand of boozy boisterousness was instantly classic. Bob and Ron ruled L.A.'s waking hours with hysterics as they came up with all of the insane bits they would later include on four top-selling comedy albums.

Bill Ballance was next, in the perfect housewife-mom midday time slot with his all-call-in *Feminine Forum*.

Bill was one of the big boys at KFWB in the sixties, but his later masterwork of the *Feminine Forum* allowed the true *entertainer* in him come out.

The stuff Ballance would get girls to say was way beyond "booger" and "hog jowls"—just on the razor-thin 1970s moral-borderline. California Senator Alan Cranston threatened to have the FCC investigate Bill when the *Feminine Forum* became the first of the "naughty" talk shows.

> *Ballance didn't even pretend to be infatuated with rock and roll, but he was in love with the English language. His vocabulary was vast, his wit dry, and his mind ever-lively.*
>
> *Ballance found an even bigger radio audience with his "Feminine Forum," a show for women that focused on male-female relationships.*
>
> *Depending upon the caller, "Billo," as he was affectionately known, could play the conspiratorial confidant, the leering boyfriend, or the affectionate grandfather. Ballance's popularity exploded, and his show was syndicated*

throughout the country. Although the callers were women, he attracted almost as many male listeners.

Feminine Forum is usually credited as being the inspiration for "shock jocks" such as Howard Stern and Tom Leykis, but Ballance was mischievous without being crude. The show was irresistible because he relied on his unscripted banter with untutored female callers, not entertainers hawking product.

—Author Dave Feldman,
eulogizing Bill Ballance in 2004

Dave's Little Black Book

Things began for me in fairly normal Hullabalooer fashion at KGBS.

I would begin my show at 3:00 in the afternoon and it would roll into the evening, ending at 7:00. The station had both an AM and an FM outlet—but they were both in the same studio. Because of atmospheric conditions, transmitter power, and other factors, during the winter months, my show would start on AM, and then at 4:45, I'd supposedly run upstairs to transition to "the FM side of things." I'd come back on the air panting hard, having just run my tail off to make a seamless shift to the "other studio"—when, actually, I'd never leave my AM control room. But it really did make things sound so mobile, active, and universal in scope!

I was perfectly comfortable in this kind of drive-time dementia, but it didn't take long for me to be pulled into a new kind of magic being spun by Hudson & Landry and Billo.

An empowered intensity in pure comedy and increased *interaction*.

My daily dial-change from AM to FM was not nearly as strenuous as I made listeners believe—*CLICK!*

In a very loud echo of the past, Ballance began promoting a big dance he was putting on at the Hollywood Palladium. It was a "Nifty Fifties" oldies dance.

Cool, Daddy-O...

It was becoming one of the most talked-about upcoming events in town, with couples deciding what clothes to wear the night of the show and what type of vintage "lead sleds" to rent- or borrow-to-impress as they cruised up to 6215 Sunset Boulevard.

Well, one afternoon a listener called into my show to tell me that his date for Ballance's big "hop" had just dumped him and he needed a "chick" to go with him.

Interaction...

"Dave, I need a name from your personal 'little black book'... I need a date!"

I told him I was a married man with a family of seven in Arcadia. I didn't *have* a "black book."

But *hmmm...*

I asked him to stay on the phone.

I had a great idea...

I became a combination therapist and lonely-hearts-club event coordinator right there on the air.

What kind of a car do you drive?

How tall are you?

What color are your hair and eyes?

Do you even HAVE any hair?!

What kind of woman are you looking for?

I found out he drove a Mustang convertible and was six-foot-three with dark eyes and hair—Wow! It sounded like I was interviewing a blend of Dean Martin and Joe Namath.

Every telephone line began ringing!

The first woman on the line told me, "I don't care *what* he looks like! I'll take him! I want to go to that dance and I can't buy tickets anywhere!"

Dial-A-Date was born!

And li'l ol' matchmaker me was an every-evening extravaganza of hullabaloo.

Dave: Tell me all about yourself. We found out you're twenty-two, you live in West L.A....

Female Caller: You want to know my measurements? I'm 36-23-35.

Dave: 36-23-35?! Hon, that's perfect! Every man wants a woman like that!! Oooh... do you have a belly button that goes out or in?

Curvy Caller: I'm an Insy.

Dave: Oooh...let me put down..."Insy" on Belly Button. That's perfect. Maybe he's an Outsy!

KCBS **PUBLICITY**

Storer Broadcasting in Los Angeles / 1020 AM / 97.1 FM
338 South Western Avenue, Los Angeles, California 90020 / Phone (213) 388-2345

He Plays Cupid—Sort Of

Dialog

CALLER: "Dave! Don't hang up on me! I've been waiting a month to get on!"

HULL: "I know! I've been waiting a month to hang up on you!" (CLICK)

There's no preplanning used to select the callers who will be matched. "Something about the voice has to click," he said, "but the guy with the best chance is one who comes on strong, unusual and interesting." Even then, it's up to the whims of Hull.

CALLER (male, crying): "I've got to get a date!"

HULL (immediately mocking the tearful voice): "What's the matter?"

CALLER (crying): "I'm all alone."

HULL (crying): "You still are!" (CLICK)

—Staff Photos by Jim Buckhouse

DIAL-A-DATE—Dave Hull engages in a bit of repartee with another person on other end of telephone in his radio program which sometimes insults people and other times matches male with female callers for blind dates.

Floyd, Ling-Su, and Confessing to Father Moriarty

The crazy pre-eHarmony let's-find-true-love nights we orchestrated on KGBS were hilarious—but we hadn't heard nothin' yet!

Out there in listener-land were two very fertile minds—two creative brains lying in horrible wait in craniums of loony imagination, cruisin' in old Volkswagens, listening to "The Tennessee Tango" and "I Saw Mommy Kissing Santa Claus."

Dennis Ousley and John "J.J." Solari became regular callers. But not as themselves.

Not that "themselves" wouldn't have been interesting enough— J.J. was a former Disney Mouseketeer gone bad, and they were both very *esoteric* writers.

But they would expand themselves and their spiky fantasies like startled puffer fish, becoming different characters. And I mean *become.* They were inner-possessed by these characters in as powerful a way as Jonathan Winters and, later, Robin Williams took on *their* many alter egos. Dennis and J.J. were engulfed and taken over—they were Linda Blair with spinning heads as they called in, fumbling their way into trying to convince California girls that they were "just right" for them, and much, much more.

Neither Solari nor Ousley knew me *or* each other before they began to call in; but that would change. As their mutual maniacal interaction became more and more central to what I was doing—and would be doing for years to come—we would all melt messily into a team.

"Floyd" was the first to call.

It was Ousley—Ousley with barely intelligible nasal speech that elicited painful pity and falling-down hilarity.

Floyd was a "salesman/mechanic" for the "Hollywood Television and Transmission Exchange," and drove an "older" VW beetle that he called (with his speech *anomaly*) a "sisty-two vote-wagon."

Oh boy, I thought, laughing. *This guy's either a nutcase or he's gonna be funny as hell!* So I decided to take a chance.

It sure paid off!

Floyd became the first "regular" (maybe *irregular* is more like it) caller.

With the nasal noise and gnashing, it often took asking him to repeat something ten times!

And he was always willing.

His main focus was always to get a girl to accompany him to see his favorite entertainer, Molly Bee.

In concert.

In Blythe, California.

Floyd worked the ever-caring nature of the California girls— they figured he was, if nothing else, sweet and sincere. They had long stopped trusting the guys who would call in with deep voices, claiming boast-profiles of being "tall, dark, and handsome, with keys to a brand new Jaguar in their Peter Cassara suit pants pocket."

> **Floyd:** When I get a date, Dave, she's gonna love my sisty-two vote-wagon. She's gonna love it. There's no back seat or nuttin', but she's gonna love it...

He just knocked me out.

"Ling-Su" was next to make an appearance in Dennis' very 1970s (and very un-politically correct) cast: an Asian female beauty looking for action:

Dave: Hello.

Ling-Su (with heavy accent): Hi, this is Wing-Su from Ko-REE-a. I show you good time for five bucks!

Dave: Wing-Su?

Ling-Su: No, Wwwwing-Su! Joe, you think me plitty? Me show you good time, Joe—five bucks!

Dave: *(hysterics)...(more hysterics)... (even more hysterics)...(finally, choking)* Pardon me—I have nothing to say!

Then came J.J.

Wait! I apologize for that *very* understated introduction.

That's kind of like looking out at the Pacific horizon and casually saying, *Then came Godzilla.*

And Gorgo.

And Gorgo's mother.

Acquainting oneself with J.J. Solari is on the same sanity-survival level as juggling vials of nitroglycerin in Death Valley in July.

© Walt Disney Productions

From mouse ears to menswear, J.J. Solari always dives headfirst into making a statement!

Solari being cast as a Mouseketeer on the original *Mickey Mouse Club* was perhaps the most blatant demonstration of irony mankind has ever seen.

Looking back, knowing what we know today, making J.J. a Mouseketeer was the entertainment equivalent of giving your three-year-old a Komodo Dragon *and* a chainsaw for his birthday.

"Jay-Jay," as he was dubbed on his official Mouseketeer t-shirt, was infatuated with the show's principal mouse-ears-on-the-head, *fully-developed* teenage star, Annette Funicello. He made no bones about his "feelings" for her at an early age.

J.J. would later develop into a writer who would rival Hunter Thompson in terms of crazed "uniqueness"—creating years of brilliant fiction for the edgy and world-famous "biker" magazine, *Easyriders*. His 2007 book, *When Bikers Meet Humans,* is a landmark in lunacy and laughs!

Well, when J.J. started calling into *my* show, he came up with a character with an Irish accent.

Father Moriarty.

A priest who called frequently to remind me that he hadn't "seen me in church lately."

Father Moriarty would also call to purge me of my sins.

"David, it's time for you to confess," he'd gently implore.

And I would—right there on the air.

Dave: Father, It's been sixty-one years since my last confession.

Moriarty (not so silently thinking): Oooh, this guy's got a lot to confess...

Dave: Father, I've had evil thoughts...

Moriarty: Ooh, ooh...

Dave: About women...

Moriarty: Oh, I know, my son...I know...I have some of those too...

Some Catholic listeners thought Father Moriarty was real and wanted to know if he would hear *their* confessions as well—because they hadn't been to church lately, either!

Then there was "Randy."

Randy would semi-holler into the phone.

And he was, well, let's just say, Richard Simmons-*ish*.

Whenever Randy was on the air, we would ring a tiny "tinkle bell" after he shouted his name.

<Ting-a-ling-a-ling!>

Solari Speaks

Bells, confessions, nowhere-near-PC Asians, and Molly Bee fans went from improv to planned.

The Ousley/Solari team was developing new characters and routines with Cecil B. DeMille precision and direction.

And with *my* blessing and help as well.

> *"My calls became more collaborative with Dave. He would call me and mention some news item that he thought was odd or ridiculous and ask me if I could come up with anything that would relate. And he used to love Father Moriarty because I think it made him feel warm and fuzzy, and it kicked in that old Catholic thing where you score points for the afterlife; in other words, do Catholic-friendly shtick on the radio and when you die God will like you—God and Jesus both being Catholics and all...*
>
> *"Me and Dennis and Dave were—are—three totally different people. But if you were to put all three of us on phone lines and have some fourth person start talking to us, in five minutes all three of us would have a complete fix on that individual's entire past and potential future. Crazy, sane, gay, messed up, delusional, pain in the butt, totally cool, trouble,*

atheist, terrorist, loser, thief, killer, psycho, amazingly normal...we would have the guy profiled more accurately and for far less money than the FBI and the CIA and Scotland Yard put together could do it."

—J.J. Solari

Even the mayor took notice of all the hullabaloo we created with *Dial-A-Date*!

Here Comes (Mrs.) Santa Claus

One of our biggest fans was superstar film and television actress June Lockhart. She would drop in at every station I worked at in L.A., bringing us organic fruits and vegetables she'd grown.

She loved to be in the studio as we all shared in the peace and harmony of God-groomed pure food while I blew up listeners on the air, tossed my crash box on the floor, and created my general hullabaloo!

And she adored *Dial-A-Date*.

What a lady she is!

June decided she wanted to be the Grand Marshal of the Lilac Festival parade in the small village of Pine Mountain, California, where my family had a vacation cabin at the time.

Great! We could make that high honor happen!

The small Kern County hamlet's business association provided June with a huge log cabin at no cost for her weeklong stay.

One day during the never-a-dull-moment Lilac Festival celebration, Jeanette and I picked up June for lunch and headed for the restaurant at our local country club.

Having lunch in there by himself while his father played a round of golf, was this twelve- or thirteen-year-old boy. The boy had just seen a movie on television the night before, which starred June as Mrs. Santa Claus. The boy took one look at June, dropped his food, and ran over and threw his arms around her.

"You're the movie lady!" he said.

Then he ran out onto the golf course screaming for his dad to come inside and see the lady they had been watching on TV last night.

June Lockhart was a true blue—and lilac—fan!

While he was gone, the hostess came by to pick up his food, figuring he was finished.

"No!" we told her. "He'll be back!"

And he was. *With* his father.

And then we *all* finished our lunches.

Together.

We got to know fans of all kinds pretty well—whether they were innocent kids or semi-psychotics like J.J. and Ousley!

The Amazing (Golf Cart) Race

"Here and now, it was virtually constant interaction with the fans..."

August 1972.

KGBS asked me to participate in a golf-cart race against disc jockeys from other stations, to be held at the old Ontario Motor Speedway.

It would be an all-star field—just like Indianapolis on Memorial Day. But a little slower.

KFI's popular morning team of Lohman & Barkley would be behind the wheel, along with more of the biggest names in L.A. radio: Rick Dees, Charlie Tuna, Russ O'Hara, Geoff Edwards, even Wolfman Jack.

And the race actually had a darn nice winner's circle at the finish line. The first one across would receive an all-expense-paid trip for two to Hawaii. *And* a battery-operated clock mounted in a full-size tire.

Publicity! Perks! Perfect!

When I arrived, hundreds of fans were already there to support their favorite disc jockey. This was it! This was California's "Brickyard," Daytona 500, and *Talladega Nights* all rolled up into one grinding sprint to the island gold.

We—*the drivers*—received our pre-race orders.

I was given Cart #2.

I already had a good feeling. The number 2 was used by legendary NASCAR driver David Marcis—now it was mine! But really, other than the numbers, all the carts were identical.

We were told to go to the clubhouse to relax until we were called. You know, to get loose, mentally prepare, and all that stuff.

I wandered around the facility and found the bar.

I also *found* an actual racing helmet that someone had left at one of the tables. I figured there was no harm in "borrowing" it for the race. It would make me look very official! (Not to mention keeping me safe in the case of a high-speed spinout or an end-over-end tumble in one of the dangerous curves!) And, certainly, I'd return it right after our big competition.

Then I got talking to the girl who was working the bar.

"Which one are you?" she asked.

"Dave Hull," I told her.

Well, that started *her* engine! She told me she had been a fan of mine since the Beatles—had been listening to me for years.

I told her that I was racing today—risking life and limb in this high-powered contest of man and machine—because my wife and I had always wanted to go to Hawaii.

"What's your cart number?" she asked quietly.

"Two," I whispered.

"You *will* win this race," she said in a voice even lower than before.

"How?" I asked.

"Don't worry about that," she said, disappearing silently from behind the bar, like a mysterious quick breeze ruffling the curtains in a haunted house.

Although the event featured no national anthem played by Al Hirt or the Purdue "All-American" Marching Band, like the previous two years at Indy, and no flyover by the Blue Angels or anything, the air was still thick and tense as the race began.

On your marks, get set, G-O-O-O-O-O!!!

The green flag!

Five laps.

Five grueling laps.

THEY'RE OFF AND ROLLING

In the hard heat of the battle, I thought about something that famous racecar driver A.J. Foyt once said: "Determination that just won't quit—that's what it takes."

Yes!

A.J., I understand! I had that determination! I had what it takes!

To go to Hawaii!

A.J. won the Indy 500 in 1961, '64, and '67. Well, when the dust and the roar and the smell of burning rubber had settled *here* at the Onty 5, I had indeed won!

And I won big.

I beat the rest of the field by a ton of lengths. I *was* A.J.; the rest of the jocks were turtles-on-a-fencepost.

And they were really mad!

AN ATTEMPTED SABOTAGE

The race disintegrated into a combo demolition derby/WWE SmackDown wrestling match! Some of the drivers stopped their slower carts and *ran* across the infield attempting to get to me in the winner's circle! They tried—unsuccessfully—to yank me out of my cart! Good thing I was wearing that helmet!

It's also a good thing that the race's sanctioning body didn't have their inspectors anywhere around, because what happened was that my *fan* on the inside had gone out to the "pits" and strategically over-inflated ol' number 2's tires just slightly, while draining a fair amount of air out of all the others. She knew her stuff.

I "glided" around that course while Dees, Wolfman, and the rest plodded along like sleepy sloths on soft rubber!

Jeanette and I had a beautiful week in the Hawaiian Islands—not to mention a cool clock-in-a-tire—courtesy of my slightly shady but very savvy "pit crew."

Dave: Elvis, how's it going up there?

Elvis: You know who ended up here? Lamborghini...the only man whose funeral was clocked at 190 miles per hour!

Dave: ...(laughter)...

Elvis: He got up here, God gave him the pole position!

The Hullmark Hall of Fame

A Shout Out to Some Very Elusive Moose

TV & Radio Commercial Voiceover Career: 1973–1978+

It was 1973.

I had been at KGBS renovating, innovating, and matchmaking with Floyd, Ling-Su, and the rest of the Solari-Ousley zoo for three years.

I had now been in radio for twenty years.

I'd also had a tempting taste of life-beyond-the-microphone in front of the TV cameras back in '66 with Monkees, Swine, and Crabs.

I guess I was in the middle of a mid-career reflective convergence. And in the middle of *that* was the decision at the Storer Communications offices to drop Hudson & Landry, Bill Ballance, and *me* in favor of a new format of current hits. KGBS-AM was finally going 24/7 powered by 50,000 watts. Actually, we had all been urging them to do that for years, but we never got our wish.

A new on-air staff would.

So as I'm leaving KGBS, floating amidst this "mid-career reflective convergence" a little voice in my head starts whispering—no, shouting—*"Stay tuned out there…it's time for a word from our sponsor!"*

With the help and persuasion of an agent I had met named Bob Colvin, I found a new way to hustle up some broadcast hullabaloo.

"Words mean more than what is set down on paper.
It takes the human voice to infuse them
with deeper meaning."

—Maya Angelou

Out there, in between the cameras and the mics is a talking–Twilight Zone where the visual impact of TV-land merges with that "human voice" infusing "deeper meaning." When this synergy occurs, wonderful things happen: people buy stuff! And people *pay* those people with the voices to get those *other* people to open their wallets as they seek that "deeper meaning" in cornflakes, toothpaste, new cars, and exercise gizmos that would make you skinny if they were ever really used, and not just bought and immediately stowed in a closet or the garage.

It was time for the Hullabalooer to enter that "dimension of sight and sound."

Stay tuned...we'll be right back...

Bamboozling and Plundering

To a great extent, agents in every facet of the entertainment industry are looked upon in the same way mainstream folks look at lawyers—with a *slight degree* of cynicism and skepticism.

Slight.

"If God had an agent, the world wouldn't be built yet.
It'd only be about Thursday."

—Jerry Reynolds

"It is well-known what a middleman is: He is a man who bamboozles one party and plunders the other."

—Benjamin Disraeli

"Let every eye negotiate for itself and trust no agent."

—William Shakespeare

Well, okay, but I had some pretty good luck in that "iffy" agent department. Bob Colvin became my first and only Hollywood agent. He was the *Colvin* of Carey-Phelps-Colvin and later was a part of International Creative Management (ICM).

"Bamboozling" and "plundering" took a backseat as Bob showed me what this entirely new (to me, at least) vocal-vocation was all about.

Auditioning for and recording regional and national commercials takes on a life of its own. Your agent must know what your strengths and weaknesses are—and not be afraid to tell you directly!

COMMERCIALS 101

WARNING: The following is very scholarly and clinical, but it will enlighten you as to just what a voiceover technician must endure!

As we entered this world of major-league commercials, it became obvious that my strength was in the voiceover commercials rather than those on camera.

No one really wants to buy anything from a "shoe salesman"—as Cher put it. (Unless, of course, you need some shoes!)

And I was quickly learning the business spin on this, too.

First, auditions take a lot of time and effort and do not bring in any money for the actor. All the expenses involved in getting to and from locations and everything else is on you.

But, once *in*, the money is great.

You get paid a "session fee" each time you come in to record. In addition, you're paid a fee for each commercial you voice during that session.

In addition to *that,* you get paid a "usage fee" every time the spot runs. You receive a check after every thirteen-week cycle.

How much you are paid depends upon what kind of a commercial it is. A "wild spot" pays less up front but is run as many times as the client wishes on as many stations as they wish.

And rates are usually set differently for local vs. regional vs. national commercials. If you're lucky enough to voice a commercial to be run on a national network, your usage fees will be much higher.

Finally, if the advertiser wants to reuse the commercials later, you'll receive "reuse fees."

Elvis: How's everybody at my favorite radio station?

Dave: We're all doing fine down here. We're still playing your songs and selling your stamps.

Elvis: I appreciate that. Now, don't forget those Elvis checks!

It's a great bank to draw from, but the draw*back* comes in having to develop a fireman-on-call readiness.

When the agent's bell rings, you'd better be prepared to talk!

Now!

"Hey, Dave, it's 12:45. You're supposed to be in Westwood at 2:30. And then we've got you going here and there and there, and then you can go home."

And you have to be able to do that consistently every day if you're going to make that "great money"—and you definitely can! Six figures for doing very little work. Because of residuals, you're making hundreds of thousands for probably only working sixty days a year in sessions. I'm sure it's more now, but even back then, for some commercials, I'd get $364 (in seventies money!) every time they ran.

Okay!

Whew!

I hope you got all of that—we'll have a pop quiz a little later!

COMMERCIALS 101: A little education for those of you who just might want to hear your own dulcet, mellow, hypnotic voice over the air convincing shoppers and buyers that *"It takes a licking and keeps on ticking"*; coaxing *"I'm a Pepper, he's a Pepper, she's a Pepper, we're a Pepper, wouldn't you like to be a Pepper, too?"*; assuring *"Mr. Bubble gets you so clean your mother won't know you"*; observing *"Sometimes you feel like a nut—sometimes you don't"*; and reinforcing *"It's so easy, a caveman could do it!"*

A Symphony in Super-Premium

This was working.

I was working.

My biggest account was Union Oil and Union 76 Gasoline. The spots I did for them were heard on the Dodgers, Chicago Cubs, and New York Mets radio and television games.

But I wasn't the first choice of the big-orange-ball gasoline guys. They already had *their* guy.

But this guy wasn't *just* the voice of Union Oil—he was also an adventurer of sorts. So when Union Oil decided to grease up a new ad campaign, he was hunting somewhere in Montana.

Somewhere in the *147,042 square miles* of Montana.

The guy's agent gets a call from the gas giant's A-list ad agency.

Agency: *We've got a whole flight of spots that have to be done. Where's our boy? Our voice?*

Agent: *He's on a moose hunt...*

Agency: *A moose hunt?! Well, call him. Get him back here!*

Agent: *Uh, yeah, okay...When's the session?*

Agency: *Early next week!*

Next call, a day later...

Agent: *I can't find him! I've tried everywhere!*

Agency: *Call the Montana State Police! Have them find out where the hell this guy is! Track him down! Find him! Do you know how much money, time, and effort is at stake here?!*

COMMERCIALS 101: A well-paid commercial voiceover actor must be prepared for an agent to call and tell them when and where they should be...

Well, Union Oil's boy wasn't exactly D.B. Cooper, but he couldn't be found out in *his* woods, either—at least not during the window that 76 Gas had open.

But Doug Hues of Union 76's agency, Leo Burnett Advertising, was good friends with Bob Colvin—*my* agent. And Bob was friends with Bill Bell, an eventual Emmy Award winner for his work in media sound. Bill Bell was about six hundred pounds and was one of the "biggest" talents in Hollywood audio work.

Hues needed a new talent, quick, to replace the lost moose-marauder.

Bell tells Hues via Colvin, "The best up-and-coming voiceover guy is Dave Hull. You ought to hire him."

And he did.

It provided a very pleasant dimension in this Twilight Zone I'd now entered.

For me to get the "feel" of the emotions Union 76 wanted to convey in their commercials—and there are many emotions in gas!—they sent me on-site to the taping of their big-production television spots.

The Union 76 commercials were filmed at a beautiful service facility in the northern San Diego County resort area of Lake San Marcos. (Yes, along with providing emotional connections, gas stations can be beautiful, too—sort of...)

In the commercials, the boss (cleverly and blue-collarly named "Murph" and played by veteran character actor Richard X. Slattery) would run to fill up a customer's car with the finest that 76 had to offer, while his young mechanic (played by *CHiPs* costar Larry Wilcox) would clean the windows and provide all the full service that now seems to have gone out the continually dirty window with pterodactyls and Justin Bieber's first hairstyle. And all of that "full service" was performed amidst a lush backdrop of the lake's gorgeous mountains, trees, and pristine water. It made the gassing-up experience as sensory-satisfying as strolling the Alps hand-in-hand with the von Trapp family.

Yes! I was getting that feel!

The emotions!

You could almost hear Julie Andrews singing, *"The hills are alive with the sound of sixteen gallons of ethyl pumping..."*

It was pastoral petroleum! A high-octane opera! A symphony in super premium!

I got it!

I understand!

I stayed with Union Oil for eight years—including 1976 when they bought spots on nearly *every* radio and TV station in the country to promote their new "safe-burning" gasoline. I made a ton of dough for these gas guys.

And myself!

And I still thank those moose up in Montana for being slippery enough to evade the sights of that other guy long enough for me to bag his job!

"Roses Are Red, Violets Are—" "NEXT!!!"

I was becoming very well-seasoned in the gainful goulash of commercial voiceovers.

The spicy, sales-persuasive voice of Morton Salt on the *CBS Evening News with Walter Cronkite* was now me!

And then I went after Santa's hold on Christmas again, like I'd done back in the sixties when I upstaged him at the parade with our Junky Float. Bob Colvin got me the best audition in town: reading for Hallmark greeting cards.

This was big.

Real big.

The producers for this account invited every major voiceover talent to the audition—which immediately intimidated me into rubber legs, hyperventilation, and tastes of bile.

I recognized just about every "voice" in the waiting room.

When my turn came, I figured I'd last a few minutes and the producer/director would scream, "Next!"

But I was there, and I was going through with it. No matter how much I felt like throwing a blanket over my head and slinking down the elevator.

I entered the room. Several serious-looking people were sitting behind a table, all holding small but very official-looking notepads. Besides conducting auditions, I figured them to also be the creative committee who came up with Hallmark's sympathy cards; they definitely looked like the *"In This Time of Sorrow"* bunch, rather than the *"Happy 1st Birthday to a Bubbly Bouncy Boy"* crowd!

I was directed to a couch, facing them. That's when I noticed that the commercial copy was placed on a short coffee table in front of me, situated far lower than the couch—along with the *stationary* microphone.

I engaged myself in simple physics.

Since my diaphragm would probably be all scrunched up if I leaned over, thus effecting my breathing, I asked if I could "drop to my knees" while reading.

I immediately noticed the writer and the director exchange glances.

Hmmm...

I read my part, got back on my feet, and left, figuring that the "we'll call you" was simply polite-obligatory.

What I didn't know was that the actual spot would feature the song "O Holy Night" and that cue for the voiceover actor to begin speaking was right after the background voices sang the words, *"Fall on your knees..."*

I soon got a call from Foote, Cone & Belding Advertising. I got the gig! I had won the audition over nearly a hundred others—and the kneeling thing had a lot to do with it.

(A tip from ADVANCED COMMERCIALS 101-A: Many writers are superstitious and feel that the talent selected for their commercials should be "different." Different, to them, translates as *better.*)

The Hallmark spot I recorded "on my knees" became one of the longest-running Christmas commercials of all time.

I Was *G-G-G-R-R-R-E-E-E-A-A-A-T-T-T*!!!

From gasoline to salt to the dignity and class of Hallmark—what was next?

Of course! Ball-point pens!

But I was in some *g-g-g-r-r-r-e-e-e-a-a-a-t-t-t* company on this one. I recorded a back-to-school spot for Flair Pens that would run on several Saturday morning cartoon shows. My blurbs for ball-point bliss were done over the singing of one the most unmistakable voices of all time: the late Thurl Ravenscroft.

The Thurl Ravenscroft.

Tony the Tiger.

"Frosted Flakes...They're G-G-G-R-R-R-E-E-E-A-A-A-T-T-T!"

Backup singer for Bing Crosby, Frankie Laine, Spike Jones, Jo Stafford, and Rosemary Clooney.

"You're a mean one, Mister Grinch..."

Disneyland's Haunted Mansion.

Yep, *that* Thurl Ravenscroft.

And the Hullabalooer!

Not long after I did the spot, all my kids were watching Saturday morning cartoons and the commercial came on.

The kids heard *me*.

And Thurl.

Wow!

I was a hero!

For a week or two, the kids' rooms were cleaned, the leaves raked in both the front and back yards, the dishes washed, and homework done on time.

Their dad was *g-g-g-r-r-r-e-e-e-a-a-a-t-t-t!*

But it wouldn't last long.

Things went back to normal as quick as the click of a Flair fine-tip. Except with Lisa; she was *always* on the neat side of things, whether Dad was a "star" right up there with Scooby-Doo and Foghorn Leghorn or not.

Professor Hullabaloo

My commercial career would overlap my return to radio in 1978. So for many years, I worked in a parallel universe—*"a dimension of sound, a dimension of sight, a dimension of mind...shadow and substance, of things and ideas."*

It was a dimension that lasted fifteen years. During that time, I represented nearly three hundred fifty different clients.

It was also during that time that I formalized my "Commercials 101" notes and began to officially *teach*.

The Los Angeles Broadcasters (LAB) knew of my success (though I don't think they knew about my lucky elusive moose!), and asked me to conduct a Commercial Voiceover class.

The class would involve history and techniques.

Students would learn how to read copy and use a mic.

The LAB had thousands of scripts I could use as a teaching tool.

Each class would have thirty students and last for six weeks.

Yes! I'll do it!

I had students read multi-voice commercials, interacting with one another. And then they had to do "spokesman spots" by themselves. They would do serious spots, humorous spots, dialogue exercises.

At the end of the course, they'd get their own tape of their production work, which they could edit and circulate to agents or agencies.

I didn't get to wear a mortarboard and robe like a real *professor,* but the class was a success anyway.

Then the LAB asked me to teach a class in Commercial Interpretation—how to interpret every line you're given; how to deliver a line in anything you read.

That, too, was a massive success (despite the continued lack of the professorly uniform!). I taught for LAB for five years and then moved to a cable radio network office in Sunland for five more.

One of my more prestigious students was my genius newsman from KRLA, Richard Beebe. It was humbling yet an honor to have Richard in my class.

Some years later, after we were both gone from KRLA *for a second time*, he wrote me a letter that I still hold so dear:

July 30, 1985

Dear Dave,

Well, I'm finally getting around to writing you about one of the highlights of my professional career.

In this business of communication, you stand out as one of the great talents! When I decided to take your classes, I felt I had the potential to succeed. But it was your ability to communicate the special techniques needed as well as the challenges ahead that has given me the confidence to proceed.

I'm sure that as I continue to get involved in doing commercials and voiceovers, I will discover more and more the value your instruction has brought to my work.

You are a super teacher, Dave. Thank you "a mundo" for an enlightening experience.

Yours truly,
Richard Beebe

Fade to End

I was working.

Richard was working.

Guys like us were doing all right.

But in a slow, frog-in-the-frying-pan kind of creep, the big-name entertainment stars with the big-name faces started to get hip to just how lucrative this stuff could be. At first they thought hawking things like gas and salt was beneath them, but that green bottom line is always persuasive. Sure, in the old days we had Dinah Shore and Bob Hope wheeling their Chevys and Buicks into ads. But not long after that things *really* got rolling.

And we're talking *stars*—not those who caught on with the occasional campaign *before* they were big-time (like Brad Pitt hustling Pringles, Matt LeBlanc Heinz Ketchup–ing a wiener, or Sarah Michelle Geller having it "her way" at Burger King).

Tom Selleck, Cloris Leachman, and Burt Reynolds were very, *very* established when they jumped on board the Good Ship *Let's-Sell-It*. Toward the end of *my* trade-and-transaction tenure, that kind of top-personality influx was killing it for us small guys.

As the years have gone by, we've seen the likes of Nicole Kidman, Sally Field, Susan Sarandon, Diane Keaton, Robert De Niro, and a surprising Bob Dylan barking out come-ons and deals. Today, even the explosive Charlie Sheen is shilling for Hanes underwear with Michael Jordan!

And speaking of Charlie, the guy may have had a few *uncomfortable* moments in his career, but amidst it all, he did say something that deserves repeating—something that relates to radio, to the commercials, to all of this: *"I still don't have all the answers. I'm more interested in what I can do next than what I did last."*

You know what, Charlie? I agree with that. I have always been interested in what I could do next.

And I've never been disappointed.

Another Way to Have a Ball

"HAVE YOU EVER SEEN AN UMPIRE THAT *WASN'T* BLIND?!"

CIF (California Interscholastic Federation): Early 1970s–Mid-1990s

Mike Tyson raises pigeons.

Angelina Jolie collects daggers.

Johnny Depp is into dolls (*really*, actual dolls—not just the living, breathing sexy kind!).

Bruce Willis loves boxing.

Robert Patrick is always on his Harley.

Hobbies and non-work, psyche-soothing, second-nature activities are important to the creative artist.

Personally, I like dressing in black and white and blowing a whistle in front of large crowds! Now, that's not as strange as it may sound, but it may take some 'splainin', Lucy.

One Friday afternoon, my son Mike caught the would-be winning touchdown for Arcadia High in a sophomore game at San Marino High. But it was called back on a questionable holding penalty against a fellow lineman way across the field. Right then and there, from my cheap seat in the stands, I knew it was time for me to get into sports officiating.

I needed to be down there on the field.

It would certainly be therapeutic for *me* and it would even more certainly be a boon to the overall fairness quotient in American scholastic and amateur organized sports!

And as I got into it, of course, I found that, as with most things in my life—from the bloody axe in Jack's dad's pickup truck, to my overwhelming political triumphs in high school, to getting virtually everyone in Detroit mad at me, to pretty much everything—a lot of hullabaloo followed me.

You know, maybe it's just because I keep my eyes open. I have a good time. I look at life not through rose-colored glasses but through those goofy ones that have the eyeballs hanging down off of springs. I seem to have a strange magnetic pull—but it's a good one. I attract the fun, the good times, and that "bouncy, bouncy" Tigger attitude of life.

There's a certain comedic-karma that engulfs a few lucky people. Thankfully, I am one of them. And that karma followed me onto the field of play.

Tigger had his stripes and I was getting mine.

I made up my mind to be a sports official and I ran right into the game. I was trained and certified by the California Interscholastic Federation (CIF), the governing body of high school sports, and began my career by officiating in Junior All-American and Pop Warner football before ever stepping on a high school or college field.

I was scheduled for freshman, sophomore, and JV games for three years before getting my first varsity game. My position would be at umpire, the official responsible for watching all offensive and defensive line play. This is the official positioned just feet away from "hard-charging" offensive linemen and "quick and punishing" defensive linebackers in the middle of all of the "violent and crushing" action.

It was like skateboarding northbound on a southbound interstate.

With your eyes closed.

At night.

I loved it.

From wax-spinner to whistle-blower: I was so proud to earn my reffing stripes!

You Got Me in Stitches!

It didn't take long, however, for those "hard-charging, quick and punishing, violent and crushing" elements of the game to get up in my face.

Literally.

Some of our better high school/college officials were used at the semi-pro level of football, too; I was chosen as one of them by the

Semi-Pro League of Southern California. One Sunday, I was working a game for them at Los Angeles Harbor College. I was at my umpire position, just behind the defensive line, when a Yeti-sized running back drove his helmet straight into my face.

BOOM!

The impact slit and split my lower lip in two, requiring twenty-plus stitches to close the wound.

Sirens and blood!

Lots of both!

I was taken to Martin Luther King Drew Medical Center for surgery, and—like on every Sunday afternoon—the place was overflowing with gore, guts, and groans.

Weekends were action-packed there.

The emergency surgeon came into the waiting room to grab the next patient and saw me in my uniform clutching a bloody gym towel to my face. He stopped and asked me what had happened. I told him that I had just been run over by a twelve-foot-tall, nine-hundred-pound semi-pro running back.

That touched him.

It brought back memories.

He had played college football himself. He looked at me, and then out into the sea of sickies in the waiting room, and then back at me. "You're next!" he shouted.

When we got into surgery I asked him if he was any good. He told me he'd closed up knife wounds day and night for years—*it was his specialty*.

You have to look really close to find the scar today—he definitely was an urban-attack *artist*!

Lacing Up the Keds

Tehachapi, California, is at the 3,970-foot elevation point up in the Tehachapi Mountains—above and between the San Joaquin Valley and Mojave Desert.

It's really out in the wilderness compared with much of Southern California—with more deer and dirt roads than cars and concrete.

I was scheduled to officiate in a high school finals playoff game up there. I was assigned to the umpire spot; the referee (the one with the white hat) was a guy named Rolf Rawl.

Now, Rolf bothered a lot of us a lot of the time. He didn't wear athletic shoes. He wore Keds tennis shoes.

High-tops.

Black.

With that old familiar Ovaltine-esque Keds logo on the side.

It just wasn't professional. We hated seeing him put on those shoes.

Well, anyway, all the officials had ridden in together. When we got within two or three miles of the up-in-the-hills field, we rolled into a blanket of Tule fog—wet soup that made visibility about what you'd have if you put your face into a bowl of oatmeal.

We had to pull over.

I had an idea—a plan that would get us into the stadium.

"Rolf," I told our Keds boy, "I'm going to have to get out on the fender of the car; otherwise we'll never find the gate! Keep the windows down so we can talk. I'll be a black-and-white-striped, whistle-blowing Kit Carson! *I* will be our guide!"

It took a while and I felt a lot like a bagged buck hanging on out there. I got real damp and cold being a trail-blazing beacon, but we eventually found our way to the field.

The shadow of an administrator from the school was waiting for us in the haze at the gate. He slowly walked with our car to get us in to park; then he helped us to feel our way to the locker rooms.

I pulled Rolf—and his Keds—aside. "We're never going to be able to play football in this! Nobody is going to be able to see the ball in the air! No one's going to be able to kick the ball, or receive it, or anything! This game *has* to be suspended. You're the only man who can do it!

"You better blow the whistle to officially start the game," I told Rolf. "Then I'll tell the kicker, 'Don't go, don't kick a thing! The ref is gonna go to the announcer booth and suspend this thing!'"

But Rolf Rawl just looked at me, shuffling side to side in those Keds. "Dave, I've worked games here before. When 7:30 comes, this fog will lift."

Right...

Now, I had dealt with weather and weathermen for years on radio. I knew that, meteorologically, the odds of this kind of fog soup lifting that quickly were close to the probability of a snowstorm in Arcadia.

In July.

Rolf was ridiculously wrong.

7:15. Nothing new.

7:20. Still foggy.

I looked at Rolf—and his Keds—and I just shook my head. We had two full football teams out here and stands full of people, and he seemed completely unconcerned.

7:25...

7:26...

7:27...

7:28. The fog began to clear.

By 7:30, you could see more galaxies in the sky above the stadium than the Hubble Space Telescope! And the game went off just fine.

I wanted to find a pay phone and call Jeanette: *Is it by any chance snowing there?!*

Down below his sock line, Rolf may have been all floppy Keds; but up above the high-tops, he had quite a head for fog!

Making a "Burro" of Oneself—LIVE!

The greatest hockey player of them all, Wayne Gretzky, wore number 99.

Manny Ramirez, Warren Sapp, and George Mikan all had 99 on their uniforms, too.

And so did a man in the black and white stripes.

Tony Corrente has worn number 99 throughout his entire officiating career—from high school games to the Super Bowl. Back in the hanging-on-the-fender-days, Tony was on our crew. Tony was a protégé of one of the big boys in the training of officials, Don McKenzie. Don was the man who assigned refs and umps for all California junior college football and baseball games. Don taught me, too. He taught me the finesse needed to become a good official.

For years I worked as Don's umpire, before I finally became a referee with my own white cap and my own five-man crew. With that white cap, *I* was the one on the field who made all the final decisions. *I* was the one everyone else reported a foul to.

But with either hat on, I always loved a big game!

Like when the Neff High School Trojans from La Mirada went spear to hoof against the Burroughs High Burros from Ridgecrest.

The finals in their division.

A big game...

The game was being played on Neff's home field, but it was being broadcast live by Ridgecrest's local radio channel back to the remote high desert city a few hours' drive north of L.A.

I was the umpire at this game; Don McKenzie was the white-hatted referee—but *I* was the official responsible for bringing the visiting team's captains out for the coin toss.

Well, the on-field coin toss was just a formality. The *real* coin toss and the choosing of whether to "receive or defer" had already occurred back in the locker room with the captains and coaches present—Neff's Trojans had won the toss.

So I'm in the process of helping stage this little on-field show for the fans, when the radio guy from the little Ridgecrest station comes up to me. "I'm broadcasting live! Can I come out to the coin toss?"

Hmmm...this could present a problem. Thank God I'm not the one in charge!

"Well, our referee is Don McKenzie," I told the reporter. "Go tell him what you want to do. If he says yes, I guess we'll do it."

He ran right to Don...and then a second later came sprinting back to me. "I talked to Don and he said that *you're* the media professional here—it's your decision to make!"

Don was an officiating legend, yes, but he was also famous for, let's just say, *easing some responsibilities* off onto others.

What could I say to Ridgecrest's version of Howard Cosell? Except, "Okay...fine..."

It was my job to prep the visiting team.
"Live broadcasts are not for the weak!" I should have warned.

In those days, mobile broadcasting was primarily a truck with long wires from the reporter back to the equipment in the vehicle.

So here we go...

I gather together the visiting captains. I have the high-desert voice of the Wide World of Sports in tow, with his broadcast gear, mic, and long lengths of wire that resemble the Transatlantic Cable. As we're all walking, I hear the on-the-spot reporting of the drama that is about to unfold!

It is a highly charged, *very* detailed, blow-by-blow saga about Ridgecrest Captains Lewis and Williams headed to face off with Neff High's finest. Trojans versus Burros—*mano-a-burro!*

"You can see in their faces that they're more-than-ready for the battle of tonight's game! This is the finals—the FINALS! This is bringing to Ridgecrest's Burros what they've been fighting for years to achieve! To the seniors on this squad this game is everything! YES! It's everything they've been fighting for during their four years as Burros! Referee Don McKenzie, head official for tonight's championship game, will flip the coin! It's almost time for the toss…"

And then Mr. Radio *whispers* into his mic, *"Let's listen to the voice of referee Don McKenzie…"*

He puts his microphone right into Don's face.

Now, I didn't want to put a damper on the most important sporting event of the century, but *we already knew who won the toss!*

I didn't know how Don was going to cover it up if the Burros won *this* toss—but it didn't really matter. Things descended into chaos pretty quickly. As soon as the future Chris Berman stuck that mic into Don's grille, Don looked in his pocket for the officially sanctioned coin. Then he looked in the other pocket…and then another…

It was an awkward few seconds.

Extremely dead air.

Just as the Ridgecrest reporter began nervously whispering, *"It appears that Referee McKenzie is having some trouble finding th—"* out booms Don with: *"Oh S**T! I forgot my coin in the locker room!"*

And every one—I mean *every* one—of Ridgecrest's 7,629 residents was listening!

"Uh…now a word from our sponsor…"

[Expletive (Not) Deleted]

Sports always has rivalries.

Sure.

And they add a lot to the excitement of games.

But sometimes they can get *too* exciting.

Montebello High and the crosstown Schurr High have always been rivals. One particular year their matchup was the season's opening game.

A big game...

Unfortunately, the previous year's game between Montebello's Oilers and Schurr's Spartans had turned into a bloody riot, suspended in the third quarter.

"It won't happen again!" was the decree from Don McKenzie and the CIF offices.

Even more orders came down to all the referees and umpires from the CIF head of all officials—a guy named Darrell Roundy: *"We're not going to tolerate it! There will be nothing tolerated that could lead to even the slightest hint of trouble! If you hear even one swear word out of a player's mouth, our offices are authorizing you to throw that player out of the game; remove them then and there. We're not putting up with anything!"*

I'm, of course, working the game.

Kickoff.

In Spanish, *montebello* means beautiful mountain.

It was fitting.

Just before the very first snap of the ball, this "beautiful mountain"–sized lineman from Montebello High looks across the field and screams out at all the Spartans: *"F*** YOU! F*** YOU! F*** YOU!"*

Out comes my rag. He's out of there!

But the rules further state that the referee must notify the coach immediately upon a player's ejection from a game.

Don, however, did have that habit of *"easing some responsibilities off onto others..."*

"Dave, you go talk to the coach," he told me. "Besides, you're the one who saw what happened."

Well, the coach of Montebello was this Japanese fellow with a butch haircut and the stance of a seven-foot fire hydrant. He looked like he'd been an ice-blooded U-boat commander in the Second World War.

Talk about nasty!

Even my old "Take a lap, Hull" coach was nothing like this guy.

The meanest twelfth-century samurai wasn't as nasty as this guy!

Now, the ball still hasn't been snapped. Other than kickoff, no plays have been made. And here I am confronting this coach who looks like he snacks on puppies and rocks. I'm explaining to him how one of his players—because of *me*—is now heading for the showers before he's even started to break a sweat.

Yes, sir!

Your number 76 is out of the game!

Disqualified!

And that's it!

No discussion!

The coach just looked at me. He had that same kind of *focused stare* that the T. rex got in *Jurassic Park* right before he ate the lawyer in the outhouse. A look that indicated his *strong displeasure* about the roster manipulation that we were imposing upon him and his team.

I ran back out on the field.

We still hadn't played even one down. Finally, we were ready. But just as Schurr was breaking out of their first huddle, Don asked me something. Now, Don wasn't the kind of ref who liked to discuss *anything* around players; but in this situation, he asked me just what it was that the "beautiful mountain" of a lineman had said.

It was getting loud on the field, so I had to shout as I repeated to Don *exactly* what the player had so colorfully expressed—and it apparently came out with a bit more volume than I anticipated:

"F*** YOU! F*** YOU! F*** YOU!"

The Spartan's center's eyes got as big as the shield of Zeus!

"Man, this game's *way* out of control now!" I heard him tell one of his guards. "Even the refs are fighting!"

The Scene of the Slime

I was still on my hiatus from radio, but using my voice remained *what I did.*

The commercial work was going well, and I genuinely loved officiating at games. This period of my life—the "halftime show" between my radio start in Casablanca, the jackrabbits, and the Beatles and all the radio hullabaloo that would come next—was a *Hull* different ball game for me.

It was highly personal.

I was influencing young athletic lives.

It was beautiful.

So why do we need to talk about something as base and gross as the Mediterranean fruit fly?!

Well, because it's time.

Because this little insect caused almost as much concern and retching-fear in Southern California as what occurred in Europe when Reptilicus ate Copenhagen.

And I was smack dab in the middle of it—because of my officiating.

Californians Take Issue with the Pesticide Malathion, Which Comes in on Medfly Wings and a Sprayer

Dawn hadn't yet touched the verdant hills of Pasadena, Calif., when Police Lieutenant Terry Blumenthal received word that six state helicopters, flying in formation, were bearing down on his community. Their payload: a 1,050-gallon dose of the controversial pesticide malathion, to be dumped on the city's houses, pools and gardens. Blumenthal climbed into his chopper and headed south to intercept the offending helicopters. "We have you flying in formation below 700 feet, in violation of ordinance No. 9.42.010," he said into his microphone as he spotted the choppers. "I have to ask you to cease and desist."

"Affirmative," came the brisk reply from the state pilot. "We acknowledge your transmission."

Yet the trail of white chemicals continued. "Are you going to keep on spraying?" Blumenthal asked in amazement. "Correct," the pilot responded firmly.

That astonishing exchange was the latest flare-up of a mini-revolt brewing in Southern California. The battle is over the state's use of malathion, a pesticide used to control the dreaded Mediterranean fruit fly. After one of the pests was discovered last July near Dodger Stadium, state officials, fearing that the medfly might endanger California's $16.5 billion agricultural industry, ordered 383 heavily inhabited square miles of Los Angeles, Orange and San Bernardino counties to be blanketed with sticky white pesticide-laced corn syrup. Eerily reminiscent of *Apocalypse Now,* more than 60 predawn helicopter missions have taken place in the past eight months.

—Susan Reed and Dan Knapp,
People magazine, April 2, 1990

The above article indeed appeared in *People.*

Yes!

The gooey grip of the fruit fly spraying that gummed up California for so long made it into top high-gossip media. And all of us who got slimed in one way or another had our stories. As usual, *mine* is just a little more *different.*

I was driving home after a game and I was in a hurry. Jeanette and I had plans, so I didn't even shower in the locker room—it was just "game over" and I'm outta there.

I'm racing down the road; but then, *there they are!*

I see them coming in from above! A flight of several "Fruit Fly Extermination" aircraft heading my way; spraying and spewing their chemicals on everything and everyone below.

My car!

My paint!

My breathing!

NO!

I hang a U-turn, and like a tornado hunter, I'm about to outrun the storm!

Until the red lights come on.

The red lights of the sheriff's car I had just made the illegal U-turn directly in front of.

I was nervous and jumpy when I pulled over—I could hear the "blat, blat, blat" of the choppers getting closer.

I could smell the hideous toxicity of the chemicals already tainting the landscape!

The deputy was female, and she was apparently oblivious to the death-from-above closing in on us.

"Do you know what you did wrong?" she asked me in a very officious, badge-heavy tone.

"Yes, but..." I pointed at the approaching 'copter pack.

"You made an illegal U-turn," she said.

"I know! I know! But really—" I now screamed. "Can't we forget this ticket for now?! You need to get under cover!"

I was pointing upward like Chicken Little with Saint Vitus Dance.

"I'm sorry, there's no excuse for..." And then she looked up.

It was very bad timing.

The helicopters were unloading. The malathion bombs were dropping. And they were on target. On her.

She took a direct strafing in the face. Her *abundant* I'm-a-cop-but-also-a-lady makeup ran like "MacArthur Park's" cake out in the rain.

The whole setting was glopped in goo. But *I* was inside and *she* was outside. That slight but important difference in physical positioning made her really mad. Furious.

Looking like a badly melted snowman with too much charcoal for eyes, she slipped and slid back to her sticky cruiser and wrote me a fifty-dollar ticket for the illegal turn.

I smiled as I finally pulled away from the scene of the slime— imagining the reaction of her fellow officers back at headquarters...

"Geeeze, what happened to your face???!!!"

If she had just listened to me...

Life, Liberty, and the Pursuit of a One-Off Cap

My football officiating took me way beyond La Mirada and even Tehachapi. In 1986, I was asked to go to Korea to train other umpires and refs.

Korean nationals were trying to learn American football. The way we were playing the game in American high schools was college level and beyond for Korea.

They really had no clue how to play on either side of the ball.

Korean ref reps got in touch with the always high-profile CIF office and asked who was the best instructor for new officials in the state.

And they said Dave Hull.

So they sent me over to Asia to train the freshman officials. They also sent Dean Crowley, who would later become the CIF commissioner, to instruct the senior officials.

And they sent a man named Bill Clark to instruct the coaches.

Our Korean audience really wanted this level-up in their games, so they were focused on us and everything we said. They wanted to suck up every bit of information they could.

We stayed at the U.S. Embassy in Seoul. We lived and ate there, and that was our headquarters. We had a driver at our command at all times.

He would never go home.

Sometimes he would fall asleep at the wheel—but that was his job; a job ordered by the South Korean government.

And then we were given Miss Park as an assistant (of course, 8.5 percent of *all* Koreans are named Park—third only to Lee and Kim). She also was assigned to us by her government. She was in her late twenties, highly educated.

"I am here to help you in any way I can," she told us.

We thought that was really neat!

But I was encountering one *social* issue that I thought she could help me with.

"Miss Park," I said, "people are looking at me with disdain and they're all pointing at me as I walk down the street. Women are laughing, men are scowling—why would they do that?!"

"Mr. Hull," she told me, "that's because you're wearing shorts. No one in Korea wears shorts in public. You can wear your shorts with the family, in the house, but you don't show your legs in public. It's very disrespectful!"

"Why didn't you tell me that when you saw me leave with my shorts on?!" I asked.

"Because it's *more* disrespectful for me to tell you that you're doing something disrespectful than it is for the disrespectful act," she explained.

Wow!

It was all coming back to me.

I thought of something I myself had said so long ago: *"Never trust anyone in short pants!"*

I put all of my shorts back into my suitcase.

And I definitely was wearing 오랫동안 바지 when we went on a day trip to the place where all the Korean scriptures were written on wooden tablets centuries ago and then kept in a highly secret well-hidden temple.

It took us hours to get there, but the locals told us it would be worth it. We made it to the top of the temple; up thousands of steps to where the wooden religious tablets were stored. People were praying and incense was burning. We stayed there at the top for a respectful amount of time (and to recuperate after all those stairs!) and then we started back down.

On our way to the bottom, we encountered a man in a horsehair Korean gat hat—shaped kind of like the stovepipe hat that Lincoln wore. And he was *crawling* up the thousands of stairs on his hands and knees.

I asked our driver why he would do that.

"He's been doing this for years," the driver told us, "to express thanks to the Americans for saving Korea."

Every time I tell this story I can see that poor man. I asked him to stand up so we could talk. But he wouldn't do that. But he did let me take his picture. And from his position, hands and knees down on those dusty steps, he thanked me directly for what the Americans had done.

♪

Our driver was *always* there with us. One evening we asked him when he ever got to go home to his family.

He said that he never did.

He was there for us.

This is my job…

And part of that job was to take us to a department store in Seoul to stock up on some things we needed. We got to the store late, as they were getting ready to close—but that all changed when we arrived.

Every clerk was dressed the same and looked the same. And every one of them came to "attention" when we walked in.

This trip was really changing my life, both in my thoughts about how Americans are viewed around the world *and* how other governments operate outside the life and level of freedom that we have here.

And that was seen so starkly when we went to the Demilitarized Zone (DMZ)—the strip of land that runs across the Korean Peninsula between North and South Korea, along the 38th parallel north. The "buffer zone."

The South Korean government specifically wanted the three of us to see it.

Each side has these huge binoculars set on tripods, and all kinds of guns and weapons trained at each other. The soldiers from each side just stand on the line and stare and glare at one another.

The whole of the DMZ and what occurs there says so much about humanity and our abilities—and *inabilities*—to get along.

While we were at the DMZ, I made the mistake of simply *pointing* in the direction of the North Koreans.

"NO! Don't do that!" the South Korean military personnel told me. "They can easily *overreact*!"

I noticed that our military hosts were wearing a unique cap.

"I'd love to have one of those," I said. "Do you think I could get one?"

No...

But I did wind up with one. I was wearing it in Tokyo one time, and a guy stopped me on the street and offered me a thousand bucks for it right on the spot. But *I still have it!*

It's a priceless reminder of just what liberty—and the frightening lack of it—means.

"Who the Heck Was That?!"

Back home, I began "switch-hitting" in my officiating—I entered into baseball umpiring.

Elvis: We just had a great big softball game the other day, baby!

Dave: You mean in heaven, they have softball games?!

Elvis: You kidding me, baby? With the people we have up here? We choose up sides—shirts and skins! The Boss recently chose Casey Stengel, and let me tell you something: He makes as much sense up here as he did down there!

My early umping brought me into a game at Glendale College. *POW!!!*

I witnessed the hardest hit ball I'd ever seen, before or since, by a college player—a straight-shot liner to the base of the outfield wall.

> *"As long as you live keep smiling,*
> *because it brightens everybody's day."*
>
> —Vin Scully

Vinny probably would have called that ball a "Polaris Missile" or another of his classic "Vinny-isms"; and I would definitely "keep smiling" as this slugging-skilled kid pulled up in front of me at third base with a stand-up triple. I later asked his coach, "Who the heck was *that*?!"

He told me he was a new young player by the name of Lyman Bostock. Bostock would go on to hit for a three-season average of .311 for the Twins and the Angels. But in 1978, Lyman Bostock was killed in Indiana in one of the most *wasteful* murders ever associated with a professional sports star. And to make matters worse, through a series of strange circumstances, Lyman's killer spent only twenty-one months total behind bars. The entire horrible ordeal did, however, lead to sweeping changes in Indiana's insanity plea laws.

A Controversial Call

Back to Glendale College.

This time I was the plate umpire, and I rolled in with no time to spare—I had a ton of duties and things to prepare for with the rest of the crew.

But the parking lot was full.

And even though we officials held an enormous amount of power, clout, and reverence, there were no preferred *parking accommodations* allotted to us.

I had a personalized plate on my car that read: *CIF REF,* which had helped get me and the crew into a lot of places.

Not this time.

The only parking space available here was, yes, a bright blue–painted, well-designated handicapped-only spot.

It was now morals and good citizenship versus duty and responsibility!

I pulled in, trying to ignore the blue grid lines screaming at me, telling me that I was a cad, an ogre, an inconsiderate boob, a swine, and someone who undoubtedly kicked the canes out from under old ladies and squirted fast-food restaurant ketchup packets onto slow old men.

I closed my ears, opened my trunk, and began putting on my equipment.

Here comes the security guard.

His direction was simple and expected: "You can't park here; it's reserved for disabled persons."

I was silent.

For a second.

It was that thick-air time, like when the number one closing pitcher stares down the opposing cleanup hitter in the box; in the bottom of the ninth, nursing a one-run lead—two outs, two men on, full count.

Just *looks* at him.

Like I looked at this guard.

He had served up a floater. I stepped in and connected.

"Have you ever seen an umpire that *wasn't* blind?!"

Ta-da!

Rimshot.

It was a brilliant line; right up there with Jack Benny's *"I'm, thinking it over!"* and Art Carney's *"Hello, ball!"*

The guard broke out laughing! He told me that was the funniest excuse he'd ever heard from anyone—a lot better than the guy who told him that his disability was "the inability to read road signs." Then he told me "not to worry" as he pulled a bunch of orange cones off his cart and placed them around my car.

He even escorted me into the stadium.

S-a-a-a-f-f-e-e!!!

Dave: What's on your mind this
morning, Elvis?

Elvis: Well, you're probably wonderin',
maybe, if there's life after death.

Dave: Yeah...is there?

Elvis: Well, here's something else to wonder.

Dave: What?!

Elvis: Where does everybody park?

My on-the-field officiating fun was definitely "another way to
have a ball." Beginning in the early seventies, it became a solid, long-
running part of my parallel universe right along with the commercial
voiceovers. I dressed in those black and white stripes and blew whistles
until well into the 1990s.

But by the late 1970s, radio needed to blast back into that
universe.

I really, *really* missed it.

That'll Be All

ORATING BY OSMOSIS

KIQQ, KIIS: 1977

I began to do some sub work on KIQQ during the week. I was back in radio—kinda—but it was more of a pop than a BLAST!

It did get me heard again, though, and I got a call from the program director at KIIS-AM. The guy who invented "Color Radio 98/KFWB" way back when was Chuck Blore; and Chuck was now the big boss at KIIS.

Chuck had left KFWB because we had pounded him at KRLA.

The KIIS program director wanted me there full-time, but Blore had to make the final decision and he was out of town.

"Would you just do me a favor, Dave," the PD said, "and take the weekends until I can get Blore in here and you can sit down and talk to him."

"Well, yeah," I told him. "But how long will it be?"

"Couple of weeks."

"Fine."

So there I was, a little KIQQ during the week, a little KIIS on the weekends, but still no BLAST!

Blore finally got back and the PD called me right away. "Come on in, Dave. Chuck wants to talk to you, to be full-time."

I go in, and there's Chuck Blore, in a chair, leaning up against the wall in the program director's office.

But the program director is not there.

"Sit down, Dave," says Blore. "I want to talk to you, to find out some feelings about you and so forth."

In front of him is this huge white dog, right there at his feet, and it's very friendly.

"Let me tell you something first," began Blore. "By a process of osmosis," he told me, "I want you to become *me*."

I stared at him. So much in my career began coming back... unfortunately, it was the negatives.

If there was one thing I could just *never* deal with, it was micromanaging.

A future here would have as strong a stench as the Alpo breath on the white pooch—and I envisioned a thick collar and leash all planned out for me as well.

Those thoughts—those realizations—sparked a bark of my own.

I leaned forward.

"Do you know what, Chuck?" I said, energized and amazed. "That's the strangest thing I've ever come across!"

Blore looked puzzled, *inquisitive*. "What do you mean?"

His chair came back down on all fours.

"You may not believe this, Chuck," I said. "But by a process of osmosis, I wanted *you* to become *me*!"

Blore was silent. He leaned back in the chair again, the dog still at his feet.

"That'll be all," he told me.

As I went out the door to leave through another office, I saw the program director; his phone was already ringing. Obediently and immediately, he grabbed for it.

I knew who it was, so I waited until he hung up.

"What the hell did you say to him?" the PD asked me. "He doesn't want you."

"Find out by way of osmosis," I told him. And I left.

It was all so weird. For the three weekends I was there, I had to play these goofy bits called "the KIIS-ettes"—little jingle things with Blore's voice:

"This is this, and that, and the music, and the winds come through the leaves, and you're listening to KIIS-AM..." or something sap-silly like that!

And these painful vignettes went every fifteen minutes or so!

Those few minutes with Chuck Blore, and that leaning chair, and that dog, and that osmosis thing were some of the worst moments of my career. That whole Blofeld/Dr. Evil-and-his-cat scene represented so much of what was—and is—wrong in our industry.

I thought back to the confrontations with Dick Lawrence at WFLA in the early sixties and what I'd felt then: *I've always believed that creativity cannot be dictated from behind a desk, but rather is a God-given gift that must be cultivated over time.*

My feelings hadn't changed one bit.

Elvis: We had a big celebration here on Easter Sunday...The Boss was in rare form—he actually told a joke.

Dave: You mean, GOD told a JOKE??!

Elvis: The Boss has one heck of a sense of humor, baby.

Dave: He does, huh?

Elvis: He made program directors, didn't he?

The Home Stretch

This period was rough for me, really. I was subbing at KIQQ during the week and KIIS-AM on weekends; doing commercials; and officiating at games. "You were just never home!" Jeanette would say of that whole stretch.

Well, I was home after that meeting with Blore. I gave up the random KIQQ subs, and KIIS was horrible-history. But I still craved that blast.

I was ready to get back behind the mic for real. And besides, I missed my friends Floyd and Ling-Su.

Someone needed to finally go to that Molly Bee concert with Floyd, and someone needed to date Ling-Su and coo into her ear that she was "plitty"!

Lovelines

"WHY DO YOU KEEP HIM ON, DOING THAT NASTY STUFF?"

KMPC: 1978–1981

"Did you Whittinghill this morning?

The good folks out there in L.A.'s radio-land heard that question for almost thirty years. KMPC morning man Dick Whittinghill was as steady as the eastern sunrise at AM 710.

As Dick neared retirement in the late seventies, Robert W. Morgan, doing fill-in work for KMPC, hoped to be in line for succession to the Radio Hall of Famer's early drive-time throne.

At that same time, KMPC also had Pittsburgh's KDKA veteran Clark Race doing a dating-advice kind of show called *Love Lines*.

Love Lines was similar to my *Dial-A-Date* in the same way that a Hyundai Accent is similar to a Maserati GranTurismo—both have essentially the same purpose, but one wouldn't fall apart if you pushed things to the limit.

On *Love Lines*, Clark teamed himself with a professional psychiatrist to analyze young people's dating habits.

Okay.

But it was *sooooo* clinical. You could almost smell the antiseptic soap and rubbing alcohol right through the radio.

What do you do for a living?

Oh, you're in education, are you?

What kind of school do you teach?

You didn't know whether to scream or yawn.

There was zero sense of humor.

Clark Race was a legend from his years at KRKD, but this gig just wasn't working. Race developed a few problems with the overconsumption of stuff that was stronger than rubbing alcohol and left KMPC to head north to San Francisco's KYUU.

Love Lines was immediately offered to Morgan. But Robert W. wanted Whittinghill's spot.

He would wait.

Morgan told KMPC's general manager, Stan Spiro, and program director, Mark Blinoff, that there was only one man for the job—and that was Dave Hull.

What he didn't tell Spiro and Blinoff, however, is that I would dump the soap and antiseptics *quick as a wink* if I stepped into Race's show.

So I was hired.

The Hullabalooer was back on L.A. radio!

And he was ready to make a few changes...

On the first night, the *Love Lines* doctor who had been working with Clark Race was "replaced" by our new *Lovelines* therapeutic team of Ousley and Solari. The debut show tweaked the old name just a little, but the new "counsel" of J.J. and Dennis tweaked everything else like a drunken plumber with a pneumatic wrench.

Old *Love Lines* listeners coming ear-to-voice with this new *Lovelines* bunch was right up there with having a truckload of squirrel monkeys and baboons turned loose in the local mall—lots of things would break, rude squishy-squirting noises would echo from Sears to Orange Julius, and gross messes would be splattered from the food court to "Monkey Wards."

A young-thinking audio engineer by the name of Bud Stalker jumped right into the position of zookeeper and helped the show take off. No station in L.A.—or anywhere else—had anything like it.

The sound effects Bud chose to use during my live commercials and while transitioning back and forth between *Lovelines* listeners were pure audio art.

Disgusting, maybe, but art nonetheless.

They were *surprising*. Even ever-so-slightly off-color. Like the sounds he chose for my live commercial-reading about an upcoming event, the Black Beans & Rice Festival in Orange County. Along with burps and belches, Bud added the sound of *passing gas*.

R-R-R-R-P-P-P-P-P-P!!!

KMPC's phones lit up for hours.

And naturally, each bodily poot and splat brought more calls from Ousley and Solari! This whole new environment of gauche glee provided the perfect vulgar vitamin boost for those two, like rude noises in a boys junior high locker room.

The animals had been caged for way too long; now they were on a stampede.

Within six months, *Lovelines* became the highest rated nighttime show in the history of KMPC. People still talk about it years later.

Dave (breathless): Hello...hello

Woman (in naughty secretary voice): I may be small, but I sure can whoopee...and boom-boom!

Dave: Oh, you do boom-boom and whoopee?

Naughty Secretary: And hotsie-totsie!

Dave: Hotsie-totsie? (laughing) A NEW ONE!!!

Dave (to new caller): Hello!

A Very "Flamboyant"-Sounding Guy: Hi, Kissy-face!

Dave: How are you?

Mr. Flamboyant: I'm fabulous!

Dave rings his little "tinker-bell." <Ting-a-ling-a-ling!>

Dave: Fabulous, huh?

Mr. Flamboyant: I hotsie-totsie, too! <Ting-a-ling-a-ling!>

Dave: You do hotsie-totsie?

Mr. Flamboyant: And totsie-hotsie, too!

Dave: Totsie-hotsie!

Dave (back to naughty secretary): Hello.

Naughty Secretary: Hi.

Dave: Hi, baby! I've never had a woman hotsie-totsie for me before.

Naughty Secretary: I am HOT-sie-TOT-sie!

Dave: I am hotsie...totsieeeeee...

Naughty Secretary: I am steaming!

Dave: Steeeeeeam-i-i-iiing. Ahhhhhh...Boy, oh boy! What are you doing around the house on a Thursday night, hon? Just steamin' there waitin' for the *Lovelines* so you can hotsie-totsie some more, huh?

Naughty Secretary: Looking for some whoopee, Dave!

(Sounds of "passionate reaction," like Dave's gonna explode)

Dave (in high-pitched voice): Yeah, yeah, yeah—don't go away. HOLD ON!!!!

Herding Tigers

One night I got an off-the-air call from Bob Hudson. He'd been in San Diego making a personal appearance with his partner, Ron Landry, and was heading home to Altadena. He was rolling! He was trying to tell me through the laughs that he was going nuts listening to Ousley and Solari—just laughing out loud. He later told his wife, Beverly, that he hadn't laughed like that in his entire life!

Dave talking to Solari, as a "Tobacco Spitter," spewing chaw at objects as he speaks:

Tobacco Spitter: Wouldn't cha wanna know what I look like or anything? <Scchpppitt!>

Dave: Oh! Well, I'd like to have you give me a rundown on that now, sir!

Tobacco Spitter: Okay...<Scchpppitt!>...I've got brown hair...

Dave: ...(obviously writing)...That's brown hair...

Tobacco Spitter: I got brown eyes...<Scchpppitt!>

Dave: ...brown eyes...

Tobacco Spitter: I got...<Scchpppitt!>...brown clothes...

Ousley, Solari, me, the listeners, the callers, everyone was just *on*! Dennis and J.J. were back with all of their characters—and more. Ousley came up with a lunatic mailman.

J.J. *became* the chief commandant of a banana republic in South America. He wanted a date, but all he kept talking about was his bumbling military. "What a stinking army I got!" the generalissimo would exclaim.

What *I* had was an army of on-air oddballs to juggle.

My on-air antics had me jumping through hoops—it even required charts and graphs!! And I could have used a lasso or two for Ousley and Solari!

A whole other world existed in these guys' minds—and it went in so many different directions! The old "herding cats" thing had to be kicked *way* up when it came to steering the feral drift of Solari-Ousley. It was more like herding tigers! Big toothy ones.

And *I* was the head wrangler.

I remember Dave used to set people up over the phone. It was like a twisted version of television's The Dating Game. *But this was different—hilarious. It was just unbelievable, because of the insults; Dave would insult people without their even knowing it.*

But the way he did it was so much better than what you can imagine because it was with humor. It was playing to people's strengths and weaknesses and talking about them in physical terms rather than emotional terms.

He'd have like five people on different lines all at once and be trying to set them up on dates. So he'd be asking them what they're looking for and what they want—you know, tall, thin, older, younger, that type of stuff. It just became absolutely hilarious.

Dave: Hello.

Female Caller (breathless): Yeah, hi.

Dave: Hi, baby. Okay, now you got a choice between semi-fat Cory, mucho-mucho-mas-grande fat Spanky, and Mr. Flubbo!

MEDIA

Hull: "How hairy is your chest?"

The Singles Bar Comes to Radio on Dave Hull's Zany Dating Game

By Stu Black

"...Yes, I'm a state governor, and I'd like to meet a pert rock star..."

"Now it's time to go to the love line and make someone sexually happy. H-h-hello . . ."

In Los Angeles, the most radio-active city in America, the legacy of Marconi stretches from Doctor Demento to Muzak, from hyperkinetic voices to Michael Jackson's king's English, from the wildly imaginative Dick Whittington to amazingly boring psychologists, psychiatrists and Christ peddlers who, amidst the commercials for disposable douches and conglomerate dentists, fill the airwaves with messages of salvation, telling you how to let the Lord into your heart or get your head together.

Dave Hull is one veteran of L.A. radio who offers neither soothing sounds nor daily deliverance during his zany six-day-a-week stint on KMPC. Instead, he offers humor and sex. Bells ring, sirens scream, horns blow and bombs detonate. His show is what L.A. is all about—irreverent, chaotic, silly, pointless and fun. It's a poor-man's dating game, upgraded by a personality hell-bent on making everyone as wonderfully nuts as he is.

"Hello, Dave. This is John."

"We've already got a john. It's down the hall, two doors on the left. H-h-hello."

"Hi, Dave. This is Bill."

"I'm looking for women now, Bill. I've got a main dude already. Call me back if there is any change in the gender. Hi, baby."

"Hi, Dave. This is Tom, and I'm really ready to boogie."

"Aren't we all? Call me back some other time, Tom, when you're available again. Hi, baby."

"Hi, Dave. This is Nadine, and I really like that first John guy."

"How old are you?"

"Twenty-two."

"But you're so much older than him."

"That's all right. He lives in my neigh-

Newspapers may have called my show a "Singles Bar" for radio, but it was usually more like a looney bin for the lovelorn!

Finally there was a girl; some girl called him and he asked her to describe herself.

"Well," she said over the air, "I weigh 170 pounds and I'm five-foot-two."

"Just a minute," said Dave. He immediately got on the phone to this other guy and said, "Hey, I got one who's fat who'll take anybody. Sounds like it's right up your alley!"

And he would do this as if the girl wasn't listening—wasn't hearing it—but you just knew she had her radio on! So you were going, "My God, he's totally insulting her!" But nobody ever got mad.

That was the amazing thing: nobody ever got mad.

—Wes Parker

Dave, talking to female with nasally, drawn-out, drawling voice, from Odessa, Texas:

Dave: Uh, listen, hon—let me see if we can get a couple of things straight here, okay.

Little Odessa: *Okaaay.*

Dave: You do have the most obnoxious voice in the history of womandom. That is true.

Little Odessa: Oh, *yeeeaah...?*

Dave: Now, you don't, besides that, seem to be too bright.

Little Odessa: *Wellll...*that's the way I *ammm...*

Dave: I'm puttin' down "Not too bright"...and your name is "Little Odessa."

Little Odessa: *Right...*

Dave: Uh-huh, so that means you're not too tall.

Little Odessa: *Right...*

Dave: Well, how tall are ya?

Little Odessa: I'm about five-*twooo.*

Dave: Five-two. Boy. You're not fat too, are ya?

Little Odessa: *Noooo...*

Dave: I'm glad. Cause I couldn't take much more of a downer!

Wow! Well, I hate to ruin Wes's perception of me, but we were actually on a nine-second delay for censorship purposes. So if I returned to the *potentially* offended caller before the nine seconds were up, that person would be talking to me on the phone and would miss everything I had said about him or her before.

"Hold on!!!"

Eventually I got both Dennis and J.J. on the payroll at KMPC—and I even bought them Christmas gifts!

"The Singing Cowboy" Meets the Hullabalooer

KMPC was owned and operated by one of the finest country gentlemen in the business—Gene Autry.

Gene Autry, "The Singing Cowboy."

A member of both the Nashville Songwriters and Country Music Halls of Fame.

The only personality to be awarded stars on the Hollywood Walk of Fame in *all five* categories—Film, Television, Music, Radio, and Live Performance.

The guy who wrote "Here Comes Santa Claus" to save the Hollywood Santa Claus Lane Parade.

Autry's executive offices were right above the KMPC studios on Sunset Boulevard. And occasionally he would *descend* the huge mahogany stairway to greet and shake hands with anyone and everyone he'd find in the hallway.

He loved his people.

"Hi, Dave," he'd say. "I heard you last night, and I laughed out loud."

Then he'd go on to Gary Owens: "Gary, you've been with me so long—I just love you!"

Gene always knew who you were and always said something to you.

I revered him.

I've worked for grand people—I really have—but Gene Autry was a prince. I don't care if you were a boom operator, if you were a cameraman on KTLA-TV Channel 5 (which he also owned), if you were a disc jockey, if you sold time on his radio or television station—it didn't matter. He would always take time to talk to you.

But he did have a confession for me: "Dave, you know *I* love you, but my wife's not too hot about you!"

His first wife, Ina May Spivey, was marvelous, but she really didn't take to me. To her, *Lovelines* was risqué!

She'd ask Gene, "Why do you keep him on? Doing all that nasty stuff?"

"He's the funniest man on the station," he'd tell her. "Leave him alone!"

Dave: Hello.

Caller: Hi. Richard here. I'm looking for one of those "Big Girls"—the ones you talk about that are little too "zaftig"... I'm a little zaftig myself.

Dave: Oh...you mean you want a muy-mas-grande, el-medium, el-gordo, chunk-chunk fatso!

Caller: Yes!

Ruining a Perfect Game

Along with KMPC radio and KTLA television, Gene Autry also owned the California Angels. And—*surprise!*—their games were broadcast over the two outlets.

During the season, *Lovelines* followed Angel baseball, and the players went nuts for the show. They'd listen as they drove home.

They loved us so much that the Angels' manager, Jim Fregosi, gave Jeanette his official team jacket.

Actually, she asked him for it.

"No, you can't have *that,* but you can have me!" Fregosi told her.

"Now, wait a minute..." I butted in!

But it was all in fun, and he *did* give her the single-edition pro-player-only red and blue satin threads.

All the guys with the Angels were really cool. Actually, they *had* to have great attitudes; up 'til then, the Angels had never played a winning season.

But despite that, their games and *Lovelines* were both hitting home runs in the ratings game. KMPC's nighttime numbers were racking up the highest scores in the station's history.

But there was always that soap bubble...

A new manager, elevated from a sales position, came in and replaced Stan Spiro. It was the first strike in a lot of bad innings to come.

The new manager called me in for a meeting. I walked into the office and Don Drysdale was already sitting there, waiting. Don, the retired pitching great for the Dodgers, was the voice of the Angels on KMPC's play-by-play.

"What are *you* doing here, Dave?" he asked me.

"I don't know..." I said.

In came Geoff Edwards right behind me—he did the entertaining "The Answer Lady" bit on his show.

Same question: "What are *you* doing here?"

What were we all doing here?

It was an old song. This new manager knew nothing about radio; he was a salesman elevated to the position. But he had the power now to let us all go. So he did. He had checks already made out for us, including our severance and paid vacations. His main reason for the massacre was that the station was getting ready to go all-talk— a harder brand of talk with zero music.

Okay. *But why?* My show had the biggest numbers in the nighttime history of KMPC. But that afternoon marked the end of *Lovelines* and the end of music on KMPC.

Drysdale, Edwards, and Hull were the first to go. What a great group to get fired with!

On our way to our cars, we talked.

We sounded like characters on the final episode of *Friends* or something—melancholy and *"interested in what we're going to do next..."*

We stopped in the KTLA Channel 5 parking lot

The group looked from one face to another...

Don, in particular, was stunned.

"I've never been fired from anything in my life!" he said.

Don Drysdale had spent all fourteen of his years in the major leagues with one team: the Dodgers. No trades. A perfect game of a career.

"But it's probably for the best," Don added in a sigh. "I've been asked to be the voice of the *ABC Baseball Game of the Week* and I've been thinking about it. I'm going to go home now and make the call."

Smiles and handshakes...

"*I* just got very lucky!" said Geoff. "I'm going to take the emcee spot for a new television lottery game show out of Sacramento."

Pats on the back...well wishes...

"Me," I said, "I've still got my commercials and I'm on my way to making a movie!"

Group hug...start the theme song!

Lovelines: The Movie

The team of Ousley, Solari, and Hull knew it had something raucously rare with the characters developed on *Dial-A-Date* and *Lovelines*, so we pursued an expansion of their demented but incredibly funny world. We attracted interest in their unique universe from motion picture studios.

This could be big! For Floyd, for Ling-Su, for all of us!

Dennis, J.J., and I would spend four or five hours a night writing scenes.

But as with every landmark classic, a lot of the details have eroded with time—like the sand and wind grinding away some key parts of the Dead Sea Scrolls! A few of the "secrets and mysteries" about *Lovelines: The Movie* are as remarkable and mythical as the Jell-O horses story from *The Wizard of Oz*.

What? You don't know that one? Well, *according to sources*, the horses used to depict the "horse of a different color" in the Emerald City palace scenes were colored with Jell-O crystals. The cameras had to roll quickly, before the horses started to lick it off!

Lovelines: The Movie had *exactly* the same "behind the curtain" cinematic enigmas.

Exactly!

To begin with, there is confusion as to just which movie studio was actually at the forefront of interest—Columbia, Warner Brothers, or Paramount.

Dennis Ousley recalls that, *maybe*, the whole reason for the possibility of a movie at all was that Barbra Streisand heard the radio show and told her then-husband, the infamous Jon Peters, "I think this show is funny." So Peters, the former head of Sony Pictures, was the guy who got the ball rolling.

One thing for *sure* is that Michael Campus, director of 1973's Richard Pryor cult classic, *The Mack*, came on board.

J.J. remembers a touch more:

Somehow Steve Zacharias and Jeff Buhai got involved, too. They were the two who made Revenge of the Nerds, *and I am convinced they got the idea for that from Dennis, because for years Ousley was often asking me, "You ever find yourself wondering what happened to all the nerdy guys in high school? What happened to them????? What are they doing now?"*

This was before the Microsoft explosion, when nobody knew who the geeks actually were. Turns out they were just "in waiting."

Well, anyway, around all these movie types, I found I was making more enemies than friends, because of my "negative energy," as Steve called it.

All of this took place at Warner Brothers, not Columbia or Paramount. But something did take place at Paramount—come to think of it—but I don't think it had anything to do with Lovelines. *I think*

Dennis snuck me onto the lot somehow and we spent the day wandering around. I had to keep telling him, "No!" He likes to explore...

The enigmas thicken!

But mysteries or no mysteries, like the Tower of Babel, Schubert's Unfinished Symphony, the Crazy Horse Memorial, and Octomom's offspring-production, the project just never got totally done.

A lot *was* completed, though. And we always had an *uncomfortable* feeling about our partial gems and what really happened to them.

Secrets and mysteries...

We would finish the scenes and give them to Campus. Campus would bring them to the studios.

We think.

But somewhere down the line we think that perhaps, possibly, they were shown to the Zucker brothers.

The Zuckers were a new group of writers working on a film project called *Airplane!*

Fine.

But...

Well, we all know that when *Airplane!* was released in 1980, it became a high-altitude hit and a long-flying classic. The movie has been in list after list of the top motion pictures of all time. But a couple of controversies have cropped up as the years have jetted by, concerning the originality of this *very* original flick.

First was the screenplay's "similarity" to a 1957 film, *Zero Hour!*, written by Arthur Hailey.

Airplane! lifted line after line *directly* from *Zero Hour!*

Both had the same plot of the plane's flight crew being incapacitated by a toxic fish dinner.

Even the lead character's name—Ted Stryker—is exactly the same.

So many of the scenes were *exactly* the same, too.

Yeah, but...

In all fairness, the creators of *Airplane!* did purchase the rights to *Zero Hour!*, allowing them to legally use the screenplay almost verbatim. And they tacked on laugh-genius punch lines to each scene's overdramatic end. And that was the point: to do a *Saturday Night Live*–tinted parody of something that took itself way to seriously.

But when *Airplane!* taxied into theaters, we recognized a lot of *our* gags, too. (For example, we wrote a scene where a guy was running after a train and ran straight into a pillar; it showed up in *Airplane!* just as we had written it—action-wise and context-wise.) This made the incompletion of our film just that much harder to swallow.

Like the tasty gems in ol' Franz' partial symphony, however, what *was* completed of the *Lovelines* movie—and what wasn't digested by others—was deserving of *Bravo!* and a standing O or two.

One scene in particular was one of the funniest pieces that Ousley and Solari ever came up with. They developed a Middle Eastern character—turbaned, of course—riding a low-powered motor scooter. He's sitting on the scooter waiting for a red light to change. Suddenly, hundreds of tough-looking biker guys surround the guy, his motor scooter dwarfed by their big bikes like a Lego building against the New York skyline.

"How would you like to join our club?" they ask him.

The guy on the putt-putt hollers, "America! I love America!"

But, yes, the bunch has "other plans" for the guy on the tiny two-wheeler.

The motorcycle "gang" takes their newfound member into Beverly Hills, where they have an evil plan to destroy most of the high-end homes there. As the group roars (and putts!) down a small incline with expansive, expensive mansions on either side, "For Sale" signs begin popping up out of the ground in front of the estates. One Hearst Castle–sized joint even has a huge, rolled up canvas façade on the roof which drops down to camouflage the entire place as a simple tree-lined street in Middle America with simple houses and store fronts on either side.

The biker vs. citizen tension builds.

The scene had the same cliff-hanging effect as Eric Von Zipper and his leathered Ratz & Mice bunch facing down the professor and his exotic martial art "Himalayan Time-Suspension Technique" in the *Beach Party* flicks.

The bad bikers...

The poor Middle Eastern scooter jockey...

The bikers surround him...

They need him to help take over Beverly Hills...

They—

Cut!

The scene ended there.

Maybe, just maybe, sometime down the road, we'll eventually find out the answers:

Does the "gang" really take over the 90210?

Does the turbaned dupe endear himself to the guys by swapping his turban for a bandana and trading in his Vespa for a Fat Boy?

Just like Franz might just come back someday, reincarnated as oh, say, the winner of *X Factor*, and finally pen in that finale to his *Symphony No. 8*, maybe Ousley-Solari-Hull will eventually orchestrate a *crescendo* for the nervous residents along Rodeo Drive and for the by-now *really* nervous جاي on the scooter.

As always, *stay tuned...*

Maybe This Was Going a Little Overboard

by J.J. Solari

J.J. Solari and Dennis Ousley were so key to my success with Dial-A-Date *on KGBS and with* Lovelines *on KMPC. And as mentioned, J.J. is also an accomplished writer with a long career in the "biker" world.*

And that fits him.

It's edgy and scary and not for everyone—just like J.J.!

He was the only Mouseketeer to grow fangs!

These thoughts from J.J. are left "reasonably" intact as far as his "unique style" goes. Much of J.J.'s writing is in the same ethereal slant as the great American poet, e.e. cummings— free from such frivolous parameters as punctuation and proper grammatical structure. And that is how it should be—with J.J. at least. He, and his work, are free-form expressions of one of the most interesting looks at life that any human being has ever possessed.

i thought of all this on the way to visit dennis in the hospital. his left hand was a bit [CENSORED!] up. so i was walking into the place and saw the "chapel" that they got there and it looked like a funeral parlor and i remembered that what got dave laughing the HARDEST was the first time dennis called into *Lovelines*, allegedly from a funeral home. he had very VERY bad organ music playing in the background and he called in tears and barely able to talk. dave knew it was dennis, of course, cause we had already been set up with our own phone line there at KMPC. but we never told dave what we were going to do. often we had to talk each other into making certain calls because one or the other of us would think maybe this was going a little overboard. so dennis is calling and talking in tears about looking for a date. so dave is going, "sure, sure, how tall are you?" "what's your name?" etc. then dave goes, "...ummmm...are you crying, sir?" dennis says weakly, "yes, yes, this has not been a good day." "ummmm..." (dave is starting to laugh and the little light is going on in his head.) he says, "ummmm...do i hear an organ playing??"

dennis says, "yes."

"ummmm...where are you calling from?"

dennis says, "a funeral home."

now, there would sometimes reach a point in an unrehearsed phone call to *Lovelines* when dave would suddenly be able to see all the way down the road of where a call was going to go, long before the journey ever started. and if what he saw all the way down the road was funny, he would not be able to wait to get there to start laughing. no, he would start laughing early. cause this was all new to him. and we knew once he started laughing, all the LISTENERS would stay glued to the radio because, well, he was probably laughing for a reason. and genuine laughter cannot be faked. so getting dave in stitches was our goal.

Dave: Hello!

Caller (in deep, serious voice): Hello, Dave...

Dave: Yeah, hello!

<CRASH!>
(Sound of receiver bouncing on floor)

Dave (hysterically laughing): The guy tipped right over, man! Fell right off the bed. It was amazing. The phone slipped from his hand and...(hysterics)...

Caller (in deeper, more serious voice): Hello, Dave...

Dave (wheezing with no sound coming out): Don't say anything, pal! I'm in the midst of a laugh!

so dave eventually says, "you're calling from a funeral home?"

"that's correct."

"i'm so very sorry, sir. is it a loved one that has passed away?"

"no."

"oh, whew, well then, who is it?"

"my wife."

this telegraphed joke actually caught dave by surprise, and he laughed naturally for a goodly while. and then of course he had to play the sincerely sympathetic well-wisher and say, "oh, I'm so sorry," and dennis nonchalantly—while still crying—replied, "no, that's okay, she's not telling me to get off the phone for once!"

and then, of course, the real reason for the call—looking for a date—would be MORE than enough material for ten minutes of fun. and of course, as the weeks rolled by, the guy in the funeral parlor would KEEP CALLING. cause this was funny. so, unlike his wife, this character could not be allowed to die. explaining all the reasons WHY he was still at the funeral home with his—now for months—unburied wife only added (more than just a little) to the hijinks. which is really understating things.

Caller (in Peter Falk/Columbo-gravelly voice):
    I'd like to speak to the Mister
    Bobbalooer. My name is Flubbo.

Dave: Is that Blubbo?

Flubbo: No, it's Flubbo, sir. F-L-U-B—you got
    your "Flub." B-O you got your "Bo."
    Put 'em together, sir, and it spells
    "Flubbo." I'm on the police force.
    Would it bother you if I smoked while
    we talked?

Dave (laughing): No! Go ahead and light up, sir,
    if you wish.

Flubbo: It's a very stinky cigar.

Dave: Yeah, it goes along with the B-O!

"Be good and you will be lonesome."
—Mark Twain

Samuel Clemens compliments J.J. Solari on his eclectic literary brilliance in *When Bikers Meet Humans.*

Hullabalooning Back to KRLA

FULL OF HOT AIR...BUT NOT QUITE ENOUGH!

KRLA Revisited: 1981–1984

October 1981.

Meanwhile, back at the KRLA ranch...

For years, the Dream-House of KRLA had been falling down. AM 1110 had seen an odd-mix parade of on-air personalities, some confusing jumps in formats, and a swirling, down-the-drain flush in ratings.

In 1976, though, KRLA looked back on those "oldies but goodies" and found an identity when Art Laboe took over the programming.

Laboe had lived out the "Angel Baby" dreams, low-riding for years and miles through the most traditional "Dedicated to the One I Love" kinds of tunes. Those "Dreamy Side/Rockin' Side" tried, true, and comfortably worn album tracks and 45s brought an instant following within the Hispanic community and among those who never did quite psychedelicize in the 1960s—those who perennially preferred old Chevys, khakis, and R & B to VW peace-vans, beads and sandals, and drum circles.

For five years, Laboe's "Sitting in the Park" soiree worked; but it was ultimately limited as far as growth and new listeners went.

By 1981, Jack "The Hitman" Roth had grabbed the wheel at KRLA, and he saw no harm in steering the station into a combination of 1110's two most productive musical eras—sixties rock and old school R & B—while highlighting their *one* most productive personality period.

Roth's first plan was to get *me* back and to add in another of the most memorable and recognizable voices of the sixties, "Humble Harve" Miller.

Except (and this sounds familiar) I didn't know it yet!

As a kickoff to the changes, on the Halloween weekend of 1981, *everyone* was coming back to KRLA for one bone-rattling reunion! Everyone who was anyone—everyone who had said *Hello, Goodbye* in the *Strawberry Fields* of *Yesterday*—was back behind the KRLA mic. We'd all be *Happy Together* one more time.

Hudson, Quillin, O'Donnell, Kasem, Eubanks, Biondi, Foster, Moreland, Hayes, the Hullabalooer, Beebe, and more—and all of us using the same heritage jingles and promos that had made us so popular in the 1960s.

Roth even brought back Bobby "Boris" Pickett to exhume his ratings-reviving scare-shows from seventeen years before.

Reb Foster actually fired up the last remaining record turntable in the broadcast booth; tape cartridges ("carts") had long since replaced the spinning, needle-stuck vinyl. Reb's rewind helped us all to *really* reminisce.

Johnny Hayes went on air and read "recollections" from past *KRLA Beat* newspapers.

Bob Hudson's weekend segment was the first one-man show he'd done since 1971 at KGBS, before teaming up with Ron Landry.

During the three-to-six p.m. slot *I* had been given, the station lobby was opened and "lost legions of the Porch People," as described by KRLA Historian Bill Earl, streamed in—all looking *just a little* older.

The weekend was a talent time machine, featuring prime-choice entertainers and entertainment. KRLA radio hadn't sounded this good in decades!

Dave (starting his show):
"This'll be me, Dave Hull, until we get sick and tired of each other at six!
<Honk, Honk!>

—October 1981 reunion, KRLA

After the last talent had left the air, I received a call from Roth. A dozen years after that final "meeting" with Doug Cox, KRLA was about to *Gimme Some Lovin'*.

They made me an offer I couldn't refuse.

A few weeks before the reunion, I'd actually been asked to sit in for Johnny Hayes on his afternoon "Countdown" show—apparently as a "practice show"/audition. It had felt so comfortable to be back as one of the Eleven-Ten Men, even if just for one day (or so I thought).

I began with, "Now, let's see, where was I when I was so rudely interrupted back in January 1969...?"

The 1981 KRLA reunion brought together such KRLA favorites as Bob Eubanks (right)...and me!

Eleven-Ten, Take 2

November 1981.

The Monday afternoon following the Halloween reunion, I was back on KRLA 1110 in the three-to-seven p.m. time slot. It was a perfect renewal of so much—for me, for the fans, and for an era that still had such a stronghold on American history and entertainment.

> *To keep with the spirit of the sixties that Roth tried to instill at Eleven-Ten, Hull's first show back featured a half-*

*hour phone call to Ringo Starr, plugging his new record...
This was magic hearing Dave Hull, "the Fifth Beatle" in Los
Angeles, interview Starr...There was no doubt a chemistry
there...and even the things about the Beatles that caused
Hull to break with them in 1967 seemed a thing of the past.*

—Bill Earl, *Dream-House*

In addition to Humble Harve and Johnny Hayes, I was surrounded
by oldies veterans like Russ O'Hara and, later, Dick "Huggy Boy" Hugg.

*Clearly the strongest man in the new lineup was Dave
Hull. He created a character called "Miss Goodbody" who was
supposedly the station's "censor," and when Hull would say
something rather "naughty" (which he did much, much more
now than from 1963 to 1969), you could hear the sound effect
of a body falling over—<BONK!>—the illusion that "Miss
Goodbody" would faint at the sound of something "blue."*

—Bill Earl, *Dream-House*

**Dave (referring to a popular video game):
"Donkey Kong...(*pause*)...that sounds
kind of dirty!" <BONK!>**

My second stint at KRLA saw me blowing double the hot air!
(With morning man Rege Cordic [left], at the Santa Claus Lane Parade.)

The Ballad of the Beefy Balloon

I was on the air, and *in the air*.

I was flying high this second time around at KRLA.

I seemed to be on good terms with the FAA now (apparently no one remembered the ugly incident with the DC-3 in 1955 when I was soloing back in Roswell)! So I figured it was safe for me to take to the friendly skies once more.

Stuart Anderson's Black Angus Restaurants asked KRLA if the station would be willing to broadcast our morning show aboard their hot air balloon over Southern California. Penny Biondi, our marketing director, agreed and started working on getting the project "off the ground"!

The time and place was set for launch!

Early in the morning, Penny and I took off with an experienced balloon pilot (cue the 5th Dimension's "Up, Up, and Away"!).

But after broadcasting live for over an hour, with hundreds of cars and trucks chasing us below, we needed to radio Mission Control:

"Pasadena, we have a problem..."

For some strange—and scary—reason, the balloon began rapidly losing altitude.

"Oh, the humanity!"

We were going down!

Onto an elementary school's playground.

There's nothing like being part of a freak disaster in front of an audience—especially a young and impressionable one. One that will remember that grisly moment for the rest of their long lives—awaking in the throes of horrendous nightmares, the image haunting them forever.

We were dropping. *Terra firma* was rising!

The monster Black Angus lighter-than-air craft wasn't so light anymore, and we were plunging directly toward the school! It was a bad scene—a brutal blend of the Hindenburg crash and the giant M&M balloon's rampage at the 2005 Macy's Thanksgiving Day Parade!

You could almost hear Herbert Morrison's dirigible-disaster newscast from back in 1937 as we careened toward the ground: *"It's crashing! It's crashing terrible! Oh, my! Get out of the way, please!"*

As our lives careened toward their possible ending, the fortunate thing was that all the young students were inside the post-recess safety of their classrooms. But all of them were looking out the windows! Still, at least no physical scars would accompany the mental ones.

The shadow on the ground of the big balloon got larger and LARGER as *we* got closer and CLOSER to the end as we knew it! It was a frightening, irreversible total eclipse of a diving balloon!

By now, all the wide-eyed kids had their little noses pushed hard against the schoolroom windows—and so did the teachers!

This was a once-in-a-lifetime—and maybe the *last* in a lifetime, for some of us—sight.

KER-PLOP!!!

Whew!

Another miracle! No one was hurt as the once-mighty and imposing Graf BAB (Black Angus Balloon) more or less *lightly* bounced down on the playground.

Actually, the kids at the school were delighted—because with all the emergency equipment, personnel, and noisy chaos that ensued, they got to get out of school for the rest of the day!

The newspapers pretty much beat everybody else there, and their accounts of "The Great Balloon Crash of 1982" were much more than just hot air. All the nosedive-notoriety the following day made The Black Angus Restaurants the most talked-about food chain in Southern California.

It definitely inflated *their* reputation.

Why Don't Men's Rooms Have Couches?

October 1982.

It was nearly a year to the day since I had been back on KRLA. Jack Roth's rebuilding of the Eleven-Ten Dream-House had been a stroke of genius. Unfortunately, another type of stroke was on the way.

Now, our airborne promotion had been great.

All of our promotions were great.

And commercially productive!

But they were also strenuous and time-consuming—and they were taking their toll on my health. Of course, like so many things, I didn't know it yet!

Just before my show ended at six one evening, right around that one-year reunion anniversary, I suffered a transient ischemic attack (TIA)—a mild stroke. I was on the air at the time, with the added bent irony of having the Ousley/Solari team on the phone right then. It was like having a piano dropped on you *while you're on fire*.

I closed my microphone right away. I knew that something very real, very bad, and *very real bad* was happening to me.

My speech suffered immediately, just as soon as the attack started. Then the loss of all feeling started at my toes and went all the way up from there.

Everything on my right side just went away!

Before a stroke, you take your sense of feeling for granted. Even the hair on your head and arms is sensitive; there for you to feel. But you never pay any attention to that daily, pleasant, alive feeling of the wind in your hair and those simple touches in life.

Until all of your feeling is gone.

It was a turning point in my personal life. I was a pretty dogmatic guy—I was the real strict one when it came to my immediate family. From my *regimentation* with Lisa's dating to really everything else at home. But my stroke changed me. It really did. Even though I'd always enjoyed the freewheeling hullabaloo in my career, I would now apply that freedom and appreciation of every second of life to my family.

But first I had to survive this.

I told the engineer to play uninterrupted music until she heard from me again. Then I called for Penny to come into the studio at once. Roth came with her. They helped me get to the ladies room where I was able to lie down.

As a side note: I had never seen the women's restroom at the station until that moment—and my first thought, even in the grip of the stroke, was: *Hey, their bathroom is a lot better than OURS! I didn't know ladies rooms have couches...WE'VE never had couches... why don't WE have couches?* And there were two of them!

The entire paralysis lasted about eleven minutes, with all sensation back within thirty.

Jeanette was called to come to pick me up. I just wanted to go home. My being helped physically into the house made an impression on our youngest son, Brian, who rushed inside to see what was happening. However, it wasn't long—just a few minutes—before Jeanette decided that she didn't care *what* I said; she'd better get me to the hospital. She took me to the emergency room at Arcadia Methodist Hospital, where I was admitted into the Intensive Care Unit.

And these guys were *serious*.

Dr. Vincent Fortanasce at the neurological center became the primary neurosurgeon with assistance from Dr. Edwin Todd. I received every test available. They injected dye into my brain to see where the stroke may have occurred and found no abnormalities. My carotid arteries were checked and no blockages were found. No definitive reason was found for my attack; and since I'd retained all of my faculties, it was essentially and objectively determined that my condition "*may* not prove incapacitating later."

But...

Dr. Fortanasce went far deeper in his assessment of my condition than the on-paper facts.

"Dave," he told me, "you've lost *something*. I don't know what it is, and you don't know what it is, but something will come up that is a part of life and you'll have forgotten it. Some attached brain cells may have been damaged or disconnected. Whatever it is will come as a surprise. When that thing comes—while you're driving or doing whatever you're doing, sitting in your office reading, on the air, whatever it is that you normally do—you will forget."

He was right.

Some weeks later, I was driving my family down the I-605 Freeway to see my mother, who was now in Huntington Beach. And as I took the off-ramp to the I-5 South...well, I might as well have just rocketed to the fourth star cluster of Andromeda. I didn't have a *clue* as to where I was or what I was doing.

So I stopped.

Dead in the water.

Right there on the freeway.

Cars were honking and whizzing around me.

I knew I was driving, but I suddenly had no idea what to do or where to go. I asked Jeanette for help. Jeanette patiently, and relatively calmly, told me to just keep going straight and to get off at the next exit; which I did.

We eventually made it to my mother's and we told her what happened.

"Call the doctor!" she said.

I did.

He prescribed an interesting therapy.

"Drive a few times to your mother's house in the coming weeks," Dr. Fortanasce suggested in a very "medical" tone. "Get into the proper lane early on that will transverse into the upcoming freeway lanes and then just concentrate on the road ahead."

The second time I tried going to my mom's, the same thing happened. But I tried it again. Then things started to work—things started to come back to me.

After a few more trips, the problem was fixed and I never had trouble again.

But...

On my next visit, Dr. Fortanasce told me something else.

"You have about twelve years to live," he informed me. "Because of what has happened, we figure that between now and twelve years from now, you will have a major stroke that will kill you."

I just looked at him. Then I looked at Dr. Todd.

"Do you agree with that, Dr. Todd?" I asked.

"Yes, I do," he answered. "That's the general rule of thumb. Ten to twelve years after something like this, well, the patient usually succumbs to a large stroke."

That was 1982.

Thankfully.

They were right about my forgetting something. Their other hypothesis: not so much!

Dave: Hi, Elvis. Could you do me a favor? Am I gonna be up there someday with you?

Elvis: Baby, eventually everybody will...let me check my paperwork...(checks advance-copy obituaries...checks "The Boss's" computer)... I don't see you down here for a while, son.

Dave: Then I can have fun down here for a while!

Elvis: Yeah, you're still doin' time down there, baby!

It was interesting—did I start to work less? Ease up on things because of what had happened? Not really. I did cut back on the commercial work a bit, but overall I think I started working even harder—both at my career and at understanding everyone in my family and what their needs and desires were and are.

"Wow, Hullabalooers—Dave seems to have come down with the flu...but he'll be back in just a few days..."

I returned to the air just as soon as I regained my strength. Really, *that* was my therapy!

Back with Beebe

It wasn't long before the station asked me to switch to morning drive time, in a move to increase ratings even further (and for a substantial increase in salary!). What do you think I did?

The *next* Monday, I was up at 4:30 and on the air an hour later. This dawn patrol gave me the chance to work again with one of the greatest talents in radio, my old pal who dropped news tapes out of the sky during my first run at KRLA, Richard Beebe.

Beebe also returned to 1110 in 1981 (after leaving in 1970). Richard's humor was *still* a current-events whoopee cushion. Just like back in the sixties, he continued to "flavor" the air of real news with his own *input,* imitating heads of state and other headline hams.

You could give Richard a premise, and he would run with that premise in incredibly creative ways; very similar to Solari and Ousley.

You'd start it by saying something like, "Richard, I'm going to be calling you in a minute. A news story just came over about the Peruvian navy; one or two or three of its boats sank, for no apparent reason. I'm going to call the newsroom and you're going to be the head of state for the Peruvian government."

"Okay," he'd say. "Let me get a couple of things out of the way here and I'll jot down a few notes."

He'd run and get the story. He'd look up the names of the vessels. The whos, whys, whens, wheres, and whats. Then he'd come on the air:

Me: *"Hello, could I speak to the generalissimo, por favor?"*

Beebe (in a Spanish accent): *"The generalissimo? Sí, he's here now. You can talk to him."*

Me: *"Hello, Generalissimo..."*

And then it would roll.

He would get into character just like that.

Doing the news with Richard Beebe was like touring the Empire State Building wth King Kong!

Cabbage Patch Bombs

One of the best characters Beebe ever played was one *I* came up with.

Hull spawned Dickie Dark to help him on his morning show. The running character, played by KRLA newscaster Richard Beebe, was the personification of all the manic-depressive qualities of an American cliché: the itinerant radio personality who is an anonymous broadcast star one day and simply anonymous the next.

"Remember the shotgun shooting at a Monterey radio station? It was about two years ago and that's how Dickie Dark began," Hull said. "Some guy came in and shot the place up and scared the devil out of the woman who was the announcer."

The real-life incident led to the creation of Dickie Dark whom Hull "called" at the Monterey station to get reaction on the shootout. After that first call, Hull followed Dickie's "career" as he was "fired" and "hired" on stations across the country.

"Dickie told us that the shooting turned out to be a real great promotion for the station. That's the kind of character this guy is."

At one station, Dickie had Cabbage Patch dolls dropped from B-29 bombers, after which Dickie was promptly fired.

> At another, Dickie held a trivia
> contest and awarded a couple a weekend
> in a New Jersey motel.

> —*Los Angeles Times,* March 5, 1985

After so many years in this business, Dickie Dark personified a lot of what I'd seen and done—and would do!

Bogey & Bacall; Beebe &...?

Romance wasn't in the air only for those lucky lovers at the 'Jersey motel. Richard himself brought some of Cupid's conjuring to KRLA.

Some listener fell in love with him. She obviously knew that he worked with me in the mornings, so she called the Huntington Sheraton Hotel and had them send over an elaborate morning breakfast for him at the studio.

> *"The way to a man's heart is through his stomach."*

> —Fanny Fern (1811-1872)

> *"A hot dog at the ballpark is better than steak at the Ritz."*

> —Humphrey Bogart

The doorbell rings: *Ding-dong, Ding-dong.* I go to the door; Beebe's in the newsroom.

"Yes?"

"We have this for Mr. Richard Beebe: his *breakfast.*"

"Hmmm...wow! Well, come on in." I'm thinking maybe I can get a muffin or something.

They set up the table. An elegant cloth goes over the top; then flowers. They light the candles. They neatly open a morning edition of the *Los Angeles Times* for Richard's reading pleasure as he dines.

The entire Bogey-and-Bacall scene was accompanied by a card. Richard read it.

An Admirer.

He looked at me. I shrugged.

Well, this pretty much sent Richard nuts trying to find out just who this "Admirer" was.

For weeks.

It turned out the whole thing wasn't by just "some listener." Richard's admirer was Ann Strohecker, a woman who worked back in a small division of the promotions department at KRLA.

Ann may have been tucked away from the immediate studio, but she was close enough to watch—with a fair amount of Cupiditious glee—Beebe's whole consternation-consumed search.

After Richard had finally squirmed and squinted around enough, Ann confessed.

Richard thanked Ann, admitting that he was very impressed with her pancakes of passion and eggs of ecstasy.

Then Richard asked her out.

Then Richard and Ann became sweethearts.

Then Richard and Ann got married!

Bogey and Bacall kiss.

The End.

Roll credits...

Pacific on the Rocks

In the early eighties, the "El Niño" effect (officially described as "a periodic rise in ocean temperatures, which could cause severe weather changes") was reported as "the strongest and most devastating of the century, perhaps the worst in recorded history... California had very high rainfall and the year was characterized by extensive flooding and landsliding."

Well, we needed to be a part of that! And maybe even *fix it*! I mean, we were, after all, trying to keep up that sixties "vibe" where we all wanted to change the world into the utopia it was meant to be! Consequently, Richard and I thought the time was right to cool down the waters off the California coast. We decided we could easily do this by leasing an aircraft and dropping huge, fifty-pound blocks of ice into the ocean along local beaches. (Just like Dickie Dark's daring B-29–Cabbage Patch Kid mission!)

We would change the course of humanity, cool down El Niño, and heat up the image of KRLA all at once!

We promoted the event for weeks, urging listeners to throw away their umbrellas and heavy raincoats, as the weather would change dramatically.

We had to secure FAA approval first, of course. *No problem,* I figured, *by now, we're buddies!* (After all, the overcooked landing of the Black Angus balloon hadn't *actually* caused any damage—except of course, to Stuart Anderson's wallet!)

So I gave them a call:

"Good morning, Federal Aviation Administration, how may I help you?"

"Yes, this is Dave Hull from radio station KRLA, and we plan to rent a plane, load it with large chunks of ice, and then drop them off the

Southern California coast in order to, you know, cool down the Pacific, get rid of this El Niño thing, and get our weather back to normal. You know, it'll be nothing more than like mixing a big salty piña colada. So, what do you say? Are we good? Are we cool?"

Miraculously, we got the permit.

So Richard Beebe and I made plans to drop thousands of blocks of ice just off the coast of Long Beach, Seal Beach, and Newport Beach. We were gonna ice this terrible weather once and for all!

Beebe (left) and I prepare for our showdown with El Niño, along with our intrepid pilot. I think her name was Amelia something-or-other...

When the Saturday morning arrived, thousands of listeners, including my own son Mike, lined the shore to watch as we ordered up a *Pacific on the Rocks*.

As every hay-bale-sized cube hit the water with an orca-diving splash, Richard and I could hear the roar of the crowd over the engine of our small rented plane.

And I think their exuberance and appreciation was rewarded! I base that on the fact that we—and California—are indeed still here!

Also, among the dirty laundry list of environmental, social, and personal calamities blamed on El Niño was "a bubonic plague outbreak in Southern California rodents." *That* quickly subsided, but I really think we had a lot to do with cleaning up those rancid rats, too!

Elvis: Hello, baby.

Dave: Oh, ladies and gentlemen, I'm sooo happy to hear from Elvis, calling all the way from heaven!

Elvis: That's right, baby—Graceland North. How you doin', son?

Dave: I'm doing so well, Elvis. Everybody feels so much happier and they have a warmer feeling when they hear your voice on the air.

Elvis: Well, that's global warming, baby. That ain't me!

Barracks and Buicks in Arcadia

November 1983.

In the fall of '83, Pasadena's Rose Bowl became the only venue west of the Mississippi to host the annual Army-Navy game. The city paid for the travel expenses of all the students and supporters of both the U.S. Naval Academy and the U.S. Military Academy—9,437 in all. The reason for the switch from the normal game site of Philadelphia's John F. Kennedy Stadium was to honor, for once, the large number of military installations and servicemen and women on the West Coast, along with many retired military personnel.

Being such a part of Pasadena, KRLA decided to have local listeners open up their homes to the cadets, saving the community money for their lodging. In addition, the station's Buick dealership sponsor had several "Olympic Edition" Buicks left in its inventory, and we suggested that they make them available to the Army and Navy cadets so they could have their own transportation.

Jeanette and I had our big five-bedroom home in Arcadia, so we brought in *two* cadets, Ted Wilson and Herb Washington. Both would become officers. What great kids!

We even got one of those Buick Olympic Editions to keep at our house the entire time they were with us.

It was a great promotion for Pasadena, KRLA, Buick, and everyone who had a hand in sponsoring the whole thing.

And, oh yes, Navy won the game, 42–13.

Offering housing and Buicks to cadets was a victorious tactical maneuver for KRLA, its sponsors, and my family! Above, our kids Brian and Lisa show support for cadets Ted Wilson (second from left) and Herb Washington who shared our home.

Drivin' in Circles

Another of our free-wheeling promotions was the giveaway of a new Ford Mustang with KRLA call letters painted all over it. And like that little Suzuki back in the sixties, I got to drive it! (I guess I had come up in the world—I was now rolling on four wheels instead of two and I didn't ever have to push the Mustang to start it!)

Anyway, listeners would try and find the car's location through secret and cryptic clues given on the air! If they found it, then they had to try to guess the number of call letters stenciled, painted, written, and stuck to it. It was the old "jelly beans in a jar" thing but with a new, custom-wheeled spin put on it. Whoever came closest to guessing the number of "KRLA's" on the 'Stang would win it!

Well, one gal got especially analytical, and she outsmarted us. She used the clues to find the car not just once, but several times. Each

I was riding both high *and* low at KRLA this time!

time, she took pictures all around the Mustang, got them developed, and then went home and counted!

She won it, too; coming within just a couple of numbers of the exact count!

Pigskin Prognostication

January 1984.

More football!

Super Bowl XVIII.

The Los Angeles Raiders vs. the Washington Redskins.

Working with Richard Beebe and me in the mornings was KRLA's sports director—a Southern California Sportscasters Hall of Fame guy who would be in the winning corner of L.A. radio forever: Rich Marotta. At the time, AM 1110 was the broadcast home for all the Los Angeles Raiders games and Rich was the color commentator.

In the 1983 season, the Raiders went 12-4, won the AFC, and were headed to Super Bowl XVIII in Tampa—so were Beebe, Marotta, and Hull!

KRLA management knew it would be risky. *We* knew it would be risky! It would be like an expansion of all the sanitarium scenes in *A Day at the Races.*

Beebe, Marotta, and Hull reporting...

One night, we recorded our footsteps walking over cobblestones, as we searched for someone with prognosticating prominence who could predict the outcome of the big game. We found a small, dingy fortune teller's shop with a sign in the window:

Everything Will Be Revealed If You Just Ask

Everything?

Excellent!

And all we have to do is ask?

Heck, let's ask!

We were greeted inside by a six-year-old boy.

"My mother will be right out," he told us quietly.

We saw Madame *Mom* look out at us from behind a curtain. She saw all the microphones and recording equipment, and it really spooked her. And *we* figured that *she* figured we might be cops.

Within the shadows of the tapestry, she called for her son.

They conferred in whispers.

When the boy emerged from behind the Shroud of Tampa, he told us that his mom was "not available for any readings tonight."

We had come this far and we needed *something*, so we asked the little kid, "Well, who do *you* think is going to win the Super Bowl?"

It wasn't exactly a séance-smooth, ghostly-gritty response, but it was effective. He screamed out, "D-A-A-A-A RAIDERS!!"

Wow!

"D-A-A-A-A RAIDERS!" was now our official battle cry for the remainder of our Florida stay.

And *"D-A-A-A-A RAIDERS!"* killed the Redskins, 38–9.

The slaughter and its blood-and-guts aftermath was just the kind of thing to come out of a prediction from a precocious "Chucky" kinda kid in a creepy back-alley little shop of horrors!

Because of the severity of the pigskin carnage, Super Bowl XVIII was from then on known as "Black Sunday"!

"D-A-A-A-A RAIDERS!"

Dave Hull, Please Don't Pick Us to Win!!

by Rich Marotta

Prior to the 1983 National Football League season, the Los Angeles Raiders decided to move their radio broadcasts from All-News KNX to KRLA. As Sports Director at KNX, I was teamed up with the legendary Bill King on the Raiders broadcasts, as color commentator. I was now given the opportunity to become the morning drive sportscaster at KRLA and continue on the Raiders games. I would be part of the morning team of famed DJ Dave Hull and newsman Richard Beebe. I jumped on it!

Keep in mind, I had only worked for news and talk stations prior to this, so it was to be quite an adjustment. I found out right away.

On my first morning at KRLA, I walked into the Pasadena studio. The Hullabalooer jumped up and screamed on the air: "*That's* what a Rich Marotta looks like?!" and then he burst out laughing. I saw my career flash before my eyes.

But I soon discovered just how much fun Dave could add to my own coverage of sports. He'd throw in his own goofy ideas, and soon I was getting off lines not usually associated with traditional sportscasts. Richard Beebe joined in, and my one-minute sportscasts became five-minute chuckle-fests. (Richard is also one of the funniest individuals I have ever met, ironic in that he was a newsman!)

Dave became more and more involved in the Raiders as the season wore on. He would go out to the games in his silver and black Raiders windbreaker and would tailgate beforehand, sometimes with my family. Then, having attended the game, Dave would throw in his own comments the following morning.

The Raiders had a tremendous team. They had a few rough moments and defeats early in the season though. And those losses seemingly coincided with our new Friday morning sports feature: "Pigskin Picks, Predictions, and Prognostications." Hull, Beebe, and I would each pick three games, the last of which would always be that week's Raiders game.

Dave was an uncannily bad predictor of games. It was unbelievable, but hilarious. He couldn't get *one* right.

"Hey, Rich," Raiders Coach Tom Flores called out to me at his weekly press luncheon, following a Raiders defeat, "tell your partner in the morning to stop predicting us to win!"

That was just the start.

Dave and I attended a boxing match in Reseda, where ring announcer Bill Caplan introduced him to the crowd at the arena. "He's been killing us and the Raiders all season long with his terrible predictions...Daaaave Hull!!"

Raiders linebacker Rod Martin, at the end of one of my interviews, made the memorable plea: "Dave Hull, please don't pick us to win this week!"

That sound bite became part of the regular weekly intro to our Pigskin Picks segment.

Raiders defensive lineman Lyle Alzado, one of the fiercest players in the NFL, was more to the point. Alzado's threats to Dave included: "If you pick us to win, I'll rip your lips off" and my favorite, "Hullabalooer, if you pick us, I'll tear off your head and spit down at your breakfast!"

So it was with all that as a backdrop that Dave, Richard, and I bravely headed to Tampa, Florida, when the Raiders made it to Super Bowl XVIII. We broadcast the morning show live from Tampa that week, during which we would play tapes gathered from the night before when we'd go out on the town in search of the "seamy side of Super Bowl city."

Dave wasn't exactly embraced by Tampa.

When we went to the airport in search of a plane that was supposedly bringing in a group of hookers, an official tourist-welcoming band refused to play anymore after Dave announced what we were doing there.

Barry Manilow's agent hung up on Dave when he inquired about a rumor that Manilow was going to lip-synch the national anthem.

A bar proprietor made it clear that Dave would be welcome to leave when he bothered a patron he was *sure* was legendary running back Jim Brown.

Driving through the city after losing huge dollars at the jai-alai fronton, Dave and I spied a gas station that had on its marquee: "Welcome Home Dave Stalls"—a salute to the Raiders linebacker who was returning to his hometown. Dave pulled in to interview a guy filling up his gas tank. He whipped out his tape recorder and introduced himself. The dude responded: "Dave Hull? The guy who makes the bad predictions? You better get outta here. We want the Raiders to win!"

The final insult: After we went to see that palm reader, whose name was Madame Lee, not only did Mrs. Lee throw us out of her parlor, but after her little boy made his "*D-A-A-A-A RAIDERS*" declaration, he handed Dave a note.

Beebe read the note on the air next morning. It said:

> *Don't ever come back here again.*
> *(Signed) Mr. Lee.*

"Turn That Guy Off!"

WHEN WILL THEY EVER LEARN?

KHJ, NBC-TV, KRLA (yet again!), KRTH, KFQD: 1985–1995

February 1985.

A new movie was about to be released: *Into the Night* starring Jeff Goldblum, Michelle Pfeiffer, and Dan Aykroyd. With these Hollywood top bananas and a soundtrack featuring tunes from B.B. King, Marvin Gaye, and the Four Tops, the flick figured to be a biggie.

During its filming, the producers called Penny Biondi and asked if KRLA would provide some on-air audio for one of the opening scenes of the picture.

Certainly!

The Setting: Cars in gridlock on a Southern California freeway. The Action: A look into several cars; the radio station each commuter is listening to is heard. We hear IDs and short clips from KABC and the Ken & Bob Company...we look into a car playing a sad country tune from KLAC as a female driver cries her little eyes out...then Rick Dees on KIIS...then KOST 103...on to a traffic report from Commander Chuck Street...

But then *I* was right there in the car with Goldblum and Aykroyd.

"This is the Dave Hull program on KRLA! But we are going to interrupt the show now for this special announcement—"

Goldblum hits the off button.

"Don't you wanna hear what happened?" Aykroyd asks.

"No, not really..." Goldblum replies.

It was another hefty plug for 1110, and this time it didn't involve crashing an aircraft—it just required my being cut off mid-sentence by a big movie star.

Being cut off by a movie star wasn't so bad, but unbeknownst to me, I was about to be cut off *completely*!

Lunch and Less, for Me and Mucho

March 1985.

Our growing listener popularity had not been seen in Los Angeles AM radio for years, and it caught the attention of Greater Media, Inc.—a New Jersey radio chain that six years earlier had purchased the L.A. FM outlet KHTZ.

Calling attention to something is not always a good thing.

Greater Media, Inc., now wanted KRLA.

And they got it.

It didn't take long for my phone to ring after the purchase-paperwork had been signed.

It was the new station consultant.

"Please have lunch with me," he said.

I met him at a fine Hollywood restaurant. We sat down and ordered. Along with lunch came small talk—where the industry might be headed, all things radio, et cetera, et cetera...

Then we got down to business.

He told me that Greater Media expected to move the KRLA studios out of Pasadena and onto Wilshire Boulevard in Los Angeles. Right away, I knew where things were going for me. Just the move would mean rising a lot earlier each morning for the extra hour of commute time.

He also told me that a thirty-six percent cut in salary "would be necessary" for me to continue working on the air.

I told him that this suggestion was "totally unacceptable."

At that point in the elegant lunch, neither of us was happy. The chateaubriand was getting cold and tough, and the asparagus tarragon was wilting under our emotional cloud.

The consultant's attitude was going south, and unlike the steak, he was steaming! His fine linen napkin hit the floor as he simply stood up and left. I watched him walk over to another table full of businessmen and join *them*!

I looked back down at my asparagus. It may have been a little less "cheerfully green" than when it left the kitchen, but it *was* part of an expensive paid-for lunch!

Twenty-minutes later, I finished my meal—alone—gave a quick and abrupt wave to the group seated across the room, and got in my car and left.

On March 1st, Greater Media hired Bob Hudson as my replacement. I, along with afternoon jock Mucho Morales, was fired.

While this KRLA firing was not as tragic as the first, a few die-hard fans revisted another oldie but goodie with a mock cry-in!

Back to "Boss" Basics

Summer 1985.

The key to "Car Radio 93/KHJ" had been turned a year earlier in 1984. Bill Drake had left back in '73, and since then, KHJ had gone through its own years of up-and-down changes (even three years as a country station with their *"We All Grew Up to Be Cowboys"* tag). This new "Car Radio" format was revving up to bring back some of the high-gear glory of the past. Its renewal engine was being fired up under the program directorships of Rick Scarry, Phil Hall, and consultant Walt Sabo.

It was a good team, but it was Rick who meant so much to me.

Rick had been a fan of mine as a young teenager, when I worked at WTVN in Columbus. Just a kid, really, he would travel to nearly every one of my dances and sock hops to help me set up my equipment.

During the winter in Ohio, most public swimming pools would be drained of water and closed. (Few people like swimming in ice water, and in all honesty, *no one* looks fashionably good in blue skin—especially in a bikini or Speedos!) But when I was at WTVN, someone got the brilliant idea that they could put down wood flooring *at the bottom of the pool*, promote some hops, and sell tickets to teenagers, who were more than willing to come out in the cold weather and dance "three to twelve feet" below the surface.

The idea was a good one. It worked, and the setup had a great meteorological benefit: most of the chilling winds would blow across the top of the pool, not affecting the hot teens boppin' below.

Rick helped carry all my heavy sound equipment and he never complained. He was so into the radio world. He just wanted to be close to the action.

And he wound up *very* close to it—very much *into* it.

When he became PD at KHJ, he called and asked if I would be interested in not only joining their nostalgic Car Radio oldies format, but also in working the morning show with a "young, talented traffic reporter" by the name of Mark Denis. KHJ was really pushing the old, literal car-radio theme. Traffic reports were a big part of that, and Denis was one of the best at it.

DAVE HULL

I had actually worked with Mark earlier at KFI. He was great then, and he had gotten better through the years. When I heard we would be teamed together in this latest KHJ model, I opened the driver's door and jumped right in.

We made another great team. The format worked, and we worked. It was another example of the power and longevity of the era. It was proven over and over: when all else fails, and this new format and that new format is tried and falls flat, go back to the "boss" basics. Go back to the music that everyone loves—and always *will* love. Go back to the personalities who helped aesthetically raise one of the most expressive generations that ever lived.

But, as Peter, Paul and Mary asked back in 1962, *"When will they ever learn...?"*

On the evening of January 31, 1986, our evening jock, Dave Sebastian Williams, had one of those one-time-only, you'll-never-hear-this-again shows. He was joined in the studio by Robert W. Morgan. Many personalities from the Boss Radio days of AM 930 phoned in: "Machine Gun" Kelly, Bobby Ocean, Jimmy Rabbit, and Boss Radio–era PD Ron Jacobs.

It was a farewell broadcast.

The songs played were pure gold—and so were the memories, emotions, and sentiments.

I had been through this before, of course, and I always felt that same way—*"When will they ever learn...?"*

But it was all part of that ever-change in radio and just another fragile ride on that bubble.

At the stroke of midnight, right after "Louie, Louie" and "Rock Around the Clock," KHJ changed its call letters to KRTH-AM to match those of its FM sister station, KRTH-FM (both owned by RKO), and began spinning in a format called "Smokin' Oldies" that featured "hits of the first ten years of rock and roll." Those were ten great years, sure; but they were pre-Beatles and a ton of tuneage was left off of the playlist—ignoring wave upon wave of the *Good Vibrations* that got the L.A.–radio generation *Groovin'* and made *Daydream Believers* out of us all.

I was one of twenty-three employees of KHJ and KRTH-FM to be erased that day, along with the pioneer-priceless three-letter call of KHJ at 930 kHz.

In a January 1986 *Los Angeles Times* article, fired KRTH-FM DJ Rick Scott was quoted: *"It's the end of an era, man; half of Los Angeles grew up with Boss Radio."*

My partner, Mark Denis, headed back to KFI and traveled a long road with them as their traffic guy.

On April 29, 2000, Mark succumbed to cancer at the age of fifty-nine. Shortly after his death, California's Route 55/Route 91 interchange was named the "Mark Denis Melbourne Memorial Interchange." It's a fitting tribute to Mark, and really, a commentary on us all; this business is a road that has no final destination. You can ride in circles on a roundabout interchange forever—get off here, get right back on there. In radio, we so often wind up right back to where we started, where we made an impact, where we completely bombed, or where we enjoyed ourselves the most.

Oh, we may finally sign off for one last time, but even then, we have people out there who remember us. People whose lives we have been blessed enough to touch and entertain and inform. Some of us are even so fortunate as to have our voices—our very essences—recorded, reproduced, and turned loose forever on that never-ending road.

Matchmaker, Matchmaker...

September 1987.

Lovelines: The Movie may not have made it to the silver screen back in '78, but the shining effect of *Lovelines*—and the first-blush bud from which it blossomed, *Dial-A-Date*—still attracted a lot of passion. Nine years after our try at an Oscar for Floyd, Ling-Su, and the rest of the bunch, a bright young media entrepreneur, Gary Kleinman, approached me. He had an amour-loaded spin-off idea to at least take my daffy dating concept to the *small* screen.

Gary's idea became *Matchmaker:* a game show long on love and really darn funny!

I was the host—the Matchmaker!

Cue opening theme music...

Six hopeful singles are in separate "booths" on the back portion of the stage.

I'm blindfolded (we'll get to just *why* and *how* in a minute!) as I'm led onstage by a beautiful woman. (One of the women proved to be our greatest spin-off success: the *lovely and talented Miss Lisa Guerrero!* Lisa would go on to become the national sideline sportscaster for *Monday Night Football* on ABC. And we had another Lisa, too—my own gorgeous daughter, Lisa Hull!)

With my back to the contestants, one of the beauties would help me uncover my eyes—removing that night's blindfold, which had been carefully selected from my full formal wardrobe of what were essentially "designer sleep masks"!

I would put on my glasses (though I'd tell the audience they might want to leave theirs *off,* because—as opposed to my hostess— I look better "fuzzy"!), then I would address everyone—explaining the enchanting experience we were all about to go through.

Dave: There they are behind me! The six people hand-picked for this encounter!

Two of them will walk out of here on the road to romance.

> Dave: Now, I can't see any of them, and they can't see each other. And that's really important because I believe anybody can make a match by looking at people. But love goes much deeper than that.
>
> I'll probe their psyches, explore their minds, and come up with the two people best suited for each other.
>
> You people at home, you in our studio audience—you can hear and see all. Lucky you!
>
> After this is all over, though, I'm sure you will still agree with me. Because I am the Matchmaker!

Next, the contestants—three guys and three girls—would all let us know who *they* were.

> Contestant 1: Hi, my name is Mark. I love the water and I'm looking for a woman to go off the deep end with.

Contestant 2: Hello, my name is Alexia and I'm looking for the perfect American man—because I'm European!

Contestant 3: Hello, my name is David. I'm a mechanic and I'm looking for a woman to tinker with...

The tittering laughter would start. But *then* I would begin my "probing" and "exploring"!

Dave: Do you like skinny-dipping?

Have you ever chased an ambulance or a police car to see what was going on?

Has your floating chair ever sunk into the deep end of the pool, thus losing a six-pack?

> **Dave:** Let me ask you all this: In the *San Francisco Chronicle* and *Examiner* recently, there were five hundred and two terms of endearment listed. Some of them were: "muffin," "snookums," "sugar bear," sweetie," and "trigger"—"trigger"???!!! Oh well, anyway—what is YOUR little romantic saying you have for guys?

From here, I would eliminate two contestants, having decided on a male or female "romantic lead." Then I'd continue questioning their three potential matches to pare things down.

> **Dave:** Have you ever thought of leaving your body to science?...You haven't gone door to door showing people samples or anything, have you?

I'd also make them answer questions while performing timed silly tasks.

Dave (to the final male contestants): Mark and David, to your immediate right, you should find your "Matchmaker sewing basket" containing a shirt, a giant button, a pin cushion, and a pre-threaded needle. Do you have all the ingredients, there?

Mark and David (less-than-enthused): Uh-huh.

Dave (to the "romantic lead"): I'm gonna find you a man that knows what he's doing—a guy who's "domesticated."

Dave: While you're doing your button, Mark, let me ask you a question...

Mark (a wavy-haired surfer dude, studiously sewing, not looking up): Yeah, Dave?

Dave: Have you ever made an obscene phone call? GO RIGHT ON DOING YOUR BUTTON, PLEASE...

And I'd decide from there!

The two perfect-for-each-other winners I'd matched would then compete for a nice weekend spin to places like San Diego, Vegas, and Mexico. And of course they'd live happily ever after.

It was truly the science of love!

Because I am the Matchmaker!

So the show concept was witty, hilarious, and perfect. But we needed to get it out there—on the air! We needed some action—and some *clout*.

Kleinman personally convinced a serious moneyman, Jim Pollard, to join us. Together, we became the newest entry into media-moguldom: Kleinman-Pollard-Hull.

Gary advanced the concept to Four Star Productions—they were actually *looking* for a television game show. And they were no minor-leaguers. Four Star Productions had been operating since 1952, formed by Dick Powell, David Niven, Ida Lupino, and Charles Boyer. They had "cred"!

And they already had hits with early TV classics like *The Rifleman; Wanted: Dead or Alive; Zane Grey Theater; Richard Diamond, Private Detective; The Detectives Starring Robert Taylor; Burke's Law; The Rogues;* and *The Big Valley.*

Gary sold them on *Matchmaker* and Four Star came aboard to coproduce the project with us. Gary then headed to Orbis Communications in New York and persuaded them to distribute the show.

Orbis would later syndicate the Sphinx–solid game show *Pyramid*—a show that featured Dick Clark and (much, much later)

Donny Osmond among its hosts and my good friend June Lockhart as one of its celebrity contestants.

Like the day I was fired from KMPC, I was always in good company!

Any project must have commercial backing to be successful, so Kleinman singlehandedly brought Proctor and Gamble products into the mix.

It's hygienically reassuring to be working on the backs of Mr. Clean and Pampers.

Next, Gary took the old retail theory to heart—*location, location, location!*—and went to work on getting us the perfect time slot.

Find me a find. Catch me a catch...

Gary felt that NBC's independently-owned-and-operated stations were in need of a nightly entertainment boost following their local *News at 11:00,* so off he went to their corporate offices and pitched *Matchmaker* to their programming division. Having NBC on board meant nearly one hundred independents nationwide looked seriously at the show.

It worked!

Matchmaker was on the air across the country.

We had a great time!

And Gary won his pick for a winning time slot—*Matchmaker* aired right after the true wee-hours "entertainment boost," *Late Night with David Letterman.*

Maybe it was the "graveyard shift" airtime, or maybe it was just *me,* but the show was such an "underground hit" that it was featured in *Rolling Stone* magazine's annual Hot List of cool and hip media stuff.

HOT JUNK: 'Matchmaker' Dave Hull started out as a disc jockey. Then he realized his true talent: matchmaking. Now he is the host and coproducer of the best worst show on TV, *Matchmaker*. In what amounts to a sort of low(er)-rent *Love Connection–Dating Game,* Hull pairs off a couple without ever looking at them—just by asking trenchant questions.

HOT JUNK : 'Matchmaker' Dave Hull started out as a disc jockey. Then he realized his true talent: matchmaking. Now he is the host and coproducer of the best worst show on TV, *Matchmaker*. In what amounts to a sort of low(er)-rent *Love Connection-Dating Game*, Hull pairs off a couple without ever looking at them – just by asking trenchant questions. "I have my little tricks," he says. "Women are more sincere than men. If you ask them what room they like to make love in the most, they'll tell you straight out, 'The bathroom.' But men hedge. Mostly it's the men who come off as dolts."

DENISE SFRAGA

"I have my little tricks," he says. "Women are more sincere than men. If you ask them what room they like to make love in the most, they'll tell you straight out, 'The bathroom.' But men hedge. Mostly it's the men who come off as dolts."

—*Rolling Stone,* May 19, 1988

Matchmaker's biggest ratings occurred, though, on shaky ground—during an overnight aftershock of the Los Angeles County Whittier Narrows earthquake in early October 1987. The initial quake and its aftershocks resulted in several deaths and caused at least $215 million in damage to over 10,500 residential and business structures.

One of those aftershocks woke up *most* of the jumpy L.A. area residents. Most of *them* immediately turned on their television sets to get some news and calm their nerves.

Most of *them* tuned to NBC.

And *all* of *them* saw *me*!

Matchmaker had just started, and there I was, hooking up singles—a *Whole Lotta Shakin' Goin' On* of a very different kind. But we got the highest overnight ratings in the program's history.

Matchmaker lasted through a run of 130 half-hour episodes; it spent one year in first run and a second year in rerun. Not quite the five years and 168 episodes of Four Star's *The Rifleman* or the near five decades of *Jeopardy*, but, you know what, *Who cares?!* The little company of Kleinman-Pollard-Hull had made it to the "big time"— at least for a while. And that's better than many high-priced comedy game-show formats that collapse even before the first thirteen weeks are up.

After the show was off the air, I received a call from Walt Disney Studios seeking a recommendation for a young man who was looking for employment with them—Gary Kleinman.

"He's great," I told the woman in Human Resources, "but are you saying Gary Kleinman's *available*?! Please give me his number— I want him back here working with *us*!"

She quickly thanked me and immediately hung up.

A few days later, I learned that Gary had been hired at Disney. He spent twenty-three years as an executive of the Walt Disney Studios in Burbank—mainly in production and technology, most recently as Vice President of New Media Technology.

In 2010 Gary founded Innovation Organization, LLC, and is the company's President and CEO. The company operates www.FirstRun.tv network, which produces "innovative entertainment content for television, the Internet, and emerging mobile media channels"—and still lovingly mentions *Matchmaker* and me in the history of what Gary has accomplished.

A Hull Lull

1986 to 1992.

Six years.

Six years out of radio.

I had enjoyed the *Matchmaker* experience, but the schedule had been tough; so tough that it cut short the teaching of my commercial classes. With seven or eight shows taped on Fridays through Sundays and the logistical planning for all of that each week, there just wasn't any more time for "Professor Hullabaloo" and the LAB classes.

I had to give them up.

Now they were gone and so was *Matchmaker.* Things were beginning to feel like they did back in the late seventies—I missed radio. But, hey, I was now in the easy-breezy world of high-time real estate!

New Realtors

Former DJ Dave Hull joins Merrill Lynch

By BRIAN HOLGUIN

Two new sales associates where recently added to the La Canada branch of Merrill Lynch and three were welcomed aboard at MacGregor Realty in Glendale.

Merrill Lynch in La Canada announced that Dave Hull has joined their sales force. A radio air personality for nearly 30 years and host of the TV show "Matchmaker," Hull enjoys people and really looks forward to being of service to clients in the Foothill area.

He is a resident of La Canada and President of the California Football Officials Assocation. This multi-talented man is very enthusiastic about his new association with Merrill Lynch.

DAVE HULL

Move-in condition!

Motivated seller!

Handyman special!

Just Needs TLC!

Walking Distance to Polliwog Park!

I was Donald Trump! On-the-edge negotiations, with briefcases full of cash passing hands every second! Ferraris and fortunes, penthouses and palaces! Sign on the dotted line and half the Hollywood Hills are yours!

But to be honest, I'd rather forget my real estate *career*—I hated those days!

Elvis: Ya know, I saw The Boss the other day.

Dave: Ooohhh...your boss up there, of course, is GOD!!

Elvis: That's right, baby! I mean I see him all the time; the Man is everywhere—you can't help but run into him, y'know what I'm sayin'? However, we do have what we call semi-annual employee performance meetings.

Dave: Oh, wow. So it's a lot like real estate!

I still had my weekends with a white hat and whistle, but again, *I missed radio!*

Vacant and Ready!

Eleven-Ten, Take 3

April 1992.

After a couple years of failing ratings, KRLA decided that they just *may* have made a mistake in letting me go. The hint may have been that they never got even close to the same ratings level as before I left.

The phone rings.

"Baby, I Need Your Lovin'…"

I'm sure you do!

I returned for a *third time* to morning drive hours—at the same salary I had made before I left. I was back with Richard Beebe and his news reports. By now the KRLA studios were indeed on Wilshire Boulevard in Los Angeles, and the Hulls were indeed in Pine Mountain, at the top of the Grapevine.

Commuting was about as practical as planning daily lunches in Bombay; so I started staying at the Holiday Inn in Burbank during the week.

After nearly six years of being off the radio air, my return certainly garnered some attention.

This one afternoon, I was in my room doing a phone interview about my bounce-back to KRLA, when I was interrupted by a knock at my door.

Room service…

I apologized to the reporter on the phone, explaining that my tasty gazpacho soup lunch had just arrived.

"Okay," I told the media guy when I got back on the phone, "we can talk as long as we want now. One thing about gazpacho—you never have to worry about it getting cold!"

12 GRAPEVINE, June 1992

KRLA legend returns
by David Schwartz

Dave Hull

LOS ANGELES — One of the most popular KRLA personalities of the '60s has returned to host the morning show on KRLA. He was first heard on KRLA from June 1963 to January 1969 and again from November 1981 to March 1985.

During his initial stint, he became known as the "fifth Beatle," entertaining listeners with his inside Beatles gossip. He was a stowaway on a Beatles charter flight during which he interviewed the Fab Four.

Hull, born in the shadow of KRLA in Alhambra on Jan. 20, 1934, graduated from Alhambra High, class of 1952.

While serving in the Air Force in Roswell, N.M., he walked into a radio station and inquired about an on-the-air position. As luck would have it, someone had just transferred out and he was given a shift that began that night playing classical music.

He bounced from stations in New Mexico to Dayton, Ohio, to Detroit to Columbus, Ohio. On June 18, 1963, it was time for Hull to come home to California and begin his career at KRLA.

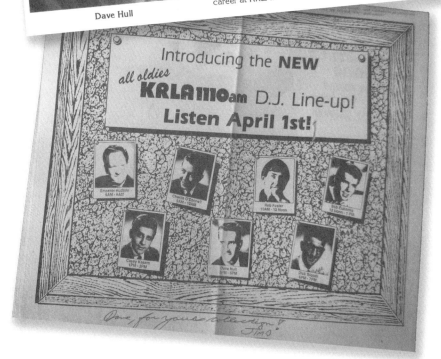

Third time's the charm: My *re*-return to KRLA brought back memories (and promo photos!) from my first time around!

"Hull-o...Elvis?"

I was back on Eleven-Ten in the morning shift—six to ten a.m.

And, yes, the trip-wire team of Ousley and Solari was still laying audio landmines. But the voice-variety of Jim Roope now officially joined in, with its own *Kid Galahad*–style punch.

I had met Jim *whilst* "professoring" at the Cable Radio Network.

Jim *was* Ross Perot—his imitations of the big-eared billionaire prez candidate were *rich*.

But he was *really* a *Devil in Disguise* with his Elvis impersonations—the best I've ever heard. I needed *him* to get my show *All Shook Up*!

It didn't take listeners long to have a *Burnin' Love* for our "Elvis Calling from Heaven" routine.

Jim—I'm sorry, *Elvis*—would call into the station directly from "Graceland North"; and naturally all of the film, comedy, and singing stars were up there with him.

He would tell us how they were all getting along, what they were doing under their "present circumstances," and even talk about what they ate on weekends while dining at their favorite raptured-up-restaurants ("We Never Close!").

Dave: Hello!

Elvis: Hello, baby.

Dave: Oh, Elvis! How are you?

Elvis: Doing just fine, baby. I just been real busy!...
          Yesterday I had lunch with Janis Joplin, Mama Cass,
          John Lennon, Jimi Hendrix, Otis Redding, Buddy Holly,
          the Big Bopper, Ritchie Valens. Then I saw Marvin Gaye...
          Bobby Darin...Roger Miller...Jim Morrison...Tammi Terrell...
          Roy Hamilton...Jackie Wilson...Frankie Lymon...Jim Croce...
          Big Joe Turner at the club last night.

Dave: At the— Oh, you have a club up there?!

Elvis: Oh, it's a big club, baby! Hell, Sam Kinison played
          last night. It was wonderful.

Dave: Well, what have you got planned for today?!

Elvis: Today, I got big lunch goin' with Mary Wells, Clyde
          McPhatter, David Ruffin, Bill Haley, Roy Orbison, Del
          Shannon, Sam Cooke, Karen Carpenter...

Dave: Wow!

> **Elvis:** ...Rick Nelson...
>
> **Dave:** Rick Nelson!
>
> **Elvis:** Rick and I are thinkin' about doing something together, baby!
>
> **Dave:** You're kidding! You mean the two of you are going to write something, or do a duet?
>
> **Elvis:** Tell me whatcha think: we're gonna do a duet of "Garden Party"...
>
> **Dave:** Uh-huh.
>
> **Elvis:** ...and then feed it to Michael Bolton in his sleep!

Listeners would call in with plenty of personal and provocative questions they wanted me to ask the King.

Are You Lonesome Tonight...?

Even my old "frenemy" Rona Barrett couldn't hold a votive candle to our insider scoops firsthand from heaven!

Elvis: KRLA and the Dave Hull Show are number one up here in heaven!

Dave: You're kidding me?!!

Elvis: No, we pipe it through all over the place, baby. Heck, everybody up here—you're playing their songs!

THURSDAY, JUNE 11, 1992 / **L.A. LIFE—3**

Only the uglies

Do you have a tie with a neat print in sequins, a hand-painted Elvis on black velvet or a tie with gawd-awful designs on it?

Send it to Dave Hull.

Hull, the morning personality at radio station KRLA-AM (1110) is looking for the tackiest ties in town for his Father's Day tie exchange, and yours will do just fine.

Maybe you *can* teach an old dinosaur new tricks, but I was still up to my old stunts, too! (Heck, I'm still wearing some of these ties!)

KRLA's ratings soared higher than Elvis' Pearly Gates penthouse. But there was always that bubble...

In 1994, KRLA management felt that an "Urban Oldies" format would be a lot better than the unholy trinity of the solid music we were playing, Elvis from heaven, and *me*.

Urban Oldies???

For the last time, I was gone from KRLA.

By 1998, music would not be heard at all on the former-classic-innovating-pioneering giant that once was KRLA. Political all-talk, featuring many "cast-offs" from KABC, such as Michael Jackson and Ken Minyard, was now heard as a dying echo in the Dream-House.

It would get worse.

In 2000, KRLA was sold to the Disney Corporation.

Next came all-*sports*-talk courtesy of ESPN via Disney, and KRLA officially and legally became KSPN, tossing away the KRLA call like dumping a Van Gogh in the Goodwill bin.

On New Year's Day 2001, the KRLA call would be "picked up" by KIEV–AM 870. Hmmm...the "Eight-Seventy Men"? It just didn't have that ring to it.

Meanwhile, sports talk didn't work on AM 1110 so the frequency got yet a new call, KDIS, and Disney's kids' programming that had been being heard on AM 710 (the old KMPC) was switched to 1110 in 2003—from the Beatles and the Stones in the heydays, to Miley Cyrus and the Jonas Brothers in the gray-days.

When will they ever learn...?

Bless Me, Father Hullabaloo

1994.

Robert W. Morgan asked me to fill in for him at KRTH while he was on vacation one year.

Robert W. and I had our battle royals in the ratings department when we were on different teams, but he had brought me into KMPC where I had some of my biggest successes with *Lovelines.*

And now, after all our years separate/together in the L.A.-radio jingle-jungle, he asked me to sub for him on what was now the biggest oldies station in the Southland.

Sure!

I brought my Hullabaloo to KRTH, and I had so much fun there for three weeks.

First of all, when I sat down in that chair at KRTH—*"K-Earth 101"*—I decided to become something that no other disc jockey had become on L.A. radio. Taking my divine inspiration from J.J. Solari's Father Moriarty, *I* was now Father Hullabaloo.

"And now, for the next few moments, Father Hullabaloo will listen to your confession. Here are the numbers to call."

Those lines would light up like the burning bush.

It was especially big with men.

"Oh, Father, bless me. I have sinned."

"And what have you done, my son?"

"...and then I went outside her house, and I looked through her window..."

"My son, you turned into a Peeping Tom?"

"Yes, Father Hullabaloo, I have sinned..."

And then, yep, Ousley and Solari got involved. They would go nuts. J.J.'s Irishman, the foundation for the original Father Moriarty, was now a *drunken* Irishman—a drunken Irishman who had more to tell you than you deserved to hear.

And the engineers loved it. They'd put a little echo on it: *Father Hullabaloo...Hullabaloo...Hullabaloo...*

"Bless me, Father, for I have sinned."

"How long has it been since your last confession?"

"Ooooo boy, Father, I'd say twenty-six...maybe thirty years..."

"WOW! You must have some whoppers, my son!"

And they did! Their soul-cleansing confessions created a Second-Coming-sized stir!

But...*for some reason,* I was never invited back.

I guess we all had *too* much fun while Morgan was gone!

And it was the *second to the last time* I was ever on the air in Los Angeles radio.

Dave: Ladies and gentlemen, on the Dave Hull Show this morning, this is Elvis calling from heaven!

Dave (to Elvis): You're dead!

Elvis: Oh, son, I'm deader than K-Earth, baby!

Hull's Hogwash

1995.

Anchorage, Alaska's KFQD–AM 750 was the first radio station in the "Last Frontier," signing on the air May 17, 1924, just fifty-seven years after the territory was purchased from Russia for two cents an acre; thirty-five years before it became a state.

The station is a 50,000-watt screamer near the top of the world. It has been heard throughout all of Alaska and Canada, and even some parts of Asia. KFQD was once one of the best full-service radio stations in the world. (Excuse the clinical, suit-and-tie scholarly definition, but a "full-service" format officially means "music, news, and sports featuring intelligent, mature personalities who can capture and maintain an adult audience.")

In 1995, KFQD needed some help.

They needed someone to run things.

Chester Coleman, a personal agent who also helped coordinate the purchase and sale of hundreds of radio stations nationwide, approached me about representing me after my days in L.A. radio seemed to have been given the Last Rites by Father Hullabaloo in the KRTH confessional.

KFQD was on his agenda.

Chester and I had worked together during my early days at KRLA, and everyone who knew him was impressed with his knowledge and generosity.

Coleman and I went *North to Alaska* to meet with the KFQD owners. After listening to their already-established format for a few days, I was convinced that, with the station's power and heritage, the format should remain significantly the same, with a few minor adjustments. I presented them with unbelievably brilliant and insightful suggestions on how to improve the station's performance and increase their ratings. I gave them a few cost-saving ideas and suggested they increase the station's news commitment, introduce some "thought-provoking" monthly promotions, and most importantly, develop an emphasis on light adult hits twenty-four hours a day.

I loved their facilities and working conditions, but most striking was being surrounded by some of the most unbelievable natural beauty I had ever seen. The Charles S. Farnsworth Park back home in Altadena was nice—what with its cobblestone community building and all—but Anchorage's 5.6-million-acre Chugach National Forest—roughly the size of Massachusetts and Rhode Island combined—was pretty darn spiffy and, as the kids say, *awesome*!

Something else persuaded me to get serious about this wild, crazy, and so out-of-the-broadcast-box job. During our stay, hundreds of teenagers had come to Anchorage as participants in an Alaskan teen-conference. They were extremely polite and engaging to grown-ups, something I hadn't seen for decades in the more "evolved" end of the continent. *Mature* outsiders were invited into their conversations; they really wanted to listen to older adult feelings about things.

That said, I had other considerations to, well, *consider...*

Number one, it was cold up there!

The station management told me that cold wasn't the *real* problem my family would face; the most difficult adjustment would be getting used to almost full-time daylight hours in the summer months and full-time darkness during the winter (Sociological Note: According to scientists with lab coats and clipboards, "Many families *never* get used to that aspect of Alaskan living"!).

But the icy pluses outweighed the more-of-the-same-in-Los-Angeles negatives, and we struck a deal with KFQD.

Jeanette and I put our house on the market, and it sold in two days with a quick-fire thirty-day escrow. We were set. We could liquidate our holdings and move everything—furniture, cars, and all of our remaining belongings—by sea and land carriers to the Last Frontier.

We were happy, *Chester* was happy...but not *everyone* was happy.

Apparently, that radio bubble is even more shatter-prone the closer it gets to the North Pole.

A woman who worked for the station in middle management dug up a corporate memo from 1986 that prescribed the station owner's official hiring policy as: *Pioneer Broadcasting will always elevate from within.*

Always.

From within...

Then she brought in attorneys to back her up.

The broadcasting group began to think...*Not only is she right about the rules, but if we interview others already in the corporation, it will be far less expensive.* "Elevating from within" would eliminate the cost of our temporary housing and the shipping expenses for our cars and a full house of furniture by pricy cargo vessel.

And some from *within* wanted the station's format to evolve into all news/talk.

But I told Jeanette that *we* had a cause of action since *we had already sold our home and had no place to go*!

"If you ever sue any of your bosses," she replied, "you'll never be able to work with them again. You know how radio circles around!"

I had to admit, she was right.

We dropped the whole thing. And in some icy irony, the middle-management busybody didn't get the position either. Instead, she was "elevated" to run some stations in Butte, Montana. She lasted six months. I heard that she couldn't take the winters!

"Seward's Folly" was how the original 1867 purchase of Alaska was referred to by some. This entire KFQD debacle may have been "Hull's Hogwash."

But both provided such crossroads.

If Secretary of State William H. Seward hadn't done what he did, the U.S. could still be looking at 586,412 square miles of valuable Russian-Soviet resources and "strategery" just 700 miles above the continental United States.

If *our* Alaskan adventure hadn't blown up the way it did, well, who knows about *that* outcome either. If we had settled in with KFQD, we would have had to face another station sale and another sure-burst of the bubble. Within just three years, Pioneer Broadcasting and KFQD were purchased by Morris Communications, along with five other south-central Alaska stations, to form the Anchorage Media Group.

Morris Communications is big and powerful, and they have a reputation for "sweeping things clean" when they execute their takeovers. My guess is that we would have been in the dustpan along with everyone else—because KFQD indeed changed their format to all-talk. I also have a strong guess that they wouldn't have paid our expenses to get us back to the "lower forty-eight."

If Hull's Hogwash hadn't happened, Jeanette might be serving "Moons Over My Hammy" at the Anchorage Denny's and I might be in a black-and-white "wise guy" suit delivering pizzas for Mafia Mike's out on Spenard Road. All of that, instead of being back on the air in sunny Southern California for another fifteen years—here, where the days are bright and it's dark at night. Here, where all this *real* hullabaloo belongs!

Matching Up with Dave

By Gary Kleinman

Growing up in the Los Angeles area, I was a huge Dave Hull fan. I honestly can't put my finger on exactly what about Dave was so intriguing, but I was *compelled* to listen every day! Maybe it wasn't so much *what* Dave said, but *how* he said it. He just made me laugh.

Early in my career, I created a syndicated radio show called *Record Report.* I'm not sure Dave even remembers that he was my first choice as host for the series. I'd had the pleasure of first meeting him as we were developing the show. But for a reason I can't recall, Dave was not available to take the job (the hosts ended up being Robert W. Morgan and Charlie Tuna at various times). But I *knew* that Dave and I would work together someday because I sensed a strong creative chemistry.

When Dave moved to afternoons on KGBS, he began doing his *Dial-A-Date* segment. In his inimitable lunatic style (and I mean that in a good way!) Dave would frantically jump from phone line to phone line, asking crazy questions and trying to make a match. Some of his questions back then might make Howard Stern blush today—but never with out-and-out crudity! It was one of the wildest and funniest running segments I have *ever* heard on radio.

His *Lovelines* on KMPC continued the lovelorn lunacy.

It didn't take long for an epiphany to hit me. I was looking to make a transition from radio to television, and Dave's *Dial-A-Date* and *Lovelines* would translate into the perfect project. Not only was it unique and over-the-top entertaining, but I was a Dave Hull fan, and it was an opportunity to finally work with him.

The events that took place after my first call to Dave went so fast and furious that it's a bit of a blur now. But we got the show sold and on the air with a new title, *Matchmaker*. Here are some of the things I can recall twenty-five years later...

We wanted to keep the TV show's format and content as close to Dave's radio show as possible, because the formula *worked*. Instead of calling in on phone lines, single men and women were place in isolated booths. They couldn't see each other, nor could Dave see them! He had to make his match based only on asking his no-holds-barred questions and assessing the contestants' answers. As each show progressed, Dave blindly eliminated guys and/or girls he felt were incompatible, narrowing down to the final couple—at which time, Dave, and the contestants, got to see each other. The viewing audience, of course, could see and hear everything that was going on throughout.

Matchmaker would be a little risqué and push the limit of what was acceptable for television in the late 1980s. Fortunately, late-night syndicated programming was in demand and that was the perfect time slot.

Dave and I found out early that trying to describe the show in writing or just by talking about it resulted in blank stares! If you hadn't heard the show on the radio, it was too unimaginable. So to effectively get the idea across, we decided to produce our own pilots, keeping true to the off-the-wall concept. We rented a huge warehouse in Van Nuys, California, built the sets, recruited the contestants, and shot five episodes—not intended for air, but to demonstrate how this unorthodox game show format would work. And that did the trick. We got the show sold.

The show immediately fell into place except for a couple of things:

1) We were teamed up with some traditional, old school *game show* production folks. Before you knew it, some elements of *Matchmaker* smacked of *Let's Make A Deal,* complete with Samsonite luggage.

2) The sponsors, distributor, and stations were too conservative to allow us to produce the *real* show. It had to be cleaned up. Dave could not be provocative nor could his questions be titillating. No blowing up the losing contestants with dynamite (yes, that was in Dave's radio show and the original TV pilots!). Dave had to be *nice* to everyone—even the losers. I don't think *politically correct* was even a term in 1987, but that's what *Matchmaker* had to be. The show became watered down.

Regardless, Dave did an *amazing* job as a television game show host his first time at the podium. *Matchmaker* was way ahead of its time, and definitely hysterical. Especially the pilot episode where Dave came out as Cupid with a bow and arrow, wearing nothing but a diaper! (Sorry Dave, I couldn't resist including that tidbit!)

I look back on the *Matchmaker* days with Dave with great fondness.

One final interesting note...when *Matchmaker* debuted in 1987, *The Cosby Show* was at its height with a 34+ rating in primetime. The same year, in its late-late-night syndicated time slot, *Matchmaker*'s ratings were somewhere around a 1.0. Not quite good enough to warrant a second season in syndication, *back then*. If you look at television ratings *today*, for a regular series, you won't see anything close to the *Cosby* numbers, but you *will* see primetime shows on major cable networks that linger with ratings *lower* than 1.0. Who knows what *Matchmaker* would do if it were on the air today with its true-to-Dave format!

Times have certainly changed, but one thing has, and always will, remain the same: Dave Hull is a true original, a wonderful friend, and one of the greatest talents around!

The End Is Near

...FOR FIFTEEN YEARS!

KIKF, KWXY: 1996–2010

We weren't exactly homeless, but we didn't have a home.

We were living at the Red Roof Inn.

At least we weren't stranded in Anchorage.

One morning, right after we had enjoyed yet another piping-hot "continental breakfast," I received a call from Art Astor. Art was the owner of the country-western FM favorite, "KIK-FM" (officially, KIKF-FM), and he was a fan of mine personally.

"Dave, will you come in and see if you can do country?" he asked me. "*And* see if you like it?"

Charlie O'Donnell and Dick Moreland always thought I should be a country DJ. Way back when, they had tried to persuade me to go into C & W and get away from the Beatles.

"No, I'm never going to do that," I told them.

I was certain.

But, yes, that was *then*.

"Sure, why not," I told Art. "I haven't *done* country, but what the heck..."

"We're going to put you on in the weekends," he said. "Six to midnight."

So it was back to weekends—*again*. But they were paying well, sooooo...

The very first country artist of the very first country record on the playlist was Shania Twain.

I had no idea who Shania Twain was.

I introduced her as "She-*nee*-a" Twain.

That's how it looked to me on the label!

And I was all alone in the studio—no one was there to offer any kind of corn-fed, NASCAR, steel-guitar-wailing, Stetson-wearing help of any kind.

She-nee-a Twain...

The phones lit up.

All of them.

All sixteen lines.

It kind of reminded me of Detroit.

I would answer one, try to get to the next one, and the first one would ring again—and there were fourteen more!

Then the program director called in on the *hot line*.

"I'm getting phone calls *here*...at my *house*...on a *Saturday*! What did you say on the air?!"

Well, they let me finish the rest of that night and the weekend, but that was the end of *my* rodeo.

It was worth a shot from the old pearl-handled six-shooter of chance, but out came a blank. My misfire on KIK-FM officially became the last time that I was ever heard on Los Angeles area radio.

My country career? In She-nee-a's words: *"That Don't Impress Me Much..."*

Bonding over Bunnies

The serious spell of "being in the right place at the right time" had taken effect in 1953, and it was still working its mojo forty-three years later when I really needed some magic.

I was still out of work.

We were still at the Red Roof Inn.

Abracadabra...

I had friends. And one of them was Scott Ellsworth from back at KFI. Scott was a radio and television personality, businessman, and jazz enthusiast. He had remained popular working on the air at KWXY in Palm Springs after he left L.A.

I called and told him the sad saga of "Hull's Hogwash," and asked if he had any ideas.

"KWXY's operation's director is Larry Collins," Scott said. "I know for a fact that he used to listen to you in L.A. when he worked at KPOL. Come right over and talk with him—*our night guy just got sick.*"

KWXY's ailing evening talent was veteran radio personality and sportscaster Roy Storey. I went to the desert, and Larry hired me to work part-time until something permanent opened up. I subbed for Roy until his health improved—and then it was back to weekends.

The same ol' song...

But a few months later, Roy Storey decided to retire. *Bingo!* I got the full-time job.

KWXY was owned by Glen Barnett, a truly wonderful guy in a business that, as we've seen, can be pretty tough. Glen was also one of the most fascinating owner-managers ever, because of his totally hands-on successes. He'd built stations in Kansas, Oklahoma, and Washington, followed by one near the U.S. Marine base at Twenty-Nine Palms, before setting up KWXY.

He and his wife, Opel, built KWXY from the ground up—from wiring the transmitter, to taking air shifts when needed, to going out in the afternoons to sell the station's commercial time.

And Glen and I had something very important in common: those Roswell jackrabbits! We had both worked for KSWS. At different times, yes, but still in reach of those long ears! Glen in a technical capacity; me, of course, on the air talking to the bunnies.

When we both figured this out, the professional closeness between us *really* began, as did the stories that no one else at the station wanted to hear.

Bunnies were just the first thing that Glen Barnett (right) and I bonded over!

Unwinding and Rewinding

The desert is peaceful.

Maybe that's why so many people retire out here. It's a great place to unwind and reflect. To think back on what you've done in your life—what your life has been.

And *who* you've been.

I was able to combine the peace of a "retirement environment" while remaining at work. I maintained a life-energy continuum that allowed me to reflect on the past while still defining things about myself in the present.

For starters, I was playing "beautiful music" for those "unwinders" out here in the therapeutic heat.

I thought back to one of the first media interviews I ever had.

A Foothill Junior High ninth-grader interviewed me for the school's paper, the *Plaid Post*, for their right-before-Christmas-vacation edition. He pitched a lot of hardball, dig-in-deep questions at me, but a specific one came to mind:

Q: *"Do you ever expect to work at a non-rock-and-roll station?*

A: *"NEVER, NEVER."*

I guess I was a little off on that one!

(Oh, and that ninth grader turned out to be Bill Earl—the future Official KRLA Historian and the author of *Dream-House!*)

As I sat behind that KWXY mic every night from six to midnight, listening to the ease of Sinatra and Mancini and Mauriat, I had the time—and peace—to reflect on so many of the people I had met and worked with, *"town to town and up and down the dial"*...

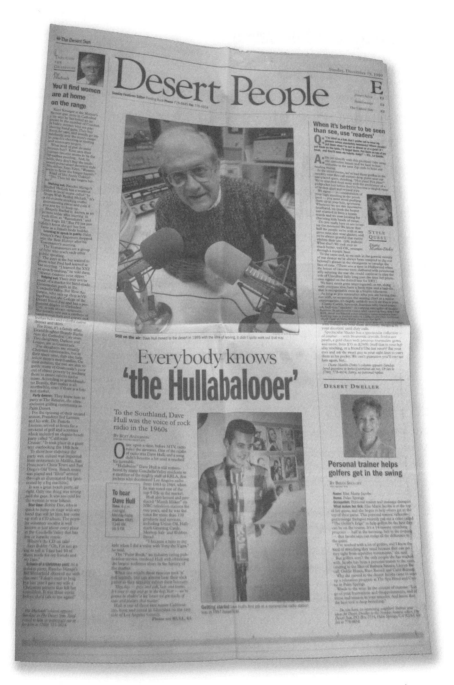

Still on the air: Dave Hull moved to the desert in 1995 with the idea of retiring. It didn't quite work out that way.

The headline was right: As the Hullabalooer, I was known. And I was blessed to know so many pioneering personalities "up and down the dial"!

Paul Moyer

Back in the late seventies, Paul had come to see me at KMPC, because, well, he was unemployed. "Can I come down," he asked, "and would you interview me so that people will know I'm out of work?"

"Sure, Paul," I said.

I mean, we do this for one another in the business. You don't go out on the air and say, "I'm available." You just say, *tactfully*, "Yeah, well, we had a problem."

And I'd say something like, "Well, if they want to know where to get a hold of you, they can call me and I'll give them your contact info."

My daughter, Lisa, was with me in the studio at the time. She was so into television then, and Paul Moyer was a big name in news. Unlike She-nee-a, Lisa was impressed!

Bob Hudson

As we've seen, Emperor Bob Hudson was an institution in this town.

As a person, he had his *issues,* but as a talent on the air, he was a killer. He really was. From these characters that appeared on his show—like Richard Beebe as Colonial Splendid and Casey Kasem as Sgt. Flippy-Floppy—to his emperor shtick, to his beyond-radio success with Ron Landry, to the completely eclectic way he did his show on every station he was on, Hudson was a hard-working fool and a creative genius.

But he was a drinker, too.

He was always funny, though—*on the air at least. That* was Bob Hudson.

Reb Foster

I told you the stories about Reb with the Turtles, Steppenwolf, and Three Dog Night. Those were all true, so help me God. And I was just astounded every time he would tell me he changed band management.

He even wound up involved with Jim Morrison and the Doors.

Reb Foster was an incredible judge of talent; he had such insight into the power of the music of the sixties.

I, of course, had the never-to-be-forgotten Palace Guard!

Ted Quillin

I've always had one line to describe Ted: "Ted Quillin was an abstract guy who talked in bizarre sentences."

A lot of what he said on the air really made no sense. But it just stuck there until the commercial was on, and you'd be sitting in your car and all of a sudden you got it.

That was Ted Quillin—a big gun, with a big, big voice.

And as I mentioned, women loved him. They would call him on the air and tell him what they wanted to do *to* and *with* him! And the problem was, they wanted to do it right then.

He had work to do!

That was Ted Quillin.

Casey Kasem

Casey was a phenomenon, and he's always been a very nice guy.

He got *Shebang*; I got *Quick As A Wink*!

That says it all!

Bob Eubanks

Bob Eubanks is really one of the princes of our business, just a wonderful guy! I thank him so much for writing the Foreword to this book. And let me say it one more time: Bob Eubanks is the ultimate on-the-air, on-camera, onstage, and behind-the-scenes Renaissance man!

Dick Biondi

This guy used to bill himself as "the Wild Eye-tralian." He was Italian, but he could never get it right on the air.

"It's me, Dick Biondi—the Wild Eye-tralian."

And he was a nutcase.

He would *scream*!

He was the first Real Don Steele.

Biondi was on a three-station call, WLS–AM 890, the big one in Chicago, before he came out to the West Coast. He lasted just three months, then cycled back East, then back here, then back East.

I'm a travelin' man...

Dick Biondi is a very diminutive man, small and thin. And a serious Type A. I mean, he was *really* Type A. He was so hyper. If you had him come over, he'd fall over the house plants, knock all the things off the shelves, spill the coffee, wander into the kitchen, break a couple of pictures, and go home.

Dick is still on WLS in Chicago (WLS–FM 94.7) from eight to midnight, and they lovingly call him "Big Mouth" and "The Screamer."

That's the Wild Eye-tralian.

Charlie O'Donnell

Charlie O'Donnell was another prince of a guy—loving and so caring; he really was. More so maybe than anyone else I ever worked with.

He cared about people, was a devout Catholic, and pronounced his faith to everyone.

I sent a letter to his wife, Ellen, on his recent passing: "If Charlie is not in heaven, there is no hope for any of the rest of us."

Even though he was out-manned, Charlie took that morning slot at KRLA after the Emperor left because we really needed help and he's that kind of guy.

We all know what an industry pioneer he was with Dick Clark on *American Bandstand;* but he was also the legendary voice of the still-spinning *Wheel of Fortune* for twenty-eight years!

Back in 1975 when he first auditioned for the Merv Griffin–produced show, he asked the director, "How do you want this approached? Do you want me to be up-tempo and out front, or do you want me to be laid back?"

"Give us both," he was told.

He did—and he got the job.

Dick Haynes

Dick Haynes at the Reins! He was one of the big ones at KLAC with country music. Haynes and Jim Hawthorne were two jocks who had this town in the palm of their hands. Those hands, by the way, were attached to two of the most completely deranged DJs ever to broadcast in this town!

Jim Hawthorne was simply crazy. Dick Haynes was expansive in his lunacy! His catch phrase was "Yucca Bean and Yucca Stew." He had characters like Gumdrop Gus and Wilhelmina Mildew, and he would play off the "side of the mic" with stuff going on in the background.

He'd be talking or reading a commercial, and somebody off the set would ask, "What time is it?"

"Wait a minute—stop everything! It's 7:26," Haynes would say, and then go right on with the commercial. The way he did the time and temperature was something we have not heard any time since.

Dick was from Beaumont, Texas; a town used to hurricanes, tornadoes, and explosive oil gushers.

Dick's on-air style was a combination of all three!

That was *Dick Haynes at the Reins*.

Hunter Hancock

Hunter Hancock was a white disc jockey beloved by African-Americans. Hunter Hancock was so Black-sounding that people couldn't believe it was a white man saying the things he said on the air.

He was on at night at KGFJ. With its relatively low power, KGFJ wasn't the "blowtorch" that KRLA, KFWB, and KHJ were, but Hunter Hancock made his mark.

Pat Sajak

Pat Sajak asked me to be a guest on a TV talk show he was hosting. (It was a Sunday show and unfortunately it didn't last too long.)

I said, "Sure, I'll come on the show."

"Just wear a jacket and tie," he told me. "Look comfortable. I want to talk about you being the Fifth Beatle."

"Oh, God! Do I have to go through this *again,* Pat?" I asked.

"Yeah, you do! We'll talk about the Beatles and have fun, and that'll be it. You'll be in and out in five or ten minutes."

"Okay, fine."

I'm on the show and he says the funniest thing to me.

"Dave, you're known as the Fifth Beatle," he said. "But what you don't know about *me* is that I was the *Sixth* Dave Clark Five."

And I tell you, that interview went right downhill from there!

Richard Beebe

Richard passed away in 1998, having accomplished so many things in his life that were amazing as far as radio was concerned. His inventiveness in the newsroom, The Credibility Gap, the tapes dropped down to me from KRLA's upstairs balcony, that great muffin I pilfered from his "Admirer's" breakfast—Richard was such an important part of not only *my* times at KRLA, but of the way broadcast news changed so radically in the sixties.

Dick Moreland

Oh, God. Dick was the person who actually promoted me at the very beginning.

I told you the story about my first words on the air at KRLA: "How do you like the show so far?" Well, *Dick* was the one who called Reb Foster and said, "Did you hear this guy, the new guy?"

"Yeah, man, I'm still trying to figure out what all this means," said Reb.

That's how I got the permanent job. And that was Dick Moreland. He was a fan of mine from that incredibly iconic "Did-you-hear-this-guy?" beginning.

Joe Pyne

Joe Pyne was the biggest talk show host here, before talk shows were even thought of. He was a pioneer. Wally George was taking calls, too, facing down controversial topics—but his rants were mostly show-fluff; he didn't have that serious *I-mean-it* kind of Pyne-punishment.

Pyne was a brutal man. Scary, to an extent. If he couldn't—or wouldn't—tolerate a caller, it was, "That's it, pal" or "Take a walk!"

BANG! He'd hang up.

Pyne was on KLAC radio and on KTTV-TV, and he was pure nails on both! He salivated over facing off with radical guests, like members of the Ku Klux Klan, the American Nazi Party, and the dregs of Charles Manson's "family." Joe felt like this brand of *guests* "exposed these violent groups to the public eye." Long before Jerry Springer, Pyne's show often involved thrown chairs and guests walking off or getting tossed out by Pyne himself—a war vet with a wooden leg.

People talk about New York and about the first "disc jockey," Martin Block, and all of these people, but they were very timid compared to the West Coast, and L.A. especially. We've always been the mecca for outlandishness on the air. Me, Hudson, Joe Pyne—you name it.

B. Mitchell Reed

Here's another one. A screwball, but I liked him. When you were one-on-one with B. Mitch Reed, he was the nicest guy in the world. And then he'd go ape. That was pretty common in sixties underground FM radio. And that is what Reed got so deeply into.

On KFWB, his show had been called *The Wide Wide Weird World of BMR*. After he attended the Monterey Pop Festival in '67's "Summer of Love," he and his show got wider and weirder. Mitch teamed up with 'Frisco-based DJ Tom Donahue, and together—with their *wild, weird* work at KPPC and KMET—they were responsible for founding underground FM here in L.A.

Roger Christian

I would describe Roger as a "nebbish with a dance show." And like pretty much all of us, he was nuts! He was also incredibly talented outside of radio. Like Reb Foster and Bob Eubanks, Roger "Hot Dog Rog" Christian was deeply into music beyond just spinning 45s. With Beach Boys genius Brian Wilson, Roger wrote several of the group's megahits like "Don't Worry Baby," "Little Deuce Coupe," and "Shut Down."

He also cowrote number ones like "Dead Man's Curve," "The Little Old Lady from Pasadena," and "Honolulu Lulu" for Jan and Dean.

Christian collaborated with Gary Usher on soundtrack-centerpiece songs for the signature sixties bouncing beach flicks like *Beach Party, Ride the Wild Surf,* and *Beach Blanket Bingo* (plus, everyone's favorite, *Catalina Caper!*)—including tunes for the "King of the Surf Guitar," Dick Dale.

He was a prolific pro in this business—*but there was an issue or two.*

Like the murky mythology that still surrounds the happenings on Hollywood's "dead man's curve," Christian had his own four-speed folklore. According to legend, Rog had suffered a fractured skull in a car wreck, resulting in a major brain injury and some medical metal in his head.

The whole *issue* with Roger was that you wanted to hire him during the spring, summer, or fall; because when winter came, this metal thing would get cold and it would *do* something, and poor Rog couldn't think on the air!

The PDs would always ask him, "Roger, are you sure you wouldn't like to take your vacation during the *winter*?!"

Stan Freberg

One of my favorite people as I was growing up was Stan Freberg.

That thing he did with the song "Day-O" (the "Banana Boat Song")...Oh my God! Hilarious!

Freberg:	Day-O!
Voice in background:	Man, I'm gonna have to ask you not to shout like that...
Freberg:	But it goes with the song.
Voice in background:	Yeah, but don't holler in my ear, man...
Freberg:	Well, it's authentic Calypso.
Voice in background:	Yeah, but try NOT standing next to me, man.
Freberg:	Well, the shout go with the bongo drum!

Voice in background:	Not MY bongo drums, man. I mean, move away!
Freberg:	Well, I don't see why—
Voice in background:	No, no, no, stand over there next to the guitar, man!

It's one of the most honest pieces of work and humor I've ever heard—he was remarkable.

Then you'd hear these footsteps and Stan's "singing" of "Day-O" would get fainter and fainter; and then the door would open.

Freberg would ask, *"How's that?"*

"It's still too loud, man."

So he goes outside, and eventually they lock him out so he has to come back in through the window!

These are the things that "banged on the bongos" of my imagination as a youngster. I thought they were great.

He did wonderful things, Stan Freberg.

The Bald Truth of It All

> *"We don't really like people our age*
> *because they're so...old!"*
>
> —Dave and Jeanette Hull

Those "what your life has been and *who* you've been" reflections became so stark out here in the desert. If you really look, these desert sunsets transcend just a pretty sky.

They prove how open and limitless this life really is.

So do grandchildren.

I've always believed there is a special bond between grandparents and their grandkids. Maybe it's because they both have a common enemy: the parents! But either way, I have learned a lot from mine.

One weekend, we hit the westbound I-10 and headed to our daughter and son-in-law's home in San Clemente, California. My grandson, Jordan, asked me if I was "old."

I told him that I was. And then I asked him why he wanted to know. He told me his dad had informed him that old people die someday.

"Well, he's right," I said.

And then I elaborated.

It reminded me of the discussion I'd had with my dad so many years ago, about life and maggots and transformation.

The "end" is the "beginning"...

I told Jordan that all things that live must someday die—plants, animals, and humans. He seemed a little less concerned about wilting hydrangea bushes and belly-up goldfish, though, and was really concerned that *I* was going to die soon.

"Don't worry," I told him. "I'm going to be around for a while to watch you grow up."

That seemed to satisfy him, and the subject was dropped.

For then...

Later, the grandkids came out to the peace of the desert. I took them to KWXY to see the station and to meet Glen Barnett.

On the way home, my granddaughter, Olivia, asked me, "Is Mr. Barney older than you?"

"Mr. Barney?"

"Yes, Mr. Barney. The man who works behind the desk back there."

Apparently "Barnett" was too hard for Olivia to say—so Glen was now "Mr. Barney"! And she was asking about his age.

Hmmm...

Figuring this was headed toward that curious and endless philosophic space where we'd once again examine the mortality of everything, I decided for the sake of time and everyone's energy, I would tell her a teeny-tiny soon-to-be-confessed-at-church fib: "No, Mr. Barney's a lot younger than grandpa."

She looked at me.

I guess she just wanted some elder affirmation of her own basic observations.

"Well, we all knew *that*," she said with that mouths-of-babes bluntness. "Because Mr. Barney has hair!"

"Unwind and reflect" with the truths of life as seen through kids' eyes.

Dave: You're in heaven, aren't you, Elvis?

Elvis: That's right, I'm dead—and I know it's tough for some people to handle the fact that I'm dead. So let me just tell those people: If you don't want to think of me being dead, just think of me as being metaphysically challenged.

Another Serious Scare

But some of those truths are not nearly as "cute."

Sometimes the peace of the desert is shattered by more than a sandstorm blanket or a rush of warm wicked wind.

Jeanette and I were returning to our Palm Springs complex late one night, and I had forgotten the automatic security gate opener.

I pulled up to the manual card reader and fumbled around for my card. It took a while, but I finally got it out and swiped it through the slot.

But before the slow-moving gate could open, this guy came out of nowhere.

And all at once, I had a gun in my face.

Another guy appeared at Jeanette's side of the car.

And another gun.

"Throw out your wallet and purse!" they were yelling.

Jeanette started screaming. Not a regular Fay Wray kind of scream, but this banshee wail that was waking the dead from Cathedral City to Indio (and parts of the Phoenix outskirts, from what I understood later!).

The men were startled! Heck, *I* was petrified!

By now, the gate had opened just enough for the car to squeeze through, so I stepped on it. I screeched away from the men, the guns, and the rudely awakened undead that I figured would soon be zombie-marching down Palm Canyon Drive.

We flew into the complex. The gate closed and we were safe. But Jeanette's *Whine of the Wild* kept on going.

"Dear!" I shouted. "You really need to stop now! You'll have everyone in the complex up and out of their beds!"

"That's the idea!" she said.

Reflections...

Every time I look back on this—and the incident back at KRLA with the threatening letters—I am grateful that in a world with so much violence, my life and the lives of my family have been relatively unscathed compared to so many.

"What your life has been..."

We've been blessed—and ours has definitely been *fun*!

Signing Off: The Final Sunset

Even when I was falling out of the sky, I was essentially having fun.

Sort of.

For the most part.

Afterward.

When KRLA did the balloon promo for Stuart Anderson's Black Angus Restaurants, I did have the privilege of meeting the cattle-beef baron himself.

Now, at KWXY, I had been set up to interview him. I hadn't seen him since that Great Balloon Crash of 1982.

We shook hands.

He remembered me, of course.

And he certainly remembered his fifty-thousand-dollar limp balloon draped all over that schoolyard.

But he didn't come after me with a Laguiole steak knife or anything. In fact, he signed a copy of his autobiography-slash-recipe book, *Here's the Beef!*, to Jeanette.

It was yet another example of those circular interchanges. *"Get off here, get right back on there...come right back to where we started, where we made an impact, where we completely bombed, or where we enjoyed ourselves the most..."*

We had "bombed" in that balloon, but it had turned into a commercial boon.

That was radio.

And so were these last fifteen years. We flew high here, too.

And never crash-landed.

With all that I have done on radio across the country—and across the world, really—working in the desert at KWXY–AM and FM was such a meaningful milestone in my career. It was the perfect setting for so many great sunsets on so many great levels.

I wound up working there longer than any one place in my entire life, including my active and inactive Air Force service and all three times at KRLA *combined*!

I worked at **KWXY** with Christopher Lewis (left), son of actress Loretta Young, and Mandy Armstrong, longer than any station in my career. Over fifteen years, Chris and I developed a strong friendship; and we shared another special bond: As a young woman, *my* mother had admired *his* mother's acting abilities so much that she had legally changed her name to Edna *Loretta* Hull!

In 2006, the AM 1340 side of KWXY was sold to Glen's close friends at RR Broadcasting, a radio group of several stations that has been in the desert area since 1956. They changed the format to political talk and the call letters to KPTR.

KWXY–FM 98.5, however, remained as a "beautiful music" station. And I remained as a "beautiful" DJ—with a little less hullabaloo than in the years before.

But in 2010, it, too, was sold and I felt it was time.

It was time to finally sign off for good—*for now.*

My old, dear friend Charlie O'Donnell (left) was always going above and beyond. He and his wife, Ellen, drove all the way from the San Fernando Valley for my final radio show. It meant the world to me, and I will never forget it.

On February 1, 2010, at 11:59 p.m., after fifteen years at KWXY, and fifty-seven years at stations from Africa to a space-alien prairie to almost Alaska, I said farewell to radio.

After a prerecorded two-minute message from Glen Barnett, I urged listeners to stay tuned for the programming of the *new* KDES beginning at midnight.

And then I said my last words on radio:

"And now, from all of us here at KWXY, thanks for listening throughout the years...and goodnight!"

Epilogue:
The Golden Age of Radio

Airwaves Never Disappear

In television, everything is done for you before your eyes. You see all the action. You see everything that's happening.

But radio must capture your imagination. There's nothing to see except what your mind experiences while you're listening. Radio *is* the "theater of the mind."

And to make that really work, radio personalities need to conjure up in their *own* minds someone to speak to.

Some *one* to speak to.

It can be anyone at all, certainly: a mother, a father, a family member, a lover, or just somebody at work. But the broadcaster must talk to that person.

That one person.

Because each and every member of the listening audience must believe that the on-air personality is talking directly to them. And you accomplish this by doing just that: talking to just one person, even though that microphone is connected to enough magic to make you heard around the planet.

And it is that singularity—at least among the true talents in this business—that often gives people in the audience the wrong impression of *"who you've been."*

Especially in my days of the most hullabaloo, everyone would say to me, "You're such an extravert!"

Onstage all the time.

On a parade float.

Sending out masks of myself.

In the company of megastars.

But, no.

Most of us on the air are introverted. An air personality goes into a studio—in most cases, the size of a broom closet—and talks, in the most literal sense, to *himself* for three or four hours, five days a week. Even the maniacal talk-radio pioneer Joe Pyne referred to himself as an "overly compensating introvert."

That is a perfect description.

Even when I began the interactive-intense radio with all the phone calls, I was still essentially alone. In there. In the studio. And really only talking to one person.

And that brings up how *talk* radio has become the titan that it is.

That old tabloid cliché about "inquiring minds" is true.

We humans are inquisitive. We want to know what the other guy thinks—even if we don't agree. And that only happens through communication and interaction. That psychic's kid back in Tampa may have done a good job predicting the Super Bowl, but true mind-reading isn't an exact science yet. Talk radio gets us closer.

It's almost like eavesdropping. The listener is getting inside the head of someone else. I mean, how many "normal" folks have picked up the binoculars and let them stray into the neighbor's house? How many "normal" people have heard the hubbub in the motel room next door and used the old water-glass-to-the-ear trick to get a little more "interactive" with the *situation*?

The person to watch out for, though, is the one who does it every day and night of the trip! The one who *always* has the high-powered Bushnells in hand!

But talk radio can be a healthy and educational *non-voyeuristic* habit.

And again, that on-air personality—if he or she is one of the good ones—is talking to *one* person.

Hullmarks to Success

Professor Hull here. For those of you who might be seriously considering—or merely toying with—the possibility of entering the always satisfying, never stressful, pure nirvana of broadcasting, I have four subjects upon which to lecture!

Ahem...

My "Hullmarks to Success" are these:

Be Dramatic

To become a professional broadcaster, you must first submerge yourself in drama. Take as many acting classes as you can—it's so important to be able to tell a story.

Don't tell me that you won't need to tell stories on the air. What do you think commercials are? They are thirty-second or one-minute *stories* about businesses with a problem who need help in a specific way.

And don't tell me the businesses don't have a problem! If they didn't, they wouldn't be advertising. Even if the only problem is that they want and/or need more sales.

Identifying the client's problem will help you understand what's important to the "story." Then you'll know how to "act" to solve the problem. I used to sell women's hygiene products. I had to *act*! (We male DJs don't do that anymore, thankfully! They have women doing it now.)

They used to have commercials for cigarettes. I did *live* spots for Kent cigarettes, where I had to *know* how "refreshing" Kents were! You've got to believe it.

Let's revisit my class in Commercial Interpretation. We'll open a script and take the line "I love you." Like the one I screamed back in that play at Granada Grammar School. It's just three words. Okay. But you have to say it in the way the script dictates. Maybe you *do* love that person. Or maybe you really *hate* that person in the script but have to make them *think* you love them!

Identify what has to be conveyed: *That's* commercial interpretation.

Speak Up!

The second Hullmark to Success is to learn public speaking. We introverts, especially, need this. Classes help, joining Toastmasters helps, and so does on-the-job training—which, of course, can lead to some embarrassments! It can also lead to success.

My brilliant early-life speech of political triumph is a perfect example. *"Do you really trust anyone who wears short pants to school?"*

is right up there with "Friends, Romans, countrymen, lend me your ears..."; "Four score and seven years ago..."; "Ich bin ein Berliner"; and "I didn't inhale" as one of the most poignancy-laden addresses ever.

Even though I wasn't as yet formally trained, the "Short Pants Proclamation" (as it is now known in oratory circles) taught me one of the most important keys to public speaking: You have to be comfortable in your own skin if you're going to stand on a stage, get behind a mic, or smile in front of a TV camera and talk to people.

Control the Conversation

The third Hullmark to Success in broadcasting is to become adept in the fine art of debate. Regular debating helps you know what people are going to say before they say it. That's super important when it comes to conducting interviews. It allows you to guide the conversation in ways *you* want it to go.

That can head off a lot of on-air embarrassment. And debating helps you to instantly think on your feet—another valuable skill to have in live media.

Find the "Key to Komedy"

The fourth Hullmark to Success is to be able to define humor. Now, if you're going to be working in the traditional starched-and-pressed mold of, say, my old coworker Dave Garroway, or some of those wingtip-wearing guys who do refinance-your-house mortgage commercials, well, then maybe you could skip this section. But most of you should consider a little less Argo Gloss in your collar.

Some of the greats couldn't fully define humor. Not Jack Benny or even Bob Hope could define it.

Well I can.

Humor is nothing more than surprise. Have you ever heard a joke that you thought you knew how it would end but it went a totally different way? That's surprise. It's the "Key to Komedy." Tell stories that listeners *think* will end one way and give a completely different ending, and you've got your surprise—like Ousley in the funeral parlor.

When asked about humor, Hope used to say, "Well, you'll know it when you hear it!" Now, I loved Bob, but his answer is clumsy to me. Jeanette and I have had long talks about what humor is, and my answer is always the same: Surprise. And that goes for sounds as well as words. The listeners expected the raspberries and the toilet flush, but they didn't expect the burp!

Elvis: Sammy Davis, Jr., has got a great new comedy act up here. And I gotta tell you something: The Boss has a great sense of humor.

Dave: Oh, God has a sense of humor?!

Elvis: He invented radio. (*Pause.*) He invented Dave Hull.

Dave: You've got a point there.

Stay in Line

Another thing to remember: You can go right up to the "line," but never cross it like so many shock jocks do now. You don't *have* to say anything "out of line." And for the most part, it's still a good idea to avoid the two subjects that used to be so taboo: politics and religion.

Your career will last longer!

Now, it's one thing to have some fun in the confessional with the good Fathers Moriarty and Hullabaloo. And it's one thing to have a Ross Perot or other leaders of the free and not-so-free worlds ranting and raving on your show. But again, there's that line.

When politics and religion get *too* serious, you can feel those big wedges of thin skin and animosity alienating you from your audience.

"Bless me, Father, my last confession was fifty years ago" will probably work for you. *"YOU'RE ALL GOING TO HELL! AND THE LOSER LUMMUX THAT HEADS UP YOUR CHEESY CHURCH ISN'T FIT TO BAPTIZE A MAGGOT!"* probably won't.

Then again, maybe it will. If for some reason, you want to dig yourself into a world that I never could understand, well, I suppose there's an audience.

But not *my* kind of audience.

Not the kind that my Hullmarks to Success could take you to.

To make it in that other world, pretty much all you have to do is to lie down in the gutter and roll around for a while until all innocence is gone.

But why?

Because it's more real?

More hard-hitting?

Maybe, but when something is hit hard over and over, it ends up being destroyed.

I loved the innocence of radio when I began—and I loved it all through my career. I even loved having those lines *not* to cross because it kept things clever and imaginative; not caustic, crass, and cliché. Digging into the dirt is too easy and it's cheap.

Groaners and corny jokes worked because they didn't offend anyone. My being nutty was just plain funnier than my being smutty.

I had that toy box full of horns, whistles, bells, and assorted junk—enough to keep coming up with "surprises" but still supply listeners with the familiar sounds of their friend, Dave Hull.

And none of those sounds ever included a "beep"—censoring out a purposeless obscenity.

I didn't need that.

And neither did my audience.

Fifty-Seven Years

The Beatles.

The Dodgers.

The commercials.

The voiceovers.

The Monkees.

Matchmaker.

Elvis Calling from Heaven.

The fun!

Through it all, though, *Lovelines* was probably my favorite—the biggest thing for me.

But at every station and venue where I worked, the fun and the big things came with my devising another "plan" that would fit the new surroundings.

New station. New ideas. New directions.

It was always like starting over, but that was always okay. The changes gave me the chance to be creative, to generate fresh material to work with and other "ways to go."

But (very personal note here!) nothing—*nothing*—could ever compare to the fun of fifty years of being married to my loving wife, Jeanette. From that first day of handing her the muddy money to getting trampled by the Rolling Stones' psychotic sweethearts to being "homeless" in Alaska to these desert sunsets, she's loved me and my hullabaloo.

Well, *most* of it.

And surprisingly, without many censoring "beeps" at all!

And the whole family has been right there with her in its support.

When I decided to retire in 2010, I naturally told my daughter, Lisa, of my plans.

A few days later, I received a note from Allison Schultz of Chicago. Allison had been Lisa's college roommate back at Cal State Northridge (the "Harvard of the West" as alumni Rich Marotta and longtime KFI morning man Bill Handel reverently refer to it!). She not only listened to me while I was on KRLA in the 1980s, but she also watched *Matchmaker* after transferring to the University of Wisconsin at Madison.

Her note to me is like these desert sunsets: it says so much.

Allison Schultz (left), the college roommate of my daughter, Lisa (right), was a longtime special fan.

It says so much about me—and it says so much about this crazy world of radio that I have given my life to.

> *As Lisa told me about your retirement, I couldn't help but remember all those days in college when Lisa and I would listen to you on the radio; and I'd always get such a thrill when you'd mention us on the air. For a girl from the Midwest, it was a big deal. You were my first real celebrity!*
>
> *They say that airwaves never disappear and that somewhere out in the universe they still exist. I'd like to think that some night, if I'm really quiet, maybe I could still hear the distinctive voice of Dave Hull on the air.*

Index

Z

Add even more HULLABALOO
to your collection!!